Retreat and Rearguard Somme 1918

To Alisha

who accompanied me on a journey
along the Fifth Army front in August 2013

Retreat and Rearguard Somme 1918

The Fifth Army Retreat

Jerry Murland

Pen & Sword
MILITARY

First published in Great Britain in 2014 by
Pen & Sword Military
an imprint of
Pen & Sword Books Ltd
47 Church Street
Barnsley
South Yorkshire
S70 2AS

ISBN 978 1 78159 267 0

A CIP catalogue record for this book is available from the British
Library

Typeset in Ehrhardt by
Mac Style, Bridlington, East Yorkshire
Printed and bound in the UK by CPI Group (UK) Ltd, Croydon,
CR0 4YY

Pen & Sword Books Ltd incorporates the imprints of Pen & Sword
Archaeology, Atlas, Aviation, Battleground, Discovery, Family History,
History, Maritime, Military, Naval, Politics, Railways, Select, Transport,
True Crime, and Fiction, Frontline Books, Leo Cooper, Praetorian
Press, Seaforth Publishing and Wharncliffe.

For a complete list of Pen & Sword titles please contact
PEN & SWORD BOOKS LIMITED
47 Church Street, Barnsley, South Yorkshire, S70 2AS, England
E-mail: enquiries@pen-and-sword.co.uk
Website: www.pen-and-sword.co.uk

Contents

Author's Note

The basic formation of the British Army in the Great War began – as it still does today – with the infantry platoon. Commanded usually by a second lieutenant or lieutenant and assisted by a platoon sergeant it was divided into four sections each commanded by a corporal or lance corporal. There were generally four platoons in a company, all of which answered to a company commander. In 1918 it was not unusual for companies to be commanded by senior lieutenants. Four companies and a headquarters company made up an infantry battalion, commanded by a major or lieutenant colonel. Within the headquarters company was the second-in-command, the battalion adjutant – the commanding officer's right-hand man – the regimental sergeant major and the battalion quartermaster. Usually the battalion medical officer was part of this group. The average strength of a battalion in 1914 was approximately 900 officers and men, by March 1918 a large proportion of battalions in the front line had been reduced to more or less 550 officers and men.

The next unit of command after the battalion was the infantry brigade, initially made up of four battalions but reduced to three in February 1918 and commanded by a brigadier general. A division consisted of at least three brigades and was under the command of a major general. Beyond that, divisions were organized into corps which were usually commanded by lieutenant generals and grouped together to form armies. The Fifth Army was one such formation. On the Western Front in March 1918 there were five British and Commonwealth army groups present along the front line, all under the direction of Sir Douglas Haig, the Commander-in-Chief.

When describing the locations of units I have occasionally referred to modern day road numbering in order to give the reader using current maps of the area a more precise location. While some of the abbreviations in the text are self explanatory others require explanation. I have used a form of abbreviation when describing battalion formations, thus after its first mention in the text the 2nd Battalion Royal Munster Fusiliers becomes 2/Munsters or more simply the Munsters. Similarly infantry brigades are denoted by cardinal numbers, the 25th

Infantry Brigade becoming 25 Brigade. So as not to cause confusion between a brigade of infantry and one of artillery I have simply added the word artillery.

German Army units are a little more complex. Within the infantry regiment there were three battalions – each approximately the size of a British battalion – and a machine gun-company. Each battalion was denoted by a Roman numeral and occasionally adopted the name of its commanding officer, where this appears in German accounts the battalion's name is identified in brackets. The four companies of riflemen were given an Arabic numeral, for example, 3 *Kompanie* – and the machine-gun company was numbered separately, adopting the battalion number. Again, I have abbreviated when describing these units, thus Infantry Regiment 31 becomes IR 31 while the second battalion within that regiment is abbreviated to II/IR 31. Within this description there are a number of other variations that appear in the text:

FAR   Field Artillery Regiment
GR   Grenadier Regiment
RIR   Reserve Infantry Regiment
ID   Infantry Division

Equivalent German and British ranks referred to in the text are as follows:

Colonel	*Oberst*
Lieutenant Colonel	*Oberstleutnant*
Major	*Major*
Captain	*Hauptmann*
Lieutenant	*Oberleutnant*
Second Lieutenant	*Leutnant*
Corporal	*Unteroffizier*
Lance Corporal	*Gefreiter*
Private	*Grenadier / Jäger / Musketier / Artillerist / Kanoniere*

Acknowledgements

In searching for personal accounts written by the men who fought in the March retreat I have scoured archive collections across the country and it is to those archivists, librarians and keepers of collections that I am most indebted. The National Archives at Kew has been a continual source of material, particularly in respect of regimental war diaries and the hugely rich source of letters and accounts that flowed between veterans and the Army Historical Branch post 1918. These accounts, apart from revealing what exactly took place and where, have provided a fascinating insight into the true nature of the fighting at a tactical level. Other sources of material have been found in the Imperial War Museum document and sound archive collections, the Liddell Hart Centre for Military Archives and the Liddle Collection at Leeds. My thanks must also go to the curators of the various regimental museums which still hold material relating to the March retreat. Of these I am particularly grateful to the Rifles Museum at Winchester and the Royal Engineers Museum, Library and Archive.

I am also indebted to Nigel Lutt at the Bedfordshire and Luton Archive, the staff at the Surrey History Centre, the Hampshire Records Office and the Leicestershire and Rutland Record Office. Special thanks must go to Laura Dimmock and Tony Pilmer at the RUSI library in Whitehall who have responded so promptly to my many requests for obscure and out of print volumes. The library – which must rank as one of the best military libraries in the country – holds copies of practically every defence review and military journal ever published, a place where one can easily lose track of time!

In gathering information I am also indebted to the host of individuals who responded to my online requests via the Great War Forum, a number of whom went out of their way to help by providing me with material. Adam Llewellyn, Chris Baker, Colin Taylor, Mark Smith, Jim Ainslie, Martin Mcneela, Al Grey, Andy Pugh and Dave Risley were in particular of immense help. Thanks must also go to Damien Burke at the Irish Jesuit Archive in Dublin for providing a copy of the Father Henry Gill diaries and permission to quote from them.

As ever it is the personal accounts of the officers and men who fought during the March retreat that make this particular story possible; to these long gone individuals I extend my thanks and gratitude for chronicling their experiences and enabling later generations to share their battlefield experiences with them. In following in their footsteps during my journey along the Fifth Army front I was accompanied for much of it by my eldest granddaughter Alisha who became adept at spotting battlefield relics and programming the satellite navigation system. Our week spent together was one that both of us will treasure. I must also thank Dave Rowland, Paul Webster, Rob Howard and Bill Dobbs who clambered around the ruins of Fort Vendeuil with me and stumbled across fields in search of numerous long forgotten redoubts in the III Corps sector.

The German accounts have been provided by Sebastian Laudan in Berlin who, when not translating German unit histories, is a serving police officer. His tireless work on my behalf has not only enabled a more balanced view to be taken but has opened the door to the notion that the initial German advance in March 1918 was not always as straightforward as has often been suggested. To my editor Jon Cooksey – a notable and published historian himself – I must again extend my appreciation of his encouragement and enthusiasm. His incisive questioning and constructive appraisal of the text is always welcome and has added much to the quality of the manuscript.

The maps have been drawn by Rebecca Jones of Glory Designs in Coventry and as usual she made several suggestions as to how my rather crude sketches could be improved. Finally, I have made every effort to trace the copyright holders where any substantial extract is quoted. Where this has not been possible the author craves the indulgence of literary executors or copyright holders where these efforts have so far failed and would encourage them to contact him through the publisher.

Jerry Murland
Coventry
2014

Introduction

The German offensive of March 1918 was the first of five major thrusts which were the brain-child of *General der Infanterie* Erich Ludendorff. Operation 'Michael' – or *Kaiserschlacht* as it is more commonly known – was followed by four further attempts to force the Allied forces on the Western Front into capitulation. Despite the sometimes breathtaking advances made in the opening days, ultimately all of these attempts failed; strategic flaws and logistical problems proving to be their undoing. Rather typically the British Nomenclature Committee saw the March offensive not as a single battle but as a series of battles beginning with the 'First Battle of the Somme 1918', a name that Randal Gray in his book *Kaiserschlacht 1918* rightly feels invites confusion with the 1916 battles which are 'forever seared into the national consciousness'. While the committee go on to add the Battle of St Quentin, Actions at the Somme Crossings, the Battle of Rosières and the British Battle of the Avre, the names themselves fail to lend any gravitas to what must be regarded as one of – if not the – most significant periods of fighting of the entire war.

The *Official British History* of the war refers to the March 1918 fighting as the Great German Offensive, and although it provides an accurate account of the fighting it lacks the tactical detail and personal accounts that allow the reader a much greater access to the battlefield. In writing about 1914–1918 I have always sought to expose the emotions of war through the accounts of those who were there – it was after all a human conflict fought by individuals no different from ourselves and whose experiences and accounts reflected the frailty of their existence. Fortunately many of these accounts still exist and bring to life the actions often described more clinically in regimental and divisional histories. These accounts shed light on long-forgotten or relatively insignificant engagements that have been either excluded from official accounts or have only briefly been referred to.

Readers may well ask why have I confined my story to the Fifth Army when the *Kaiserschlacht* offensive also involved the Third Army? There is one sound principle reason for this; the Fifth Army sector saw the greatest collapse of command and control and – arguably – some of most intense and bitter fighting of the twentieth century. However, I have referred to the Third Army where necessary particularly as it was its actions and the poor communication between the two armies that largely contributed to the gap which opened up between them and later enabled units of the German 1st Division to threaten the Rosières pocket; a situation that Sir Walter Congreve, commanding VII Corps, attributed solely to the Third Army's stubborn retention of the Cambrai salient. Similarly the involvement of the French cannot be ignored or overlooked, but while the overall strategic picture has been furnished where necessary, the text is largely confined to the rearguard actions of the Fifth Army between the eleven days of 21 March and 1 April 1918.

Another area that has been omitted from this book is the often overlooked work of the Royal Flying Corps squadrons of V Brigade which was attached to the Fifth Army. This omission does not in any way denigrate the contribution of the men involved; it is simply that the lack of space – which does not allow the full story of their role in the battle to be told as fully as I might have liked – prompted me to concentrate on the ground battle. Their exploits in the air, together with those of III Brigade who flew over the Third Army sector, are worthy of a book in itself and may well be the subject of a future project. Needless to say, 15 Wing under the command of Lieutenant Colonel Ivo Edwards with his five squadrons of aircraft, together with the seven squadrons of Lieutenant Colonel Felton Holt's 22 Wing, were frustratingly only able to get off the ground when the visibility improved later in the morning of 21 March, circumstances that also affected the Imperial German Air Service. But as the retreat moved west both German and RFC pilots quickly adapted to the changing pattern of operations as bombing and ground attack became the order of the day.

As far as the ground war is concerned the difficulty has been not in deciding which actions to describe but in finding accounts that provide that all important individual perspective on events. To put it simply, if there is no story to tell, it can't be told and as a consequence many of the rearguard encounters portrayed in the book have virtually chosen themselves. Some of course have been included because of the place they have already forged in history; the action at Manchester Hill is one of these as is that of Racecourse Redoubt. Two posthumous Victoria Crosses were won in these locations on 21 March being early contributions to the thirteen of Victoria Crosses awarded to individuals in the Fifth Army sector between 21 March and 1 April.

There were of course hundreds of individual and unit encounters during the March retreat that never found their way into any written format and sadly remain untold to this day. Typical of these is the story of the forward posts and redoubts in the British Forward Zone on 21 March. Many of these so-called strong-points were overcome extraordinarily quickly. If they had not been subdued by the preliminary artillery bombardment then the first waves of attacking German infantry quickly overwhelmed them, often surrounding them in the fog before they had any opportunity to retaliate. Where we do not have reliable personal accounts detailing what actually took place, we can only speculate as to the exactness of the fate of those outposts and their garrisons.

Many of these small garrisons may well have surrendered rather than continue the struggle in the face of what they saw as a futile resistance; others, we know, chose to fight on to the last round or until most or all of their officers and senior non-commissioned officers (NCOs) had been killed or wounded. Still more were rendered incapable of fighting by the intensity and ferocity of the initial German artillery bombardment as recounted by *Gefreiter* Wilhelm Reinhard of IR 227 at Fayet. In attempting to identify particular units which did not fight as well as others, some historians have analysed casualty and prisoner of war figures and used them as a yardstick by which to measure the effectiveness of the fight they put up – the higher the casualties the greater the resistance. Using such data has to be regarded as an unfair and imprecise measurement of overall success or failure; as every soldier is aware, casualty figures can be an unreliable indicator of the true nature of an engagement.

One such division was the 14th (Light) Division which has long been tarred with this brush. However, there are at least two accounts from commanding officers of King's Royal Rifle Corps battalions in the Forward Zone which suggest this was not the case across the whole of the divisional front. Lieutenant Colonel Charles Howard-Bury commanding the 9th King's Royal Rifle Corps held out in his headquarters redoubt until 4.00pm – as did the 8th King's Royal Rifle Corps – before both battalions were finally overwhelmed. In the sector of the Battle Zone held by the 14th Division, Lieutenant Colonel Julias Birch was still fighting hard until midnight with the remnants of the 7th Battalion King's Royal Rifle Corps, having lost 75 per cent of his strength in the opening bombardment that morning. While a number of regimental and divisional histories have achieved notoriety for embellishing the truth I find it difficult to believe men such as Julias Birch and Charles Howard-Bury would do the same. Their conduct, and that of the much maligned 8th Battalion KRRC, goes some way in vindicating the performance of Major General Victor Couper's 14th Division.

What has become clear is that the Fifth Army Forward Zone was over-manned in a number of divisional sectors and the German opening bombardment was very skilfully zeroed in on many of the forward posts and redoubts. Guilty in this respect was Couper himself who was amongst a number of divisional and corps commanders who simply did not understand the concept of defence in depth, a number that unfortunately included the Fifth Army commander, Hubert Gough.

Any student of the March offensive will before long come across the question of whether or not the thick early morning fog that was evident on the 21 March aided the German infantry attack. German opinion is divided on this. In the IR 31 account of the attack across the Oise valley at Travecy, their historian complains bitterly about the difficulties they had in overpowering the British strong-points in the fog, a task they felt was by no means going to be easy even in good visibility:

'The dense fog hanging all over the Oise valley does its best to split up all advancing units into fragments. It is impossible to cling to written plans; everybody is on his own. German troops turn out to be English and vice-versa, rattling machine guns can't be localised, let alone identified. When a village seems to have been taken, it either turns out to be full of English or it is pounded by their own artillery. Very lights and dispatch runners disappear in the dense fog.'[1]

Two days later – when the early morning fog was just as thick – *Gefreiter* Georg Maier who was serving with one of the Bavarian units attacking Jussy, felt the fog assisted their attack. 'Thanks to the fog', he wrote, [the enemy] 'was not able to hit us hard, and our infantry stormed the position where the firing was coming from.'

Although Maier's experience on the Crozat Canal was a relatively positive one there are numerous accounts of German infantry forced to advance using compass bearings while others reported becoming detached from their units and stumbling into British-held positions. German artillery too found it all but impossible to put down counter-battery fire on British gunners who were still able to return fire and with the inability of any aerial reconnaissance to get off the ground, could make no corrections and only fire along previously-established fixed lines.

British military opinion – expressed in the accounts of officers who were present on the front line on 21 March – strongly supports the argument that the fog aided the German attack significantly. Brigadier General Frederick Dawson commanding the South African Brigade reported, 'an exceptionally thick fog, it being impossible to see more than 30 or 40 yards and in consequence every arm of the defence, namely artillery, machine guns and infantry, was at a great disadvantage'. Captain Geoffrey Peirson, a staff officer at Épehy, was a little more specific, he maintained that the initial attacks were carried out by what he termed as the 'advanced guards' allowing the main German attacking force to move in columns up the valleys and roads before they deployed using machine guns and trench mortars at close range. 'Had it not been for the fog this method of attack would have ended in disaster, as all those natural approaches were covered by machine guns and field guns.'[2] His is a view supported by another officer in the 21st Division who maintained that across the entire divisional Forward Zone, 'direct shooting was rendered impossible', adding that in his opinion this was not an isolated case.

Without the cover of a thick fog the battle may have had a different outcome for the Fifth Army, certainly the unsuccessful 'Mars' assault on the Third Army on 28 March did not have the benefit of the cloaking effect of fog but it is highly unlikely this was a significant factor in its failure. The Mars offensive floundered in the face of strongly-held positions and a more flexible understanding of the three zones of defence. However, a hint of what might have been on the Fifth Army Front is provided by the IR 31 account of their attack in the Oise valley. While drawing attention to the confusion it also makes reference to the difficult nature of the task they might have been faced with had the weather been more favourable to the British. We hear the same complaint from IR 227 in Gauche Wood where the fog made their task doubly difficult, 'neither man nor trunk is distinguishable from each other' wrote their historian. Certainly the fog made life difficult for both sides but in the opinion of the author, the presence of fog on 21 March – and on succeeding days – was only part of the reason why the Fifth Army collapsed so dramatically.

There is a body of evidence to support the view that the collapse was due to the combination of fog *and* the failure of the British to fully understand and exploit the new concept of defence in depth. There appeared to be a worrying difference in opinion between corps and divisional commanders as to the role the Forward and Battle Zones were to play in delaying any enemy attack, exacerbated no doubt in some sectors by incomplete defences. It has to be said that in many sectors the Forward Zone simply failed to slow the enemy advance and its collapse precipitated what became a general retirement. Fog certainly allowed the enemy to pass unobserved between redoubts, but even without that covering blanket, reports that some redoubts were handicapped by the ground on which they were sited and the distance that existed between them is disquieting. What is perhaps even more disturbing is the apparent British inability to recognise a German attack may in fact approach from an angle – as it did on the 14th and 16th Divisional sectors and completely cut out the Forward Zone.

Yet even without the fog factor I feel the Fifth Army Forward Zone defences would probably have suffered the same fate, a notion which begs the question of whether the Germans would – in those circumstances – have been held on the Somme. Martin Middlebrook in his analysis of the first day of the offensive believes that had there been no fog on the morning of March 21 many of the German attacks would have faltered against the weight of British machine-gun and artillery fire. If he is right then the enormous casualties that would have been inflicted on German infantry by the British positions in the Forward Zone may well have taken the sting out of the advance and held the attack in the Battle Zone or at worst along the line of the Somme.

However, what is certain is that as the retreat gathered pace more and more emphasis was placed on the ability of regimental officers to provide leadership and command in the absence of the wider brigade and divisional structure that had been largely devastated by the speed and intensity of the enemy offensive. In the 1914 Retreat from Mons it was the regimental officers and NCOs which took on the mantle of responsibility for maintaining the integrity of their units; four years later the same demands were being placed on a new generation of officers and NCOs many of whom only had experience of the confines of trench warfare. It may have been this factor that escalated into a general retreat as the Forward Zone was overwhelmed and the hapless British soldier was forced out of his hole in the ground and thrown into a war of movement that was almost as foreign to him as it was to many of his commanders.

With the evident inability to adapt quickly to a war of movement becoming increasingly apparent it wasn't until the Fifth Army was on the line of the River Somme that units began to respond more effectively to the swiftly moving German assault. It was almost as if the basic tools of the trade had been forgotten and had to be learned over again. These 'on the hoof' learning curves were aggravated by the failure to co-ordinate the destruction of vital bridges and the Somme causeways into the work of the Royal Engineers. All too often we hear the despair in the voices of fighting units as they realize vital bridging points had not been destroyed and their defences – so often held at a huge human cost – were compromised by enemy infantry outflanking them.

Further censure for the Fifth Army collapse is frequently placed on the lack of manpower and the resulting emphasis on completing the construction of dug-outs and redoubts above all else. In this respect the Fifth Army commander was between a rock and a hard place. He had little choice but to build the three-zone defensive line without which there would be no defence against a German offensive, yet at the same time it appears that he did not respond – or have the time in which to respond – to the opinions of his senior advisers, all of which was not helped by Gough himself giving out mixed messages as to the state of the Fifth Army defences. We know, for example, he had boasted to Douglas Haig on 13 February that a further month would see his front able to resist an attack, yet at the beginning of March he was complaining he had no resources to work on his defences.[3]

Enmeshed in the politics of the manpower question is the reduction of the number of infantry battalions in each brigade and how this might have affected the performance of the soldier on the ground. The political manoeuvring on the Home Front, orchestrated by David Lloyd George, was aimed at reducing the influence and control exercised by the Commander-in-Chief, Sir Douglas Haig. One catastrophic result of this was to drastically reduce the flow of men to the Western Front and in so doing reduce each brigade of infantry from four to three battalions. Not only did this have an immediate effect on the rotation of battalions to and from the front line but, perhaps more importantly, it disturbed the cohesiveness that units had built up over a period of time just days before the German offensive began. Exactly what effect this had on the fighting ability of the British soldier and his officers is impossible to gauge, but it was a reorganisation that took place at an inopportune moment.

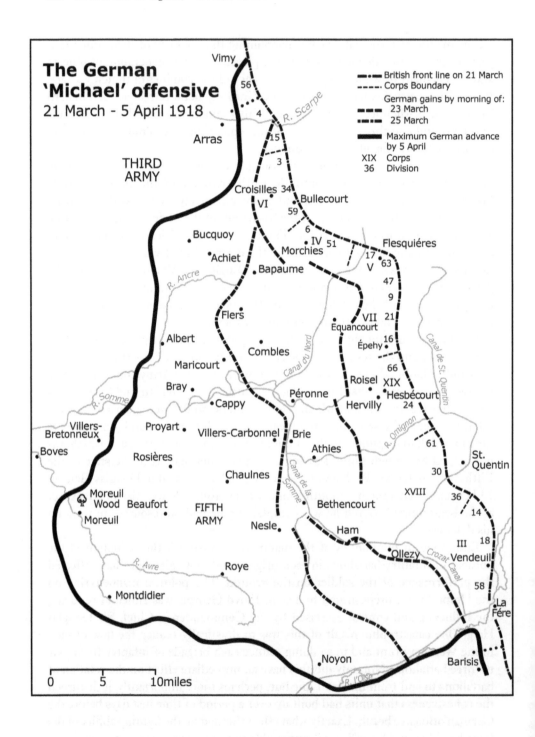

**The German
'Michael' offensive**
21 March - 5 April 1918

▬▪▬▪	British front line on 21 March
-----	Corps Boundary
	German gains by morning of:
▬ ▬ ▬	23 March
▬▪▬▪	25 March
▬▬▬	Maximum German advance by 5 April
XIX	Corps
36	Division

Vimy

56

R. Scarpe

4

Arras

15

THIRD
ARMY

3

Croisilles 34

VI   Bullecourt

59

6

Bucquoy

IV 51   Flesquiéres

Achiet   Morchies   17

Bapaume   V   63

47

R. Ancre

9

Flers   VII 21

Equancourt

Albert   Épehy 16

Combles

Canal du Nord

Maricourt   66

Bray   Roisel XIX

Péronne   Hesbécourt

Cappy   Hervilly   24

R. Somme

Villers-   Proyart   Villers-Carbonnel Brie

Bretonneux   Athies   61

Boves   Rosières   30   St.
Quentin

Chaulnes   XVIII

Canal de la Somme   36

Moreuil   Bethencourt   14

Wood Beaufort   FIFTH

Moreuil   ARMY   Nesle   Ham   III   18

Ollezy Crozat Canal Vendeuil

R. Avre   Roye   58

Montdidier   La
Fére

Canal de St. Quentin

R. Omignon

Noyon   Barisis

R. l'Oise

0   5   10miles

However, despite Ludendorff's optimism and weight of resources, the Fifth Army line did not break. It may have fractured occasionally and been twisted beyond recognition in others, but the patchy defence of 21 March, bolstered by the French in the south and an influx of reserves from the north, increasingly held firm and at Rosières on 27 March the German assault suffered its first major setback. Ludendorff's indistinct strategic priorities and the lightening success of the first two days saw the initial objectives of rolling up the British line to the north redirected into a drive on Amiens to separate the French and British armies. In creating a huge salient which incorporated much of the ground his armies had laid to waste in 1917, he in fact laid the foundations for the successful Allied attack which came five moths later.

On paper the March offensive should have crushed the British. It did not and ran out of steam as more and more men were pushed into the south at the expense of those in the centre and north. This betrayal of the original battle plan was the Achilles heel that ultimately broke the back of German aspirations; Ludendorff had expected to break clean through the British defences on the first day, an objective that was only really achieved in the III Corps sector where the line of the Crozat Canal was used as a fall back position. Elsewhere the Battle Zone had largely held – albeit rather tenuously in places – and the expected encirclement of the Flesquières salient had not taken place. The Fifth Army may have fallen back in some disarray but the disappointing first day for the Germans had already made huge inroads into men and resources that could not be replaced, circumstances that were set to continue over the coming weeks. It may have been a period of great uncertainty for the British but in reality the March offensive was doomed from the start.

Chapter 1

Soldiers and Politicians

'In mid-February 1918 we started back to the line, a fine battalion stronger than it had ever been, nominally indeed over strength, though with men on command, on leave, on courses and detached elsewhere, we should probably muster only about a hundred and fifty per company in trenches.'

Captain Guy Chapman – 14th Battalion Royal Fusiliers

The failure of the last great offensive directed by Erich Ludendorff in 1918 stands as one of the most important of the whole conflict; its demise sealed the fate of the Central Powers and provided the catalyst for an Allied victory a little over seven months later. On 21 March 1918 the prospects for a German victory on the Western Front looked bright. Reinforced by the transfer of troops from the Russian Front and motivated with a new confidence, Germany rallied behind Ludendorff with an optimism similar to that seen prior to the beginning of the 1914 campaign. The dilemma facing Ludendorff was whether he could defeat the allied forces before the seemingly limitless manpower of the United States became a significant force to tip the balance in their favour on the Western Front. If he could break through the trench lines, hold the French and bottle–up the British Armies with a determined thrust to the Channel ports, Germany would be in a powerful position to dictate the terms of any armistice – just as they had on 3 March 1918 at Brest-Litovsk on the Eastern Front. The humiliating Brest-Litovsk Treaty not only marked Russia's withdrawal from the Great War but signed over territory to Germany that included a quarter of the Russian Empire's population, a quarter of its industry and nine-tenths of its coal mines. A similar fate awaited France and Belgium in the event of a German victory in the west. But first the seemingly impregnable allied fortifications on the Western Front had to be broken; a daunting prospect but one which, after successful German offensives at Riga and Caporetto several months earlier, had moved towards the realm of the possible.

On 1 September 1917 after a five hour hurricane artillery bombardment, eight German infantry divisions and two cavalry divisions under the command of General Oskar von Hutier attacked the Russian Army at Riga. Paralysed by the sudden and ferocious bombardment, the Russian defence collapsed under the weight of the German infantry onslaught which took full advantage of a demoralized and disorientated enemy. Three days later the treaty of Brest-Litovsk was signed and the war on the Russian Front effectively came to an end. Just under two months later a second offensive, this time in co-operation with their Austrian allies, was opened on the Italian Front around Caporetto. After a six-hour bombardment using gas and high explosive, the infantry assault – operating under a similar pattern to Riga – began at 8.00am. The Italians buckled in the face of fierce infiltration tactics that pushed forward in outflanking manoeuvres and precipitated a retreat that was only held on the banks of the River Piave. Caporetto was a humiliating defeat for the Italians; its shock waves so widespread that they were felt on the Western Front, prompting the urgent despatch of an Anglo-French force to shore up the efforts of the hard-pressed Italians.

Both offensives provided confirmation to the German High Command that they had perhaps finally resolved the problem of breakthrough which had long haunted British and French commanders on the Western Front. For the British, the belief that a tactical breakthough was possible was amply demonstrated – albeit rather belatedly and to the surprise of many – by the attack on Cambrai on 20 November 1917. Totally unconnected with Sir Douglas Haig's Third Ypres offensive towards the Passchendaele Ridge, the British offensive clearly caught the Germans on the back foot as tanks and infantry penetrated what was known to the Germans as the *Siegfried Stellung* and to the British as the Hindenburg Line. British success was swiftly reversed with a classic German counter-attack using the tactics employed at Riga and Caporetto. Heavily armed *sturmtruppen* supported by aircraft and a barrage of smoke, gas and high explosive aimed, not just at the British defences, but at the all important lines of communication. Where pockets of solid opposition were encountered by attacking troops they simply changed direction to find a gap elsewhere, leaving the enemy stronghold to be surrounded and dealt with by the next wave.

Cambrai could hardly be considered a victory in terms of casualties and territory, the British had taken a slice of the German line and, before their subsequent counter-attack lost its impetus, the Germans took an almost equal amount of the British line leaving only the salient around Flesquières as a reminder of success. There were, however, two important lessons to be learnt from the Cambrai affair, lessons that both sides failed to capitalise on. By far the most important was the successful use of tanks on the battlefield, a lesson apparently lost on the Germans at the time and later lamented in March 1918; the second was the acute breakdown of British command and control during the German counter-attack, a costly lesson in failure to which GHQ did not respond and one that would be replicated three months later during the open warfare of the German March offensive.

Ludendorff knew only too well that an offensive early in 1918 was the last throw of the dice for the Central Powers if they were to have any chance of winning the war. In the seven weeks that elapsed between the Brest-Litovsk Treaty and the signing of an armistice on 16 December 1917, Germany moved a multitude of men and material to the Western Front. This transfer of men continued into 1918 and by the end of February, Ludendorff had over seventy divisions ready for his assault in the west. For perhaps the first time since the trench lines were established at the end of 1914, Germany was in a position to break the deadlock on the Western Front.

The 53-year-old Ludendorff had risen quickly during the war years. With no 'von' to prefix his name his rise was the product of ability and hard work. In August 1914 he became Chief-of-Staff to Field Marshal Paul von Hindenburg on the Eastern Front and was very much to the fore in masterminding the defeat of the Russian Armies, a task that provided a platform for his elevation to joint head of the German Imperial Army with Hindenburg. This military partnership effectively established a dictatorship to offset the growing incompetence which appeared to cloud the judgement of Kaiser Wilhelm II. By 1917 Hindenburg and Ludendorff had already reached the inevitable conclusion that the Western Front was where overall victory would be decided, a view shared by their British adversary Douglas Haig, even if it was one that his political masters in Britian were still struggling with.

Despite the apparent 'consultation' process embarked upon by Ludendorff with his army commanders and their chiefs of staff, he had his own ideas on where the offensive should fall, his mind being fixed on the sector around St Quentin. If the line of the Somme from Péronne to Ham could be reached, then, by resting his left flank on Péronne and advancing northwest, the British line to the north could – in theory – be rolled up.

There was of course another agenda behind the offensive. By the end of 1917 Germany came face-to-face with the inevitable conclusion that the war could not continue for much longer. The British naval blockade had become one of the most efficient in modern history and consequently Germany was close to collapse. Food and raw materials, particularly rubber and oil were in short supply and there was a worrying increase in industrial unrest and strikes amongst munitions workers. Worse still, the civilian population was edging ever closer towards starvation. A group of influential industrialists had already declared that to continue the war into 1919 would place an intolerable strain on the economic situation as well as on the popular will of the people to continue the war. Already the mainstream press, led by the powerful *Frankfurter Zeitung* supported the view that the popular will was crumbling and the country was on the verge of demanding peace at any price. Even as late at February 1918, Germany's political leaders were urging a rapid peace, reminding Ludendorff of the unrest at home and the precarious economic situation. Opinion was already divided in Germany on this issue, both the Crown Prince Rupprecht and Kaiser Wilhelm were convinced that a military victory for Germany was almost impossible and even if it meant giving up Belgium, they both felt a negotiated peace was more acceptable than further fighting. To Ludendorff this alternative was incomprehensible and his obduracy over Belgium ensured any possible negotiations were condemned to failure.

To make matters worse, the Americans were beginning to arrive in force on the Western Front and if there was further delay in offensive action Germany would be swamped by the American build-up. Ludendorff felt he was left with little choice, a conviction he emphasized in his post war memoirs, 'the condition of our allies and of our army', he wrote, 'all called for an offensive that would bring about an early decision ... the offensive is the most effective means of making war; it alone is decisive'.

Ludendorff's final plan for breaking the Western Front deadlock adopted the codename 'Michael' and was focussed on either side of St Quentin along a fifty mile front from Gouzeaucourt in the north to La Fère in the south. In the centre Georg von der Marwitz's Second Army would thrust towards Péronne and encircle the Flesquières salient from the south, while to the north, Otto von Below's Seventeenth Army would pinch out the salient from the north and link up with the Second Army before advancing on Bapaume. In the south, Oskar von Hutier's Eighteenth Army would drive towards Ham on the Somme and form a buffer along the river against French reinforcements arriving from the south. A second attack some days after 'Michael' – codenamed 'Mars' – to be undertaken by the Seventeenth Army would take place on the Third Army around Arras.

Unlike his German counterpart, the British Commander-in-Chief Sir Douglas Haig was set to fight the battle of March 1918 on two fronts. Haig not only found himself under-fire from the weight of German forces that Ludendorff was gathering on the fronts held by his Third and Fifth Armies but also from the political hierarchy at home intent on eroding his authority in the field. It was a testing time for Haig and one which came after a year of disappointing offensives and soaring casualty figures.

1917 had promised much and delivered little and for British Prime Minister David Lloyd George the Battle of Cambrai was the straw that broke the camel's back. The heavy losses already suffered by the British Army in 1916 and 1917 had convinced him that Douglas Haig was not to be trusted and that to send more men to France would only encourage the Commander-in-Chief to send them to what Lloyd George described as the 'slaughter house of the Western Front'. Like Ludendorff and Hindenburg, Haig was convinced that the Western Front was where the final victory would be won, a view implacably opposed by Lloyd George, who felt that more effort should be devoted to the theatres of war outside of France where there was more evidence of success. Such evidence, he argued, was plain to see in Allenby's campaign in Palestine where Jerusalem had recently been taken, and on the Mesopotamian Front where Baghdad had recently been secured. Even in East Africa, he told parliament, things were going well. But rather than work with the military leadership, Lloyd George chose to confront and conduct a battle of intrigue which largely ignored the unshakeable display of facts and figures presented by the Chief of the Imperial General Staff, Sir William 'Wully' Robertson.

It was this increasingly confrontational stance with the military establishment in general and Sir Douglas Haig in particular which led to the culture of distrust and conspiracy that characterized the relationship between the two men. As much as Lloyd George wanted Haig's resignation, however, it was a step too far for the politician to dismiss him, a step that he was not prepared to gamble on given that his view of Haig was not universally shared nationwide. The consensus of opinion – which included that of the King – was that Haig, despite the casualties, was doing a good job in what were extremely difficult and trying circumstances. Not only that, Haig had the confidence of the army he commanded and there was simply no-one in the higher echelons of command in the Army who might be considered a suitable replacement.

As a result of his failure to unseat Haig, Lloyd George was forced to resort to alternative methods of imposing his authority over the Commander-in-Chief, and that included a tighter control over military strategy. If he could not directly replace Haig then the wily politician was content to employ political manoeuvring to achieve his aim, an opportunity that first arose at the Boulogne Conference of 25 September 1917.

At Boulogne strong pressure was exerted on the British Government by the French for the British Army to take over a larger proportion of the Western Front. It was a request that Lloyd George later recorded in his memoirs as 'one we could not refuse to consider'. On face value this was an entirely transparent response, however, in arriving at a decision he deceitfully neglected to consult Haig – whose attentions at the time were focused firmly on the Third Battle of Ypres. With yet more front line to manage, and given Lloyd George's blinkered understanding of matters military, an opportunity now presented itself to emasculate Haig's offensive intentions for 1918 by diluting the forces at his disposal.

Understandably Haig was furious over the decision to extend the line south to beyond Barisis, a decision taken by politicians which, despite an earlier promise that no discussion 'regarding operations on the Western Front would be held with the French without [his] presence', had happened anyway. Nevertheless, Lloyd George was quick to point out that Haig's fury over the extension to the front only betrayed the Commander-in-Chief's intentions for 1918 – a resumption of the campaign in Flanders – and in preventing this, the politician had achieved his aim. He was, of course, correct in this assumption. There is little doubt that given the men and materials, Haig would have resumed his Flanders offensive in the belief that one more push would break the deadlock on the Western Front.

The French case for an extension of the line centred on the principle that the share of the front line held by each of the two armies should be calculated on the mileage of the total front. On their portion of the line the French had adopted a passive defence, relying heavily on the strength of their artillery as a deterrent to German offensive action. On the other hand, the British had taken a more aggressive stance, characterized by frequent attacks and trench raids and as a consequence there were a greater number of German divisions opposite the British sector. Not only that, but the distance between the front line and the coast left little room for retirement, even a relatively modest German advance would bring the vital ports of Boulogne and Calais within range of German artillery.

In limiting the control exercised by Douglas Haig, Lloyd George and his War Cabinet now took steps to control the flow of manpower to the Western Front. From December 1917 the supply of reinforcements became the remit of the Cabinet Manpower Committee, a committee chaired by Lloyd George. The question of reserves generated debate within the army and at Westminster, the argument focussing upon the future direction of the war and how the increasing manpower shortage should be dealt with, giving rise to two opposing schools of thought. The first supported the use of the new technology on the battlefield in reducing manpower while the other argued for maintaining infantry numbers on the ground.

While the technologists advocated a greater use of tanks and aircraft they also drew attention to the use of gas, smoke and mobile trench mortars which together with the increased firepower of machine guns had begun to revolutionise the fighting on the battlefield. Those who supported a more traditional approach still advocated that the number of infantry – or rifle strength – a commander could put into the field was the all pervading factor and manpower should be increased accordingly. What was needed of course was a balance of both and although Haig appeared to agree that 'an insufficiency of infantry cannot be compensated for by a development of machinery beyond a certain point', it is more likely that he held fast to his belief in the classic infantry battle of attrition.

On 24 November 1917 GHQ advised that infantry manpower would be some 250,000 below establishment by 31 March 1918 and the subsequent request for an additional 615,000 reinforcements met with an almost predictable negative response from the Manpower Committee. In the event only 10,000 men were sent to France, which led to the accusation that Lloyd George and the Manpower Committee had failed to recognize the essential difference between ration strength – the number of men a battalion had 'on its books' – and rifle strength – the number of men available to fight. Sickness, training, men away on leave and casualties, not to mention stretcher bearers, signallers, cooks and other headquarters staff, all served to reduce the rifle strength of a battalion and it was not uncommon for a battalion of some 800 men only being able to put 500 fighting men into the front line.

But whatever the mechanics of the argument were, it still served to emphasize the basic flaw in Lloyd George's thinking: his failure to realize that by retaining reserves in England he might be postponing a new offensive in Flanders. In so doing he was limiting the army's ability to defend itself effectively against a possible German offensive by reducing the ability of commanders to call upon reserves when they were required. This denial of sufficient numbers of reserves would reach crisis point in March 1918.

Underlying this response lay Lloyd George's undoubted belief that the war would only be won after American forces had arrived in strength in 1919. But again, the Prime Minister's analysis for 1918 was unsound; the one factor he had not calculated in his equation was the presence of Ludendorff, a man who had no intention of waiting for the Americans to appear and tip the balance. Certainly by December 1917, as the number of German divisions in the west gradually increased, the overall significance of the collapse on the Eastern Front became clear to Haig and his staff. The predicament facing Douglas Haig was not necessarily how many divisions were arriving from the east – although this was undeniably an important element of the strategic reckoning – but where exactly the German offensive would fall along his line.

The protection of the channel ports was vital to the BEF's survival and the distance between them and the front line in the northern sector around the Ypres salient was tiny by comparison with distance between those same ports and the front lines held by the Third and Fifth Armies. In his appreciation of the wider strategic picture Haig concentrated the greater part of his reserves in the north and if the Germans did attack his Fifth Army front, as indeed many suspected, it was becoming obvious that the Fifth Army would have to bear the brunt of any assault for several days before they could expect to be reinforced.

Haig had already lost five British divisions which had been despatched as part of a Franco-British relief force to Italy in November 1917 after the Italian defeat at Caporetto in October. Now, despite his vigorous protests over the withholding of reserves, there was little to delay the decision taken in January 1918 by the Army Council to re-organize and reduce the strength of infantry divisions on the Western Front. Divisions would be reduced from twelve to nine battalions as a counter-weight to the crisis in manpower. Since the declaration of war in August 1914 British Army formations had been based upon divisions comprising of three brigades, each with four battalions of infantry. Now, on the eve of the German offensive this was to change by reducing the strength of each brigade from four to three battalions.

Like many brigade commanders, Brigadier General Hanway Cumming, commanding 110 (Leicester) Brigade, was of the opinion that the impact of this reorganization would be felt largely by the men themselves. With only three battalions in a brigade, the traditional rotation between front, support and reserve lines in effect extended the time each battalion would spend on front line duties.

Lieutenant David Kelly, the intelligence officer with 110 Brigade mourned the loss of the 9th Battalion Leicestershire Regiment, a battalion which had landed in France in July 1915. As the junior of the four Leicestershire battalions in the brigade he felt it was a case of last in first out:

'Our 9th Battalion was accordingly sacrificed and distributed among the other depleted battalions and henceforth we had to base our arrangement on a three battalion organization, making the relief of the battalions in the trenches much more difficult ... thus when the Germans began their last great throw of the dice on March 21st our left flank battalion (7th Leicesters) had been on duty in the front line during a period of anxiety and suspense for more than twenty days.'[1]

In other divisions the disruption was not quite as pronounced. In the 24th Division, for example, the 8th Battalion Queen's Royal West Surreys (8/Queen's) were moved to 17 Brigade and the 8th Battalion Royal East Kent and the 12th Battalion Royal Fusiliers were disbanded. In its turn the 9th Battalion East Surrey Regiment benefitted from a draft of nine officers and 100 other ranks from its sister battalion, the 7th East Surreys in the 12th Division. In the 30th Division Major Robert Gibbon, the acting commanding officer of the 16th Battalion Manchester Regiment, met the draft of men from the disbanded 17th Manchesters personally, going out of his way to make them feel at home:

'Your battalion is part and parcel of us. You were formed at the same time that we were. You trained in England in the same areas that we did. When the 90th Brigade was formed it consisted of the 16th, 17th, 18th and 19th Battalions and we came out to France in November 1915 in that formation ... I will therefore, conclude by giving you on behalf of Lieutenant Colonel Elstob, who is at present on leave, and on behalf of all ranks a most hearty welcome to our battalion.'[2]

A number of those men were destined to be with Colonel Elstob in the Manchester Redoubt west of St Quentin when the Germans attacked on 21 March 1918.

There were some divisions, such as the 9th (Scottish) Division, which were relatively fortunate when it came to reorganization. Brigadier General William Croft reckoned that they 'were one of the lucky divisions which only had to pass battalions on to someone else, and did not have to disband any, except in the case of the 3rd South Africans; but as their recruiting difficulty was always with them that didn't matter too much'.

Nevertheless the loss of some 175 battalions across the whole of the British Army undoubtedly disrupted morale and left little time for displaced drafts of officers and men to adapt to new battlefield structures and unfamiliar battalions. For the 'Tommy' in the front line his world tended to revolve around his section, platoon and company. It was an existence which was inevitably affected by the mass transfer of men to new units, a factor which also disturbed the stability of command that existed between officers, NCOs and men and which may have contributed to the apparent confusion and panic that was prevalent in some British units during the first forty-eight hours of the German March offensive.

The British soldier of March 1918 was the product of a four-year evolutionary process that had begun in 1914 with the professional Regular Army – the Old Comtemptibles. When war was declared in August 1914 those who had been born in the 1880s and 1890s responded to Lord Kitchener's call for volunteers and signed up for the duration; the famous recruiting poster depicting Kitchener above the words 'Wants You' was part of a very successful campaign which ultimately recruited over three million volunteers for the armed services. These men were the cream of their generation, men who had grown up hearing the tales and traditions of the British Empire, men imbued with a clear sense of duty who had no cause to doubt that a British victory was assured.

However, the casualty lists that cut swathes through Kitchener's New Army divisions in the battles of late 1915 and 1916 were probably the first indication for the general public that this was a war unlike any other. A generation of young men was slowly being consumed by a slaughter on the Western Front which was beyond the nation's experience. The five months over which the Battle of the Somme was fought accounted for over 513,000 men killed, wounded, missing or taken prisoner; a national catastrophe that touched almost every home in the country. In 1917 the Battles of Arras and Third Ypres were responsible for another half a million casualties with the Cambrai episode adding to an increasing number of killed and wounded. Yet amid all this sacrifice the front line hardly altered, the dead were buried daily, the wounded treated and those that could – a total of 1.5 million men were permanently disabled in the four years of war – were returned to front line service to continue the fight. Increasingly the front-line soldier found himself on a conveyor belt of chance that appeared to have no end.

The resulting manpower shortage and drop in the number of volunteers was partly relieved by the 1916 Military Service Act which introduced – for the first time in British history – conscription for men aged between 18 and 41; but a further two amendments were needed to extend the liability for military service to married men, and to increase the upper age limit to 51. Thus the soldiers who faced Ludendorff's divisions along the Fifth Army frontage in 1918 were not only part of the largest citizen army ever to leave our shores and fight on mainland Europe, but a blend of Territorials who had been deployed at the front since late 1914, Kitchener's New Army volunteers who had survived the Somme and the battles of 1917, conscripted men who began arriving in late 1916 and a smattering of the original 1914 regulars. Apart from the men of the Regular Army, which had arrived in France in August 1914, the remainder of the British soldiers of the early 1918 vintage had largely been trained in the troglodyte arts of trench warfare on the British-held sectors of the Western Front which had gouged its way across northern France and Flanders.

Hubert Essame, who served with the 2nd Battalion Northamptonshire Regiment in 1918, felt the mood of the 1918 soldier could be summed up as:

> *'One of stoical endurance combined with an element of bewilderment. Any desire they had ever had to attack the Germans had long since vanished ... Fifty years later the impression which remained of them was above all one of immense mutual loyalty and good nature. Order them to go forward and they would stoically advance, however intense the fire, order them to stand fast and they would stay till told to go or to the end. For the most part they were kind, sociable men ... they were unselfish and generous, as quick to go to the aid of a wounded enemy as of a wounded friend. They had one supreme quality, a capacity to endure without flinching prolonged bombardment and exposure greater than that of many soldiers of World War Two.'*[3]

Yet despite the fact these men were hardened to the realities and yes, to the horrors of war, there remained one major shortcoming, one which would bring them close to an unprecedented battlefield disaster. Unlike their German adversaries, they – and their regimental officers – were almost completely untrained in open warfare. The years of fighting from established trench lines had in effect de-skilled the soldier who was more at home in a hole in the ground than with the mobility of fire and movement that characterized the opening months of the war in 1914.

The great battles of attrition which took place in 1915 and 1916 had practically exhausted the pre-war regular and territorial officer corps, the greater proportion of those that had survived to see 1918 were now either serving on the staff or commanding battalions. Promotion was rapid for those of ability who were fortunate enough to survive, particularly amongst the young professional men who had volunteered for service in 1914; many of these men had also risen to battalion command and in some cases were even commanding brigades. One such individual was Lieutenant Colonel John Crosthwaite, a 1914 volunteer who found himself, at 26 years of age, in command of the 7th Battalion Royal West Kent Regiment after a rapid rise through the ranks, contrasting sharply with Lieutenant Colonel Basil Crockett, a 31-year-old regular officer in command of the 11th Battalion Hampshire Regiment, who at just five years older than Crosthwaite, was considered by many to be past his prime.

By 1918 the wave of public and grammar school boys who joined up in their droves had long since dried up; being the first to volunteer, their ranks had been devastated in the battles of 1916 and 1917 where the casualty rate for junior officers was disproportionately high. Now the platoon and company commanders were almost without exception second lieutenants with temporary ranks. Many were the product of promotion from the rank and file, men who had proved their worth under fire and were commissioned after a short spell in an officer cadet battalion. Typical of these 'temporary gentlemen' was Lieutenant Geoffrey Lester of the 2/4th Battalion London Regiment, a former clerk with the Standard Bank of South Africa who enlisted in November 1914. Wounded on the Somme in 1916 he served nearly two years at the front before he was commissioned at the end of 1916.

Subalterns such as Geoffrey Lester were the vanguard of the new breed of officer that would ultimately break down the pre-war class-ridden barriers that prevented able and courageous young men of less affluent backgrounds from taking on battlefield leadership. Hubert Essame believed that these young officers met the need of the hour:

> *'For them courage was the highest of the virtues; it was better to die than betray fear; as officers they must set the example, their duty to their men overrode all other considerations, suffering must be endured in silence. It was simple as that ... With their men they formed a cross-section of the tougher elements in the British people.'*[4]

Remarkably, despite the set-backs and failures of the previous three years, the vast majority of soldiers manning the front line in March 1918 still possessed an enduring determination to not only 'bring down the Hun', but had a faith in their ability to match the prowess of their German counterparts. It was a faith which was about to be tested to the extreme.

Chapter 2

The Battleground

'*Machine guns should be distributed in depth and sited for flanking fire so as to form impassable belts of fire.*'

Instructions from BEF General Headquarters.

The German offensive on 21 March involved a colossal attack by over thirty German divisions along fifty-four miles of the British front line between the River Scarpe in the north and the River Oise in the south. Known loosely as the Somme sector, it encompassed a stretch of the front that approximates the line of the modern day A26 Motorway.

As far as obstacles to an attacking enemy were concerned the only significant geographical barriers to a hostile advance were the River Somme south of Péronne and the Canal du Nord north of it. The Somme – Crozat Canal runs from the River Oise at Tergnier via St Simon to St Quentin in the north, the Crozat Canal being that section of the St Quentin Canal between the River Somme and the River Oise running roughly from St Simon to Tergnier.

The Somme itself is canalized from St Simon via Péronne to Amiens in the west with the numerous branches of the river and their associated marshes passable only on causeways. The River Somme between Péronne and Ham is a complex waterway with the river and canal running parallel through a wide shallow river valley; the canal, which lies west of the river, forms the principle navigable waterway some 58 feet wide and 6 feet deep. The only practical method of crossing the network of waterways and marshes was by the use of causeways and bridges. Lieutenant Claude Piesse, an Australian officer serving in the 8th Battalion Queen's West Surrey Regiment, (8/Queen's), thought the narrow causeway and bridge at St Christ Briost was just wide enough to take two lines of horse traffic and wondered if there would be a 'jam when a big battle was taking place and extra large quantities of ammunition, wagons and ambulances used the road'. As far as the other waterways were concerned – the Rivers Germaine, Omignon and Cologne – these only served to restrict lateral movement as they ran predominantly east – west, almost at right angles to the front line.

To the military eye much of the area was ideally suited to rearguard actions. The undulating nature of the terrain, consisting of small valleys and sunken roads, gave rise to areas of dead ground which was hidden from ground level observation which offered advantage to the defending forces. Furthermore, the area had a number of quarries dotted across the landscape where local inhabitants had sought building material; these in particular were ideally suited as defensive strong points or redoubts, such as the Enghien Redoubt and Cooker's Quarry. However, apart from the area west of a line running roughly from Arras – Albert – Roye, it was in effect, one endless area of devastation. The German retreat to the Hindenburg Line in March 1917 had reduced the ground to a desert.

The scene that met the British as they advanced in pursuit of the Germans almost a year previously was one of total desolation. 'The larger towns were literally razed to the ground. In hundreds of villages virtually every building was either blown up or burned down, trees were felled across roads, huge mines were exploded at important road intersections, every bridge over the Somme and other rivers was destroyed, railway lines were torn up, no supplies of any sort were left behind.'[1] Paul Maze, a French liaison officer attached to the Fifth Army, spent much of the period prior to the March offensive criss-crossing the area on his motorcycle visiting the various divisional and brigade HQs. His journeys left him in no doubt of the extent of the devastation. 'The only indication of a village', he wrote, 'was its name written on a large board and a few ruins, hardly showing above the overgrown weeds. The pavé road through the village was banked on both sides by mere heaps of bricks. There was no life about.'[2]

On the eve of the German attack the Fifth Army, under the command of 47-year-old Lieutenant General Hubert de la Poer Gough, held a front line of forty-two miles from Gouzeaucourt in the north to Barisis in the south where it joined General Auguste Duchêne's Sixth French Army. An outspoken individual, Gough was a general who was either loved or hated by those he commanded, a facet of his character that became only too clear in 1914 during the retreat from Mons when his maverick and insubordinate behaviour as commander of 3 Cavalry Brigade very nearly resulted in his dismissal. Haig intervened on his behalf and from the moment Gough came under the patronage of Haig's influence, his career rapidly progressed to that of army commander by 1916. He may have been an individual who possessed an abundance of optimism and decisiveness but his reputation had been scarred by a less than satisfactory performance on the Somme in 1916 and a year later during the Third Battle of Ypres. Certainly Lieutenant Claude Piesse was not one of his most ardent fans, describing him as the 'best hated man in France'.

It was the length of the Fifth Army frontage that had been the subject of so much political acrimony between Lloyd George and Douglas Haig and would bear the brunt of the German attack on 21 March. After the Third Battle of Ypres Gough and his Fifth Army had been placed in general reserve for a short period before being deployed to a new sector of the front running south from Gouzeaucourt to the River Omignon, a sector which had previously been the domain of the British Third Army. Almost a month later in January 1918, the Fifth Army relieved the French Third Army south of the Omignon to a point just south of St Quentin, a front that was extended two weeks later to the village of Barisis, south of the Oise River, which included nearly ten miles of the front running along the wide valley of the Oise. This sector, which was overlooked by the German front line, was, according to the French, 'inaccessible to the enemy, owing to the marshes'. Unfortunately, as the 2/2 London Regiment historian remarked, 'very little rain fell between 1st January and 21st March; the marshes dried up, the water channel narrowed and became shallow and fordable; and thus the river line had very little defensive value'.

Commanding the Third Army was 52-year-old General Julian 'Bungo' Byng. He was another cavalryman who rose from command of the 3rd Cavalry Division

in 1914 to command of IX Corps during the Gallipoli campaign of 1915, where he supervised the withdrawal of British Empire forces from the peninsula. By May 1916 he was commanding the Canadian Corps and, along with Major General Arthur Currie, led the Canadian capture of Vimy Ridge in 1917. In June of that year he was promoted to general and took command of the Third Army. Byng's Third Army held a front line of twenty-eight miles from the left of the Fifth Army at Gouzeaucourt to Gavrelle, some six miles northeast of Arras, a line which included the Flesquières salient which was all that was left of the ground captured during the Cambrai battle, ground that Byng would cling to stubbornly in March. To defend his sector Byng had fourteen divisions and some 1,200 guns for a front that was fourteen miles shorter and – in terms of the number of guns per mile – could muster forty per mile of front compared to thirty-seven per mile on the Fifth Army front. There was a further disparity: Gough had at his disposal twelve infantry divisions and three cavalry divisions together with just over 1,500 guns and was struggling to maintain two infantry divisions in reserve, while Byng was able to hold four divisions in reserve. Mindful of time and distance Gough was keen to bring his reserve units closer to his front in order for them to be deployed effectively should they be required but GHQ felt his request to be without foundation and refused. The effects of this short-sighted decision would become only too apparent as these divisions were flung into the battle too late.

The picture as far as the state of the Fifth Army defences was concerned was a mixed one and was hardly an ideal situation for Gough and his corps commanders to inherit. Even if the new system of defence in depth – framed by GHQ Instructions dated 14 December 1917 – was going to be implemented, the Fifth Army would be hard pressed to complete it in time to repel a German Spring offensive. In truth the British were struggling with the entire concept of defence in 1918; having been largely on the offensive for most of the war, senior officers and the units they commanded were now faced with implementing a scheme of defence in depth without any real understanding of how it worked in practice. The result was a patchwork of defensive positions and an extremely *ad hoc* approach to defence. 'They paid the Germans the compliment of copying the methods used against themselves in 1917', wrote Corelli Barnett, 'Unfortunately they copied the letter not the spirit.' The rigid top-down command prevalent in March 1918 appeared to stifle the flexibility of deployment. In the German system of defence in depth, infantry were deployed in support of the machine gun with two thirds of the troops retained as a mobile reserve for counter-attack. In the British version the proportions were reversed, with the machine gun subordinate to a defence that was based on the infantry.

Defence in depth relied upon three separate zones of defence. First and foremost was the Forward Zone in which defensive outposts depended largely upon the tactical features of the ground they occupied. There was no continuous front line here; troops were deployed either in what Paul Maze describes as 'lightly held outpost screens', or in redoubts which were situated behind the first line of defence. The Forward Zone – sometimes referred to as the outpost or advanced zone – was designed primarily to delay an enemy advance and force him to deploy in strength and, as some divisional orders made clear, was not to be reinforced. Troops in the Forward Zone were quite simply expected to hold on – or were they? Evidence suggests that there was considerable inconsistency in the orders given to troops in the Forward Zone by divisional and corps commanders. Orders depended very much on an individual interpretation by corps and divisional commanders of how the zones of defence should be used; the inconsistencies in these directives underlining an overall lack of understanding and an inability to coordinate the three zone defence in depth system. Tim Travers cites the example of instructions given to men in 140 Brigade:

> *'The Brigade Major of 140 infantry Brigade, in 47 Division, of Third Army, was told to fight for the front line and hold it at all costs. But on their immediate right 26 Brigade [9th Division, Fifth Army] was told that in the event of a serious attack, they were to fight for the battle zone and not for the forward zone.'*[3]

This apparently contradictory approach between the Fifth and Third Armies perhaps originated from GHQ's evident acceptance that in the worst case scenario the Fifth Army would have to fall back on the line of the Somme. Conflicting orders such as these would inevitably cause confusion – as indeed they did. But it went further than mere contradiction. According to Colonel Edmund Ironside, Gough had apparently been ordered to place at least 50 per cent of his machine guns behind his front line, an order he failed to implement, preferring, as Ironside later commented, not to do this, deriding 'the idea of not fighting for the front line'.[4] It was Gough's over manning of his Forward Zone – which was again in complete contrast to Third Army directives – that contributed much to the disintegration of the Fifth Army on the first day of the German offensive.

Behind the Forward Zone was the Battle Zone which, like the Forward Zone, was organized in up to three parallel defensive systems with inter-connecting communication trenches. Built into the system were further strong points designed for all-round fire. But in effect this was never really achieved. Each strong point was designed to have interlocking arcs of fire with those on either flank and although this was completed in some sectors, much of the work was negated by the dense fog that covered the ground on 21 March. The Battle Zone was the area in which an attacking force was to be held – in effect a killing zone that could be reinforced quickly and where the main battle would be conducted and won – except there was one fatal flaw: there were very few reinforcements to be had.

The third zone, dubbed the Rear Zone, was designed to be another battle zone but, particularly in the Fifth Army sector, it had not actually been completed.

The Royal Engineers' (RE) historian described the rear zone as merely spit-locked, 'or at best, excavated to a depth of one foot, but subsequent experience showed that troops retreating in the dark – or even in daylight – could not be directed to halt on a spit-locked line, if indeed they ever saw it'.

One staff officer serving with the 14th Division was dismayed that all the divisional defence preparations were continually under scrutiny from the air:

> *'Day after day I saw German aeroplanes fly low over our positions as and when they pleased. I have personally seen German airmen wave their hands at our people and have seen them dropping bombs on our working parties digging trenches in the Battle Zone. You must therefore understand that every trench that was dug by us was at once photographed by the Germans and was, on 21 March, blown out by shell fire ... in consequence every strong point and platoon post on 21st was drenched with gas to start with and then shelled to blazes.'*[5]

When III Corps took over the southern sector of the line from the French on 29 January they found a well-prepared Forward Zone but nothing behind it. Their answer to constructing a Rear Zone was to make strong points at the rear of the Battle Zone which accounted for the close proximity of the 2/2 London's strong points to their Forward Zone outposts opposite La Fère. In fact this was hardly a defence in depth at all; both the Forward and Battle Zones were confined by the line of the Oise-Sambre Canal on the right, and the St Quentin Canal on the left – a distance which, in places, was not much in excess of two miles. Compare that to the situation west of Gouzeaucourt in the 9th Division sector where the Forward Zone near Vaucelette Farm was nearly two miles in depth and the Battle Zone occupied a further three miles. To be frank, the Fifth Army Battle Zone – like the Rear Zone – was still incomplete on the opening day of the offensive, particularly in the sector south of St Quentin down to the Oise.

Understandably there was considerable uneasiness amongst the troops over this new defensive system. Many of the 'old hands' referred to the strong points as 'birdcages' and grumbled about the lack of a continuous trench line. Soldiers will always find something to grouse about but in this case their protests had foundation. As we know, the British Army on the Western Front had been used to fighting from two lines of parallel trenches since the end of 1914 and was totally unprepared for the fundamental change that was brought about by defence in depth. The worst of these uncertainties was perhaps with regard to the distance between redoubts in the Forward Zone. In many divisional areas there was no communication between battalion headquarters and the redoubts and, often or not, they were not sited to be mutually supporting. Where communication lines were in place, the opening German barrage on 21 March destroyed many of these vital links and isolated the redoubts from their forward posts, and, as it turned out, there was very little to prevent enemy infantry from breaking through between strong points and continuing the advance almost unhindered. But what was more disquieting was that some divisional and brigade commanders, while conscious that their troops were being asked to fight in unfamiliar circumstances, were also unsure themselves how to conduct a defence in depth.

North of St Quentin the three brigades of the 24th Division held the sector around Le Verguier. Lieutenant Claude Piesse found himself in command of a number of outposts in the Forward Zone and his description of the headquarters post at Shepherd's Copse did not inspire confidence:

'All the posts were badly equipped for defence, the HQ worst of all. The field of fire over the 180 degrees towards the enemy varied from 25 yards to nil over about 160 degrees, the remaining 20 percent, though much better, also enabled the enemy to infiltrate the entire position. On arrival at the post I examined the supplies – there was a limited amount of rifle ammunition, not a single grenade, a number of drums of water, which I had the curiosity to open and found them so tainted with petrol as to be undrinkable ... it was under these conditions that I had written orders not to return and fight it out.'6

Although Piesse's experience was by no means representative of the whole picture, it was one that was replicated in many brigade areas. The shortcomings in Piesse's sector were without doubt exacerbated by the acute shortage of manpower, which, together with a lack of time in which to prepare defences, was beginning to raise the issue of defence to crisis point. In the III Corps sector for example, RE units in the shape of 4/Siege Company and 365/Forestry Company were in place by 1 February but 182 Tunnelling Company took another week to arrive. The entrenching units were delayed until 14 February and the final RE units only arrived on 7 March, a mere two weeks before the offensive began. 'It was a pity,' lamented Major General Noel 'Curly' Birch on 10 February, 'that we ever had to take over the extra front.'

In his position as artillery adviser to GHQ, Birch's concern lay not only in the lack of guns per mile of Fifth Army front but also with the deployment of artillery batteries in the new defence zones. Rather than deploy in more formal gun lines, artillery commanders were obliged to adopt a more mobile framework to give each of the battle zones sufficient coverage. Major Kenneth Cousland commanding 462/Battery, Royal Field Artillery (RFA) recalled filling his 'days and nights preparing main battle stations that were to be held if the front lines were overrun, reconnoitring reserve positions and OPs, registering targets and working out barrages'. Battery positions such as Cousland's that were within 3,000 yards of the front line were strongly wired in and prepared as defensive positions which the infantry could fall back upon if necessary. Great importance was given to Forward Observation Officers (FOO) having a good all-round view of the ground ahead so as to direct observed fire, particularly as the threat of

German tanks was considered to be a very real one. So much emphasis was given to this, that around 10 per cent of the 18-pounder stock was installed in the forward areas for use as anti-tank weapons. In the event this proved to be a complete waste of resources and, as Birch acknowledged, such a deployment 'created a greater set of communication difficulties'.

For the troops on the ground this 'new fangled' defence meant only one thing, each brigade – now reduced to three battalions – would deploy one battalion to the Forward Zone and a second the Battle Zone, leaving one in support with each battalion of the brigade taking their turn in each of these positions. It was a system of defence that Chaplain 3rd Class Father Henry Gill, who was attached to the 36th Division southwest of St Quentin, had serious misgivings about:

'There was no system of communication trenches between the forward area and [the Battle Zone]. *In fact there was no question or possibility of the battalion holding the front line being supported or relieved – or of getting away – except at night. I understand the forward battalion was expected to hold out for at least forty-eight hours before there would be any question of relief! It is not surprising that the people in the front trenches had anxious views on the whole position, and as the time of the attack was, of course, unknown, everyone in the division had an interest in the matter ... it was quite clear to me that anyone who might happen be in the front line when the attack took place would never get back alive ... it was a toss-up as to which battalion of each brigade would be sacrificed'.*[7]

'Sacrificed' was a word used by Lieutenant Colonel Charles Howard-Bury, commanding the 9th Battalion King's Royal Rifle Corps (9/KRRC) in the 14th (Light) Division. Charles Howard-Bury clearly felt quite troubled over his battalion's limited prospects should it find itself in the forward zone on the day of the German attack; it would, he predicted, be wiped out without any hope of assistance from the remaining battalions of 42 Brigade. With the possibility of counter-attack apparently ruled out – which was contrary to the German view of defence in depth – Howard-Bury understood the dilemma facing those troops in the Forward Zone:

'The troops of a Forward Zone or Outposts, or whatever you may choose to call those in front of the main line of defence, may accomplish their task in one of two ways. They may fall back fighting, in which case they are certain to mask the fire of the troops behind them, a very serious matter in these days of complicated artillery barrages; or they may stick it out to the last man. Now, no-one will deny that there are occasions when one part of a force must be sacrificed to save the rest, when troops must be expected to stick it out until the last man; but is it wise to make it a matter of routine?'[8]

Knowing his men and understanding what he called 'human frailty', he recognized instantly that if a soldier knows there is even a remote chance of relief he will generally stand fast and fight, but if there is no chance of relief the temptation to surrender before the last round has been expended is often an overwhelming one. A similar sentiment was echoed by Captain Charles Miller, a company commander with the 2nd Battalion Royal Inniskilling Fusiliers (2/Inniskillings):

'The British army has certain shibboleths, one of which, and it has cost the lives of scores of thousands of soldiers, is that when you are attacked in overwhelming force you mustn't run away. The French, who are much more logical than we, and who consider results and not prestige, invariably run away under such circumstances, and when the right moment comes run back again and deliver a counter-attack.'[9]

Many senior officers harboured serious doubts about the distinct lack of reserves that were available for counter-attack purposes. Lieutenant Colonel Thomas Mudie, on the staff of the 9th Division, felt it was 'suicidal' to have no strong reserves, a factor he felt was responsible:

for the rapid disintegration of long stretches of the Fifth Army front and the loss of whole battalions, who sacrificed themselves heroically, but who have done much more good had they been in touch with one another and retired fighting.'[10]

Exactly how many of the surviving units in the Forward Zone actually did run away on the morning of 21 March will never be known, but 'human frailty' would have ensured there were plenty who preferred captivity to a battlefield death unless, as Claude Piesse remarked, they were under an officer who was willing to hold out until the bitter end himself – but, as Piesse himself acknowledged, many of them did not do so.

The manpower question continued to raise its head again and again as the need to dig and prepare the defensive line became the prime task. Despite Lloyd George's assertion that the labour force was quite adequate for the task in hand, it was obvious to those who were actually in the front line that the labour force would have to be supplemented with troops. It was a source of much discontent amongst battalion commanders who, intent upon training their men and coping with front line duties, were constantly distracted by the need to supply digging parties. Writing to his wife on 5 March 1918, Lieutenant Colonel Rowland Fielding, in command of the 6th Battalion Connaught Rangers (6/Connaughts) who were positioned just south of Épehy, despaired over the amount of time his battalion had spent in front-line duty:

'The battalion wants a rest. It had been up for forty-two days when, last night, it was relieved, and even now I doubt if the rest is in sight, since an order has just

come in to go up to-morrow for the day to dig. I leave you to imagine the state of the men's bodies and clothing, after so long a time in the line, almost without a wash'.[11]

No-one, it appeared, was immune from the constant demands of the working party. Lance Corporal William Sharpe, serving with the 2/8th Battalion Lancashire Fusiliers, was in charge of a wiring party in the 197 Brigade sector, north of St Quentin. Since 15 March he and his detail had been regularly wiring their positions:

'Each night when it was dark, 12 nice lads and myself got gingerly over the parapet and took iron stakes and spools of barbed wire and constructed nervously, and as quietly as possible, barbed-wire fences, getting into all sorts of tangles, dropping down when the 'zip-zip-zip' of machine gun bullets came too close (i.e. when one 'felt' the whistle), and standing stock still like tree trunks when the firework display (Very lights) went up.'[12]

Charles Miller, recognizing that time was against him, attempted to keep up the spirits of his men by delivering a lecture on what he called 'this new idea in defence', but much to his annoyance the four days spent in so-called 'reserve' was generally taken up with digging the defence lines. He recounts an occasion when Brigadier General William Hessy, commanding 109 Brigade, decided in his wisdom to alter the positions of several strong points the battalion had been working on for several days:

'The appalling and crass stupidity of it all! Putting up barbed wire entanglements at night time is a hard enough job in itself, but we reached the point where we had to uproot the entanglements we had previously erected on abandoned sites, cart them off and erect them on new sites, which is simply Herculean labour. And all this had to be done on the nights we were supposed to be resting.'[13]

But there was a far more serious outcome to a scenario that working parties on other divisional fronts would have instantly recognised. Miller evidently understood the need to find a balance between training his men to fight in the new defensive zone and that of preparing the defences. It was an unenviable task and one he felt was in great danger of tipping in favour of the enemy:

'In the first place the men were tired to death; in the second place, since the position of the strong points was constantly being changed it was impossible to organize a regular drill by which every man knew his strongpoint and got there in the quickest possible time when ordered to do so; lastly, instead of being deeply dug, strongly revetted and wired it was quite obvious that when the moment came to use them, the strong points would hardly be strong enough to keep out a well-aimed snowball.'[14]

What really concerned Miller, along with Piesse, Charles Howard-Bury and others, was that when the offensive actually began, it was highly unlikely the Germans would be armed with snowballs. Had they been asked in hindsight, all three would probably have lent their support to the argument that one of the key contributory factors to the German success on 21 March was the failure of a defensive system that was incomplete and not fully understood and implemented by senior commanders.

* * *

Apart from the infantryman, the remaining fighting troops of an infantry division in 1918 were made up from the artillery and 'sappers' of the RE Field Companies. The sapper was a fighting soldier whose qualities had been demonstrated during the retreat from Mons in 1914 which had begun unexpectedly after a single day's fighting and, except at Le Cateau, heavy fighting was generally avoided. The four infantry divisions at Mons had two companies of RE per division and a supply of explosive material that was limited to what could be carried on the field company carts. Despite this, the field companies excelled in what were extremely trying circumstances. After the trench lines became established at the end of 1914, the RE settled down to the drudgery of trench warfare along with the rest of the army and for many of the young soldiers serving along the Third and Fifth Army fronts in March 1918 – and indeed a good proportion of the sappers themselves – the RE were perceived as a builder of dug-outs and the provider of trench-boards and revetting materials. The German offensive changed all that, and to use the words of Lieutenant Colonel Reginald Butterworth, the Chief Royal Engineer Officer (CRE) with the 16th Division, 'the sapper came into his own again, laying down his shovel to pick up a rifle'.

Towards the end of 1917 when GHQ considered the notion of demolition schemes, discussion inevitably stumbled across the thorny question as to who was responsible for preparing the destruction of French controlled railway bridges, track and rolling stock. Anxious not to tread on the toes of the French, GHQ fudged the matter, accepting that when the time came the French would, if it became necessary, carry out their own demolitions. Sadly this did not always happen, and when the time did arrive it was left to the Fifth Army engineers to destroy over 250 bridges for which their ally had responsibility while others were left intact and fell into enemy hands. Typical of this 'misunderstanding' was the failure to completely demolish the railway bridge at Pithon, allowing German infantry to cross the Somme Canal at that point. It was, in the judgment of many RE officers, an example of where the 'British should have retained the responsibility of dealing with all the bridges in their fighting area'.

Those RE officers who fought at Mons and during the subsequent retreat would all agree that the nature of demolitions carried out in 1914 were substantially different to those of 1918. For a start there was a demolition plan in existence in 1918 and bridges and supply dumps had been reconnoitred and numbered; there was even a list of demolition arrangements lodged with the CRE of each division. But the plan was incomplete, particularly as a number of bridges had been constructed after the plan had been completed! Writing with the benefit of hindsight in 1933, the Fourth Army Chief Engineer, Major General Reginald Buckland, highlighted what he saw as the basic shortcoming in the plan:

> '*Defence works were pushed on as labour became available, and many additional bridges were built to improve communications, causing constant additions to the schemes for demolitions ...* [even when] *an attack on a vast scale was felt to be imminent, there seems to have been no apprehension that the battle zone and rear zone might be overrun before reinforcements from outside of the army would arrive. Consequently we find complete schemes of demolitions prepared back to the line of the Somme and the Tortille, but behind those rivers little work of that nature was done before the fighting began.*'[15]

Buckland also drew attention to the tactical necessity of keeping bridgeheads and crossing points under fire to prevent the enemy's bridging equipment from being brought into use. The CRE to XVIII Corps, Lieutenant Colonel John Craster, had also raised this issue: 'there was no bridge over the Somme, or the canal, the demolition of which need delay the enemy's field artillery for more than two hours, unless the bridge was kept under rifle or machine gun fire at close range'. It appeared that no-one was listening at the time or perhaps no-one was prepared to put his head above the parapet and shout loud enough.

Bridges and their destruction were usually the responsibility of the corps concerned but to make matters more complex, some bridges were under the control of Army Headquarters. As the retreat unfolded the hierarchical command structure that the BEF insisted upon, broke down as positional warfare gave way to a rapidly moving warfare. In these circumstances some Corps commanders failed to carry out their responsibilities while others felt constrained by army orders which failed to materialize in time for demolition to be carried out.

The bridges behind the Fifth Army front were either of British construction or built by the French after the German retirement to the Hindenburg Line in 1917. The larger British constructions were supported by steel girders but the vast majority were timber bridges of all patterns and sizes. Very few were more than a few feet above the water level which in March 1918 was very low. Lieutenant Colonel Arthur Walker, CRE to XIX Corps was concerned that bridge demolition alone would have a limited effect on an advancing enemy:

> '*I am of the opinion that a great deal of the destruction herein arranged for can be easily made good by the enemy, owing to the width of the streams being small and*

the beds of the streams being merely a few feet below the bridge roadway. I think the enemy could be held up to an equal degree by blowing several large craters in roads as that through the marshland at St Christ.[16]

It was a point that Fifth Army Headquarters did consider briefly before deciding that all available tunnellers were better employed in the construction of dugouts, a move that might be considered as short sighted. Causeways and roads across the Somme marshes, such as those at Brie and St Christ Briost, could have been easily cratered and the potential disruption to the enemy was one that was even obvious to the infantry. In his role as battalion Transport Officer, Lieutenant Claude Piesse had visited the St Christ Briost bridgehead before the offensive began:

'No arrangements had been made to blow the earthen causeway [at St Christ Briost]. *The wooden bridge would be replaced by the enemy in probably a couple of hours, but if the causeway had been properly blown, it would probably have been a two day delay.*'[17]

Piesse had no way of knowing that his view was shared by Major General Gerard Heath, the Engineer in Chief at GHQ, who even tabled the importance of the destruction of roads and causeways on 28 February; sadly his advice, and that of Piesse, who forwarded his observations to Divisional Headquarters, were ignored.[18]

* * *

Much has been written of the German preparations for the March offensive of 1918 and the use of storm troops or *sturmtruppen* and the battlefield tactics employed by them. These cutting edge troops were certainly effective – as had been seen at Cambrai during the German counter-attack – but their tactics were not developed on the Eastern Front as is often supposed. The first *sturm-bataillion* was formed under *Hauptmann* Wilhelm Rohr – *Sturm Bataillon Nr. 5 (Rohr)* – who famously led the battalion in taking the *Hartmannsweilerkopf* during December 1915. Typically each *sturm-bataillon* would consist of three infantry assault companies, a machine-gun company, a mortar company and an infantry artillery battery – armed with up to four 37mm guns – and a *Flammenwerfer* section. Ian Passingham and others agree that storm battalions were both a blessing and a curse, pointing to 'their more elite status [which] led to the stripping out of the best infantry soldiers, NCOs and officers in many line infantry battalions for specialist training, so that the parent unit was weakened'.[19] It also appears that the term storm troops was one loosely applied to high quality troops on both sides, German sources prior to 1918 occasionally referred to attacking British units as *sturmtruppen* although these references may have been aimed at Dominion troops who also utilized speed, aggression and fire-power as their *modus operandi*. One of the great myths of the March offensive often focuses on the superiority of the German *sturmtruppen* and the inadequacy of the British troops. Clearly the German front line attacking troops were of very high quality and extremely well trained but we should certainly not dismiss the number of exceptionally good British divisions and brigades who fought just as well and about whose exploits this book is primarily concerned.

German units were trained to advance at speed, taking full advantage of openings in the British defence lines. The artillery creeping barrage was designed to maintain pace with the infantry and the forward units were under orders to advance until they were exhausted. No daily objectives were set for these units, Ludendorff quite rightly assuming that if daily tactical objectives were set, troops would be inclined to dig-in once these had been achieved, slowing the impetus of the advance. It is practically impossible to put an accurate figure on the numbers of storm troops taking part in the 21 March 1918 attack but somewhere in the region of 6,000 is thought to be a reasonable estimate. Another of the myths of the March offensive was that every attack was spearheaded by storm troops, an impossibility given the limited numbers of these troops which adds weight to the consensus that storm troops were allocated to sectors where a particularly strong defence was anticipated. In other sectors German commanders did what their British counterparts would do in similar circumstances; allocated their best divisions to lead the attack.

Apart from the veteran 'Easterner' Oscar von Hutier, whose reputation followed him to the Western Front, Ludendorff brought in *Oberst* Georg Bruchmüller who is sometimes credited – quite incorrectly – with masterminding the whole of the German artillery plan for 21 March. There was in fact no single artillery commander and while important to von Hutier, Bruchmüller was not the key figure he is often made out to be. However, he did introduce a new approach to artillery offensives and his experience did – with Ludendorff's backing – influence the Seventeenth and Second Army barrages, but in effect he was only directly responsible for the Eighteenth Army artillery.

For much of the war artillery bombardments prior to offensive action had achieved mixed results, any element of surprise was immediately lost by the protracted and intense bombardment on enemy lines which only served to loudly announce the forthcoming infantry attack. Serving on the Eastern Front on the staff of the 86th Infantry Division, Bruchmüller introduced the short 'hurricane' bombardment that was designed to take out all the enemy defences from the front line emplacements to the gun lines at the rear. In short he advocated a saturation barrage using a mixture of high explosive, gas and smoke which would neutralize the enemy's defences, prevent or inhibit counter offensive action and disrupt the effectiveness of command and control centres. Firing ahead of the infantry in what was a totally predicted timetable, the infantry were able to advance with the guns. Such a bombardment preceded the infantry assault at the Battle of Lake Naroch in March 1917 and again at Riga six months later. Both battles were a complete vindication of his methods and earned him the nickname of *Durch-Bruchmüller*.[20] Bruchmüller's artillery preparations and methodology may well have influenced the other two artillery commanders as by 20 March the German front from Arras to La Fère boasted 6,473 guns and 3,532 mortars in support of Ludendorff's three German armies that were spearheading the attack.

Incredibly the Germans managed to conceal their offensive intentions from the French and British with remarkable skill. For months the withdrawal of divisions from the front line for training and reorganisation had taken place without attracting attention, attack divisions had been assembled in the rear of the line, well beyond the reach of observing aircraft, while the more obvious dumps of ammunition and gun positions had been well camouflaged. Finally towards the middle of March the huge concentration of men and materials began moving up to the front, marching by night and concealing their movements by day.

By way of contrast to the meticulous preparation that went into the infantry and artillery attack, the more mundane but essential aspects of transport appears to have been neglected by Ludendorff. Randal Gray's observation that 'Ludendorff had no arm of exploitation beyond his men's feet, the hooves of insufficient and underfed horses and motor transport often on iron tyres (owing to the rubber shortage)', is a crucial one and points to the shortages of basic raw materials. Horses were in short supply as were motor vehicles, and those that were in service were more often than not fitted with iron 'tyres'. These would prove to be practically useless in crossing the battlefield as would the nine tanks prove to be ineffectual against the greater numbers possessed by the allied forces. Yet the March offensive did see Germany's first A7V *Sturmpanzerwagen* in action, five of which were deployed north of St Quentin – although two had broken down before the attack. They would be in action again near Villers-Bretonneux when three A7Vs met three British Mark IVs in what has been declared as the first tank versus tank battle in history.

On the night of 20 March Charles Miller received word that the expected German attack was imminent and there was to be no question of retreat: 'I had time to make a visit to one of the points occupied by my platoons. I hated the look of it: a couple of dug-outs, hastily made and inadequately wired, and I wished I had disobeyed orders and put them in one of the previously discarded strong-points'. It was only a matter of hours before *Kaiserschlacht* would be unleashed and Miller along with thousands like him would soon be tested to the limit of their endurance by a revitalized and powerful enemy intent on ending the war once and for all.

Chapter 3

173 Brigade and the Defence at La Feré

I still hoped against hope that we should be reinforced, as the colonel had kept rubbing it in at conferences before the battle that we had to stand fast at all costs.
Lieutenant Geoffrey Lester – C Company, 2/4
London Regiment at Triangle Post.

Lieutenant General Richard Butler began the war in command of the 2nd Battalion Lancashire Fusiliers; rapid promotion saw him take up his appointment as General Officer Commanding (GOC) III Corps just as his three infantry divisions were moving into the line on the extreme right flank of the Fifth Army. It was his first corps command. Moving into position in the La Fère sector was the 58th (London) Division, commanded by Major General Albemarle Cator. Cator's ten battalions took over nine-and-a-half miles of the front line extending from just north of Travecy, where it joined the 18th (Eastern) Division on its left, to the junction with the French south of Barisis. Beyond Travecy to the north the 14th (Light) Division held the line to Itancourt, some three miles, southeast of St Quentin. The whole III Corps sector covered seventeen miles of front line which Butler had to defend with twenty-seven below strength front line battalions and three battalions of pioneers.

Had the preceding months been wet, the level of the water in the Oise Canal and their associated marshes may well have presented a natural defensive obstacle to any enemy incursion south of Vendeuil. Unfortunately very little rain had fallen since December reducing the defensive value of the river line to the extent that Lieutenant Colonel Archibald Richardson, commanding 2/2 London Regiment, 173 Brigade, dismissed the Oise marshes as an obstacle that was more apparent than real. More worrying to Richardson was the inability of the battalion to bring any significant weight of firepower on the canal to prevent the enemy from bridging the waterway or indeed to check a determined enemy from crossing the marshes.

Richardson was the archetypical territorial officer; he fought with distinction in South Africa as a volunteer, returning home to study for a first class honours degree in mathematics. Commissioned into the Territorial Force in 1909, he was assistant professor of mathematics at Imperial College London from 1912–14 and although he was clearly destined for an academic lifestyle, it was one he shared with the demands that came with his 'part-time' soldiering. Richardson was appointed to command 2/2 Londons in January 1917, four months later he won a DSO for his leadership at Bullecourt, an engagement in which the battalion lost eight officers and 168 other ranks killed, wounded or missing. The battalion historian, Major William Grey, noted that Richardson was a 'hard taskmaster' that 'always demanded that his battalion should be efficient in the one thing that really mattered more than all else – its ability to attack'. It was now about to experience the confusion of retreat.

On the night of 15/16 March 2/2 Londons relieved the 3rd Battalion in the Forward Zone who then went into brigade reserve at Viry-Noureuil. In deploying his men to the four fortified areas of the Forward Zone he must have hoped that the German attack would come after they had been relieved. The zone was approximately 1,000 yards in depth and relied on small company strength redoubts interspersed with machine gun positions; on paper the defences looked good but in reality the length of frontage they defended was far too much for one under-strength battalion. Despite the enormous amount of work that had been put into strengthening these defences they were in no position to hold the four divisions of Georg von Gayl's *Gruppe Gayle* who were now massing opposite them.

Whatever fears Richardson may have had as his battalion moved into the Forward Zone he kept them to himself as his companies took over the main defensive redoubts. D Company was on the right flank around the Japy steel works, sandwiched between the St Quentin Canal and the Chauny-Laon railway line. In command was Captain John Howie who joined the battalion in July 1917 as a second lieutenant and won an MC three months later during the Third Battle of Ypres. North of the railway line situated in and around the Luzerne Quarry and the ruined artillery barracks on the D338, was the Main Keep where Richardson and C Company were based. B Company, commanded by Captain Leonard Bindon, held the Brickstacks locality which took its name from the nearby brickworks on the D55 and stretched from the bridge at Faubourg St Firmin north towards the village of Travecy which was held by A Company and Captain Maurice Harper. Between the main posts of defence were smaller platoon-held posts such as Railway Post which was south of the Main Keep covering the railway bridge which was one of the few Forward Zone posts that could fire directly onto the canal crossings.

The Battle Zone was the preserve of 2/4 Londons and occupied a depth of some 2,000 yards and consisted of isolated redoubts which were wired in and benefitted from interlocking fields of fire. Commanding the 2/4 was Lieutenant Colonel William Dann who took command of the battalion in November 1916 after being transferred from the Bedfordshire Regiment. Dann's headquarters was at Fargniers at the junction of the Crozat and St Quentin Canals close to A Company who occupied the Fargniers South sector while B Company, less two platoons, was positioned further north in what was known as Fargniers North. Further north still, around Rouge Farm – marked on present day maps as Tournevelles – Captain Charles Clarke commanded the men of D Company. Here the ground opened out towards Triangle Post which was over 1,000 yards further north and had been dug into a triangle of sunken roads on the D557. Commanding the Triangle and the men of C Company was Lieutenant Geoffrey Lester. Lester was typical of many regimental subalterns in 1918 in that he had served his time in the ranks before becoming commissioned. After enlisting into the 4th Battalion he found himself in Gallipoli as part of the Royal Naval Division, a sojourn that would keep him away from the Western Front until he joined the 2/4 Battalion in February 1917.

The two remaining platoons of B Company were divided between Distillery Post – near the junction of the Crozat and St Quentin Canals – and Condren, where Lieutenant Brown's platoon and a party of fifty-eight officers and men of the Oxfordshire Hussars held the line east of the canal. South of Condren the line was held by the two remaining 58th Division brigades. A little to the north of Fargniers on the eastern side of the Crozat Canal, Brigadier General Rivers Worgan, commanding 173 Brigade, had established his HQ in the château at Quessy where there was also a company of divisional pioneers in the form of Captain Harry Staddon and the 4th Battalion Suffolk Regiment.

The initial German bombardment – *Trommelfeuer* – that broke over the British lines on 21 March destroyed communications and effectively paralysed command and control on the battlefield. It was a paralysis that contributed significantly to the almost total disintegration of the Fifth Army as it began to fall back towards the line of the Somme River. Remembered by all who experienced it, the opening barrage seared the memories of men along the whole front line. Second Lieutenant Geoffrey Lawrence, serving with A Company, 1st South African Regiment in the 9th (Scottish) Division, had just returned from leave and spent most of the previous day nervously waiting for the storm to burst. His experience was one that was shared by practically every unit along the forty-two miles of front line held by the Fifth Army:

'*The next morning at a quarter to five the German barrage came down with a thunderous crash from thousands of guns of all sizes. We lit our candles and burrowed as close as we could get to the ground. First a shell blew one door in and then the other near me. The candles went out and we groped for our gas helmets in the dark. Splinters of metal were making sparks as they fell through just above us and the din was quite indescribable. Soon amongst the high explosive shells falling all around we heard the unmistakeable plop plop, as gas shells mixed with the others and the burnt potato or onion smell warned us it was time to put on our gas helmets.*'[1]

Evan Lloyd, commanding the 9th Manchester Regiment, 198 Brigade, in front of St Quentin recalled 'a terrific bombardment opening all down the line, it sounded like the bubbles bursting in a huge cauldron of boiling oil. The smell of gas is overpowering'.

On the III Corps front the fog began to rise long before the opening barrage, increasing the sense of loneliness and isolation that crept along the Forward Zone outposts. On the afternoon of 20 March the order to 'prepare for attack' had been sent out to all III Corps units and for the previous fourteen hours they had been waiting. When the bombardment did begin it was almost a relief for the 2nd Londons:

> *'The German guns rent the air, and shattered the stillness of the dawn, the long threatened attack had come at last. The bombardment was stupendous; great columns of flying earth shot skyward as the shells burst in sheets of orange flame; the ground shook with the continuous explosions; the noise rose in volume until it became deafening, and the opening of the British guns in reply passed almost unnoticed.'*[2]

To this concentration of artillery – roughly 100 guns per 1,000 yards of front – were added the trench mortar batteries which had been brought well forward to take out the Forward Zone outposts. The bombardment lasted until sometime after 7.00am but the first enemy units were crossing the Oise Canal in several places with floating bridges before it finally concluded.

The actual time of the infantry attack is indefinite but from the scant evidence available it would appear to have been between 6.30 and 7.00am. There is little doubt that the presence of a thick fog which lay over the Oise marshes aided the enemy in infiltrating the Forward Zone, indeed the general consensus of opinion was that it masked all local landmarks and rendered any co-operation between strong points practically impossible. The artillery was also similarly handicapped in that it was unable to direct an accurate fire onto the advancing enemy. Many accounts tell of redoubts that found themselves surrounded before they had even taken up their firing positions and were in complete ignorance of what was going on around them. However, German accounts lament the loss of direction experienced by many units and state emphatically that but for the fog their first day successes would have been greater than they actually were. They may have been right but there is little doubt that the fog did prevent the British Forward and Battle Zones from functioning effectively and in the opinion of many officers and men, contributed extensively to German success.

At 7.10am a message received from Colonel Richardson in the Main Keep to the 2/4 Londons' HQ confirmed the enemy was in Jappy Keep. The battalion historian described the events that overtook the Forward Zone units in the Fargniers sector:

'All communication was cut at an early hour; and each garrison was left to fight its own fight against odds entirely unsupported. It is established beyond any question that the defences of all posts in this area save Railway Post alone, were destroyed by the fierce preliminary bombardment, and those garrisons that had no shelter to go to, were either wiped out to a man or rendered quite incapable of serious resistance.'[3]

The hastily-scribbled messages sent by Richardson to Brigade HQ reveal a grim story of resistance as, one by one, the redoubts around the Main Keep fell to the attacking infantry. By noon, with little hope of a counter-attack, Richardson realised that there was little left to do but attempt to withdraw to the Battle Zone. Shortly afterwards the mist began to lift and he and the survivors of C Company took up positions near the communal cemetery at Fargniers where they fought on until Richardson was badly wounded. Surrounded and without hope of rescue a small party of men managed to slip away across the Crozat Canal with Company Sergeant Major Herbert Boag before the remnants surrendered.

Further north at Travecy village, however, Captain Maurice Harper and the men of A Company were still holding out. Like many of his fellow officers in the Londons, Harper had begun his military career as a private soldier before being commissioned. A born soldier, Harper's uncanny ability to avoid the fate that befell so many of his brother officers led to rapid promotion. In March 1917 he joined the battalion at Boisleux as a second lieutenant and in the space of six months was a temporary captain commanding A Company. His award of the Military Cross came in October 1917 while the battalion was fighting north of Poelcappelle, an occasion that reduced his company of over 200 officers and men to a mere 18 survivors.

The story of A Company at Travecy is one that is often used as a shining example of the heroism and endurance of the British soldier in defence. They held out against overwhelming odds until the evening of 22 March having expended some 18,000 rounds of small arms ammunition, 400 mills grenades and 200 trench mortar shells. Harper had certainly drawn the short straw when he found himself along with the 200 or so men of his company in the Forward Zone on the morning of March 21.

The village of Travecy sits on the west bank of the Oise between the canal and the D1044, a distance of just over a mile-and-a-half north of the Brickstacks strongpoint. From the D1044 the ground falls away towards the river which in March 1918 would have provided very good fields of fire – not only for the various posts Harper had established in the village, but also for Harper's battle headquarters in Travecy Keep which was probably situated on the D1044 close to the junction with the D555. The morning of March 21 began with the German bombardment, Harper's personal account of the action gives some idea of the confusion and isolation he and his men must have felt:

'*At 7.00am the mist was so thick that we could not see 10 yards. All phone communication was cut and we couldn't see the visual lamps on account of the mist. At 7.05am a heavy barrage fell on my sector and lasted an hour. Immediately it lifted I went to my battle headquarters at the keep. At 8am I received a note from the battalion on my left saying their right had been driven in. I moved a platoon to cover my left flank. I sent two runners to battalion headquarters but discovered later they had been captured. A few minutes later came a runner from Mr Gibson (my right platoon commander) saying he was being attacked from the front, south and north – at the same time hostile machine guns opened up on the keep from the rear. From this I gathered that, taking advantage of the thick mist, the enemy had succeeded in getting through the gaps in our line and encircled our posts. I had no news from the centre post (Mr Dixon) and runners were unable to get through.*'[4]

Quite where Harper was during the bombardment is unclear but he joined Lieutenant Stuart Clapham in the Main Keep as soon as it was safe to do so. Shortly after he had moved half a platoon of men to cover his left flank, the three posts in the village came under direct attack from enemy infantry advancing in mass formation. Given the advantage of good fields of fire, particularly from the ridge of high ground that ran through the village, the Germans were largely held off on the right flank until 10.00am when Lieutenant Gibson was forced to fall back on the Main Keep, reporting that enemy forces were now in possession of the southern and eastern edges of the village. Gibson's platoon of twenty-five men had been virtually annihilated leaving only himself and another man to escape. However, despite Harper fearing the worst, the remaining posts in the village under Lieutenants Dixon and Roberts were still fighting and holding their positions with sustained and accurate Lewis gun fire. At some point Dixon and his men were overwhelmed leaving Roberts and the survivors to fight on before they too were forced to seek the comparative security of the Main Keep.

By 7.00pm Harper received confirmation from his runners that he was completely surrounded. The enemy had penetrated several miles to the north on the 18th Division's front and were close to the banks of the Crozat Canal to the south. Harper's men comprised of three officers and sixty other ranks and it was with this meagre garrison that he fought off the next attack which came shortly before dusk. Nightfall brought a relative calm although all through the hours of darkness there were continuous efforts to bomb the garrison out of their trenches. Dawn on 22 March was greeted by thick fog again and little relief in the relentless attacks that came from all sides. In the rare intervals between these attacks several men, including Corporals Alfred Shilton and George Ansell, were still able to creep out into the village and open fire on enemy machine-gun teams and sniper positions and on one occasion Harper's account describes how they were able to bring fire to bear on an enemy transport column on the St Quentin to La Fère road. 'About 500 Germans were observed on the road across the marshes.

We opened up on them with Lewis guns at 1,500 yards range and inflicted many casualties.' Both Ansell and Shilton were awarded the Distinguished Conduct Medal for their work but sadly 28-year-old George Ansell's decoration was posthumous.[5]

But Maurice Harper knew their stand was coming to an end, particularly as 'our ammunition had got very low and the men were thoroughly exhausted'. Whether he was aware that III Corps was now across the Crozat Canal is unclear but at 5.00pm the keep was bombed by a British aircraft which had wrongly assumed anyone this far behind the enemy line must be German. 'This had a great effect on the men', wrote Harper, 'making them think that we were quite deserted and beyond help.' It was also becoming apparent that the Germans would soon close in for the *coup de grace* which could only result in a further loss of life:

'After repulsing an attack at dusk, I found the last box of ammunition had been used. At 7.30pm on 22 March, I had a council of war with my officers and CSM [Pascall]. We summed up our situation as follows: Our ammunition was exhausted, we were entirely cut off from the rest of the Army, and there was no prospect of a counter-attack reaching us, the men were so exhausted they could hardly stand, we were outnumbered by at least fifty to one, our casualties were exposed to the enemy's fire and our further resistance could in no way help our Army. In consideration of these points I decided, when next the enemy attacked, to hand over the position rather than attempt to resist them with the bayonet, which would have meant the needless sacrifice not only of the garrison, but probably of the casualties also'.[6]

Surrender came some time later when the Germans were massing for another attack:

'Very reluctantly I gave orders for a white flag to be put out. When this had been done, the enemy ceased fire and called for us to come out. An officer was called for and I went to meet the enemy. I was armed but dropped my revolver as I advanced. A German private, who would have bayoneted me, was stopped by an NCO and I was told to call my men out. They came, with their hands above their heads – the most heart-rending sight it has ever been my lot to witness.'[7]

Exactly what time this occurred is again unclear, several accounts have times ranging from late evening to 1.00am on 23 March, but whatever time it was when Harper and his men surrendered, their capture brought the total losses of the 2/2 Londons since 21 March to 21 officers and 550 other ranks. On the day the offensive began the battalion mustered 22 officers and 585 other ranks. Harper and Gibson both received the Military Cross, Harper's citation which appeared in the *London Gazette* on 1 July 1919 was a fitting tribute to the men of A Company – nearly all of whom were volunteer soldiers:

'For most gallant conduct and devotion to duty whilst commanding an outpost company at Travecy, March 21/23rd, 1918. His example inspired the remnants of his company to a desperate resistance when surrounded and without hope of relief. In addition to beating off several heavy attacks, he dispersed enemy transport, battalions in close order, and rendered excellent service.'[8]

* * *

As with the Forward Zone, the bulk of the defences in the 2/4 Londons' Battle Zone were concentrated on the right flank where, should a breakthrough occur, the road to Chauny and Noyon lay open. The precise time the German bombardment began differs in the various accounts of the battle, but 2/4 Londons in the Battle Zone record it as beginning at 4.20am. The brigade signal centre at Quessy was almost immediately knocked out with a direct hit and Lieutenant Colonel William Dann did not receive any orders to 'man battle stations' until long after the battalion were actually in place. Quite why the main battle station garrisons were not already in place is strange, particularly as the whole brigade had been forewarned of the attack the day before! Martin Middlebrook's suggestion in his *Kaiser's Battle* that some seventy or eighty battalions suffered in a similar manner whilst en-route to their Battle Zone stations may well be correct, certainly many of the initial casualties sustained by 2/4 Londons occurred in the rush to their battle positions.

As the fog lifted slightly around noon the Battle Zone redoubts had the first sight of the Germans who were advancing in large numbers all along the line. At 2.00pm Dann received word that the platoon holding Distillery Post had been overwhelmed and that the Farm Rouge and Triangle Posts were under heavy attack. Triangle Post was situated on the D557 just under a mile east of the Travecy Keep – which at this time was still holding out – and was under the command of Lieutenant Geoffrey Lester. Dug into a triangle of sunken roads and garrisoned by C Company, its strength lay in the fields of fire it enjoyed and the volume it could bring down on an advancing enemy. By 3.45pm Captain Charles Clarke's men had been pushed out of the Farm Rouge redoubt and the assaulting enemy columns were moving in the direction of Quessy and the Crozat Canal isolating the Fargniers sector in the south and Lester and his men in Triangle Post. By way of response Brigadier General Worgan immediately ordered a company of 3/Londons to counter-attack and lift some of the pressure from the retiring men of D Company and fill the gap between Triangle Post and the Fargniers North positions which were still intact. Only two platoons ever reached their objective – most were killed or wounded crossing the Crozat Canal.

By 7.15pm Dann's battalion was in serious trouble but continued to fight back against the odds, but it was clear to all that unless the remnants of the brigade fell back they were in great danger of being outflanked and overwhelmed. The orders to retire west of the Crozat Canal came soon afterwards and Dann – by this time in overall command of all troops in the Battle Zone – skilfully withdrew his mixed band of men over the canal to positions along the railway, aided significantly by a company of the 4th Battalion Suffolk Regiment (4/Suffolk) and 24-year-old Captain Harry Staddon. The 4th Battalion had been in France since November 1914 and had fought in many of the major engagements on the Western Front, but by January 1918 had been relegated – as many of the officers and men saw it – to the role of divisional pioneers. When the offensive began Staddon and A Company were positioned on the canal at Quessy and were soon in action covering the withdrawal of Dann's Force over the canal, positions which they held all day against increasingly heavy attacks. Finally Staddon withdrew what was left of his company across the remaining canal bridge which was then demolished by Second Lieutenant Ernest Bilham and his section from 303/Field Company.

Harry Staddon was an officer who had enlisted in the ranks of the East Anglian Field Ambulance before he was commissioned in 1915 and turned his considerable talents to soldiering. Although his defence at Quessy was one that was typically repeated all along the British line that day, it was in itself a superb feat of arms that went unrewarded in terms of official recognition and mustered only half-a-dozen lines in the regimental history. Unfortunately we know little more of what took place but suffice it to say that Staddon survived the war to return to civilian life.

With the brigade across the Crozat Canal, Triangle Post was now completely isolated along with its near neighbour at Travecy Keep. Captain Clive Grimwade, who wrote the battalion history in 1922, felt the ensuing battle was 'a magnificent example of stern courage again overwhelming odds'. The initial bombardment had taken its toll but the Triangle Post garrison was not closely engaged until the Forward Zone units had been overwhelmed. As soon as the fog lifted it was clear that C Company faced a very strong and determined enemy:

'*From this time onwards no orders or messages of any kind reached Lester from battalion headquarters or the adjoining companies, and he was left to fight his own battle. The advancing enemy were hotly engaged by rifle and Lewis gun fire, and large numbers were killed. Already D Company were losing their grip on Farm Rouge, but Lester decided the only course open to him was to await reinforcements. These never came, and probably, owing to the utter severance of communications, it was never realised how urgent his need was. The only support to this gallant company was one 18-pounder gun firing over open sights from near Quessy. All the afternoon the unequal fight was maintained, though the defenders were much harassed by low-flying German planes. With the approach of dusk the mist came down again, surrounding the company with an impenetrable curtain. Again and again Lester sent out runners and patrols to seek connection with the adjoining troops but these never returned.*'[9]

Surrounded on all sides and with the fog thickening Lester realised this was going to be his only opportunity to break out and get his men back to the Crozat Canal. It was the last move in what had been an extraordinary stand against the enemy but the odds were stacked against them and only the remnants of two platoons under Lieutenant John Blair managed to get back, the others being killed or captured. Geoffrey Lester was one of those captured and spent the remainder of the war in a German prisoner of war camp. The 2/4 London casualty figures for the two days of 21/22 March are difficult to ascertain with any accuracy, but casualties sustained by the battalion between 21 March and 3 April amounted to fifteen officers and 712 other ranks.

When the 18th Division withdrew across the canal that night the bridges at Liez were blown by sections of Sappers from 79 and 92/Field Companies while 80/Field Company tackled the canal bridges at Mennessis. However, in the confusion regarding who was responsible for what, the bridge over the railway west of Mennessis remained intact as did the two railway bridges west of Jussy. Although the Jussy bridges would be demolished on 22 March, the fears expressed by Major General Reginald Buckland over bridge demolition looked very much as if they were beginning to haunt the retreat.

Chapter 4

It's Difficult to Kill the Blighters

I had many long conversations with the German doctors who stated that they were receiving three times the number of wounded which they had been ordered to prepare for and that the men coming back from the front were generally of the opinion that the casualties were much too heavy to allow the advance to succeed.

Lieutenant Colonel John Crosthwaite – writing in 1931.

The 18th Division held the centre of III Corps with the 58th Division on its right and the 14th Division on the left. The division held another extremely long front line running from Lock Post on the canal north of Travecy for over five miles to Alaincourt, a small village less than a mile north of Moÿ-de-l'Aisne. The sector was separated from the German lines by the Oise Canal which flowed through the marshy Oise valley – in places over one mile wide – between the roads that flanked the valley on either side. The Oise marshes in this area had also suffered from the dry weather and no longer constituted an obstacle, indeed as early as January 1918 Paul Maze noted that they were now 'passable for infantry'. The 18th Division arrived at this 'peaceful' stretch of front line in February after a seven month tour of duty in the Ypres Salient; the contrast between the muddy morass of the Houthulst Forest and their new location was reflected in the distinct lack of casualties, Paul Maze remarking that any that did occur 'were mostly due to the persistence of the men in fishing in the River Oise'.

But the preparations for defensive positions were paramount and having inherited such a long sector of front line Major General Lee had little alternative but to maintain two full brigades in the Forward and Battle Zones and keep one in reserve. While he was able to some extent to utilize the former French positions, a great deal of work remained to be done if the division was to hold an attacking force in the Battle Zone. Thus on 20 March 1918 when the order to 'prepare for attack' was passed down to all units, Brigadier General Harold Higginson's 53 Brigade held the northern sector and 55 Brigade, commanded by Brigadier General Edward Wood, held the southern sector which included the old Vauban fort at Vendeuil. In reserve was 55 Brigade which, at the moment the bombardment commenced, were at Caillouel and Rouez with brigade headquarters located in the small village of Faillouel, just west of the Crozat Canal. Two brigades of artillery were deployed in support of the units in the front line, 83 Brigade in the north and 82 Brigade in the south.

The German bombardment drenched the whole divisional area back to the Crozat Canal in high explosive and gas, a bombardment the divisional historian noted dryly, which had three distinct objectives:

> 'For the first two hours their gunners were searching for our guns; next, their objective was to bombard our infantry positions with gas and high explosive; afterwards hundreds of mortars assisted in a culminating crescendo of shelling that acted as an escort to the advancing German infantry and continued to ravage our positions and road approaches.'[1]

Captain George Nichols, the 82 Artillery Brigade Adjutant, was asleep in the headquarters dugout when the first shells woke him:

> 'A rolling boom, the scream of approaching shells, and regular cracking bursts to right and left woke me up. Now and again one heard the swish and the plop of gas shells. A hostile bombardment without a doubt. I looked at my watch – 4.33am.'[2]

The order to man 'Battle Stations' went out at 5.12am but by this time all lines between Higginson's headquarters and his three 53 Brigade battalions were cut by hostile shell-fire as were those to the 83 Brigade artillery batteries. In the Forward Zone the 7th Battalion Queen's Own Royal West Kents (7/RWK) and the 8th Battalion Royal Berkshire Regiment (8/Berks) were holding a series of small redoubts with the 10th Battalion Essex Regiment (10/Essex) in the Battle Zone at Caponne Farm and Ly-Fontaine. The first indication that the Germans had crossed the canal under cover of the fog was from 55 Brigade which reported Lock Post had been overwhelmed; frustratingly Higginson had little idea as to what was taking place in his Forward Zone although from the noise of battle which emanated from the thick mist, it was clear his units were being heavily engaged.

The same difficulty that plagued Higginson was also causing Lieutenant Colonel Robert Dewing similar problems in that he had completely lost contact between his headquarters at La Guingette Farm and the forward companies of the 8/Berks. Robert Dewing was the son of a Suffolk vicar who had been commissioned into the RE in 1909. His capacity for leadership was recognised in 1916 when he was awarded the DSO for his dogged determination in 'sticking to his post all day'. Arriving in his present position in July 1917, the 30-year-old Dewing brought a dynamic and determined style of command to the Royal Berkshires, a style which he was about to demonstrate once again.

Some indication of the seriousness of the German attack arrived in the form of a wounded Lieutenant Thomas Baker with the news that D Company at Magpie Wood had been all but wiped-out and Lieutenant Walter Hannay was holding on with the remnants in the sunken road on the right flank, but of the nearby B Company and Captain John Footman there was no news. Baker was the only officer in the immediate front line to escape. By 10.30am groups of German infantry from III/IR 32 were seen moving along the St Quentin to Moÿ road heading towards battalion headquarters and Dewing ordered C Company to hold the trench line immediately behind the farm. Lieutenant John Randall commanded 9 Platoon:

> 'The Bosche seemed very reluctant to advance from the main road at this stage and we could hear his officers and NCOs shouting loudly and obviously trying to reorganise. Had we had sufficient men at that moment I believe we could have re-established our front line ... In the meanwhile we were putting an unceasing hail of bullets across the road and it must have been a very unhealthy spot. It was still impossible to see for more than fifty yards and we eventually saw a few German scouts loom out of the mist. These were promptly killed.'[3]

Undeterred, the main body of German infantry from IR 147 attempted to rush the company line, a tactic which failed in the face of the Berkshire Lewis gunners who 'rolled 'em up in heaps'. But they were well aware that they were now isolated and enemy units had advanced well beyond their flanks and judging from the direction of the most recent attack, had now got in behind the redoubt. John Randall again:

> 'The next move of our attackers was to send men to crawl forward into shell holes as near as possible to us. These were obviously picked shots and, making good use of cover, they were difficult to spot. The result was that we began to lose men rapidly. In every case they were sniped through the head. It was at this stage that we lost [Second Lieutenant John] Gordon who was using a rifle with good effect. [Lieutenant Norman] Williams was also killed by a sniper's bullet. This officer observed one of the Huns who had crawled forward and was about to shoot him with his revolver when the man put his hands up. Williams went out on top to bring him in, pushed him down into the trench and was getting ready to jump in himself when he was shot from another direction. Captain Fenner [Captain Harold Fenner, commanding C Company] was also shot in the head but fortunately it was not fatal in this instance and he was eventually officially reported as 'wounded and prisoner'. It was quite impossible to get any away who were severely wounded. The Germans co-operated with their snipers by sending forward a large bombing party which secured a footing in the left flank of the redoubt and also by worrying us with enfilading fire from a light machine gun.'[4]

With the attacking infantry continually being reinforced Dewing realized the position was untenable and at 1.30pm ordered the company to retire down Seine Alley, the narrow communication trench that ran for two miles back to the Battle Zone at Ly-Fontaine. Lieutenant Randall was with them:

'This meant moving in single file and we had not proceeded many yards before we encountered another large bombing party who had evidently been posted to cut off our retreat and to try to force us out of the trench. Some of them were actually in the trench and others lining either side. [Lieutenant Stanley] Harvey, the works officer, was leading the retirement at the time and he showed wonderful pluck in dashing straight at this party and shooting the first one he met at point blank range. Unfortunately he was shot by another of the enemy at almost the same second and we also had the misfortune to see Major [Douglas] Tosetti meet his end in the same way. This was indeed a blow for this gallant gentleman was a great favourite with all ranks and greatly beloved by his fellow officers. Those following took up the fight with such vigour that the remainder of this Bosche party took to their heels and we carried on at top speed towards the battle zone. The mist was now lifting rapidly and, on glancing back, we could see hordes of Bosche passing over our old positions. Messages were being continually passed up from the rear for us to 'double up in front'. We were moving as quickly as possible, but doubtless the presence of large numbers of the enemy, almost on the heels of those behind, literally gave them wings.'[5]

Dewing had got his men back but the cost had been a heavy. From a rifle strength of 24 officers and 773 other ranks on the morning of 21 March, only 5 officers and approximately 182 men were left standing at roll call.

A similar story was being unfurled along the 7/RWK sector to the south of La Guinguette Farm. At 10.30am A and C Companies had been completely surrounded and no word had been received at battalion HQ where B Company and Lieutenant Colonel John Crosthwaite's headquarters was sited at Durham Post. It was not until 11.00am that a runner from Durham Post finally reached Higginson at Brigade Headquarters with an urgent request for an artillery barrage to be put down on the St Quentin road (the modern day N22).

'Holding out at 12.30 pm. Bosche all around within 50 yards except rear. Can only see 40 yards so it's difficult to kill the blighters.' Signed J D Crosthwaite.[6]

26-year-old Lieutenant Colonel John Crosthwaite joined the 1st Battalion City of London Regiment in 1914 and rose rapidly through the ranks of the Londons to the command of the 8th Battalion Norfolk Regiment, a unit he joined on 22 November 1917. It was to be a short tenure of command as the battalion was one of those that fell to the axe barely three months later, the officers and men being redistributed within 53 Brigade. John Crosthwaite, already the holder of the Military Cross and bar, was moved to the command of 7/RWK, taking over from Charles Cinnamond on 19 March. It was to be another brief period of command.

Crosthwaite's request for artillery support was immediately responded to by the 82 Artillery Brigade guns:

'[My] *message calling for artillery barrage sent by runner was replied to very effectively by heavy guns and although the actual position of the enemy could not be seen, the flashes and the bursts could be seen through the fog and indicated they were just about on the line where they had been called for.*'[7]

Situated to the west of the main St Quentin road, Durham Post was a little under a mile south of Dewing's battalion HQ at La Guinguette Farm. When the opening bombardment began Crosthwaite kept his men below ground, noting that 'the gas-proof curtains to the dugouts were quite efficient' and although much of the ground level fortifications were badly damaged he reported no casualties. It was a different story in the battalion outpost further east. Apart from a few wounded very few of the men of A and C Companies got back to the Battle Zone. At 8.00am the outpost platoon of C Company, positioned on the canal line, was ordered back to company headquarters which held a fortified redoubt on the western edge of Moÿ. Fighting hard to fend off the swarms of German infantry they found the company post practically surrounded which, by 11.00am, was being attacked on two sides. Ordering a break-out Captain Watts and the C Company survivors managed to reach Durham Post which was more that Lieutenant Edgar Thomas' platoon at Le Vert Chasseur Farm managed. Thomas was wounded early in the day but his platoon sergeant took command and held the enemy at bay until the Lewis gun had been disabled and he was killed. Three survivors got away.

Despite the advanced companies being knocked out, Durham Post was still relatively intact. As soon as the shelling died down Crosthwaite made a personal reconnaissance across the St Quentin road and found no sign of enemy movement:

'*Runners were sent back as every form of communication was broken, but apparently they did not get through as the Brigade Major arrived at about half past six having been hit on the way up and reported that no news had got back to Brigade. Runners were the only means of communication as visibility was not more than 50 yards and pigeons when released appeared to merely flutter and stop again. I think they were probably gassed.*'[8]

Sergeant Fred Hubble, the signalling sergeant, repeatedly went out under shellfire to try and contact the forward posts laying new telephone lines right up to the canal posts. On his last foray he came up against advancing German infantry forcing him to make a wide detour in the fog, only regaining friendly lines later that day. Back at 'Durham' Crosthwaite's men were first attacked soon after 10.00am when German infantry almost fell over the wire in front of the Post. 'An attack was made on our right front but the Germans seemed to come up against our wire without seeing it in fairly close formation and naturally everyone was shot down on the wire.' The next attack was made from the sunken road which ran forward from the post. Using the fog as cover Crosthwaite's adjutant, Captain Harold Rapson, and a Lewis gun team got outside the wire and brought their fire down on the German infantry in the road, Crosthwaite noting that, 'the next day there were about 50 Germans lying dead in an area of 20 yards under the bank'. Rapson was badly wounded during this action and died of his wounds two days later.[9]

But Durham continued to hold out, the 82 Artillery Brigade barrage helped somewhat but the post was now completely surrounded and any thoughts of breaking out had long gone. A lesser man would have surrendered his garrison, but as Crosthwaite pointed out:

> *'Visibility was always sufficient to control our wire and at no point did the enemy ever penetrate. Machine gun fire was very heavy and there were a considerable number of casualties without our having any really effective target to fire on, About half past twelve we saw some of the Royal Berks pass on our left retiring but decided that we had better hold our positions at least until nightfall.'*[10]

The fog began to lift around midday enabling the attacking force to bring a more accurate fire onto the beleaguered post and soon after 4.30pm Crosthwaite was hit, a wound that rendered him unconscious until the next morning. It is unclear at exactly what time the post surrendered but from Crosthwaite's own account of the action it would appear that it was later that evening or early the next morning although as he says himself, 'I am afraid I heard nothing as to the details of the surrender.'

With the West Kents and Royal Berkshires now virtually wiped out, the 10/ Essex were holding fast at Caponne and Moulin Farms in the Battle Zone, ably supported by the guns of C and D Batteries of 83 Artillery Brigade. Commanding C Battery (C/83) was 27-year-old Captain Leslie Haybittel whose guns were in position near Caponne Farm. C/83 had been in action since dawn firing on fixed targets behind the German line but with the fog obscuring the surrounding area Haybittel had no confirmation that his battery was even on target, although by 11.15am the fog had lifted sufficiently for the battery to see the dim outlines of the advancing German infantry heading in their direction. Gunner Walter Lugg had his first sight of the enemy through a telescope:

> *'We had this chap Charlie Drake [who] had very good eyesight, marvellous eyesight, and he was looking over, and all of a sudden he shouted to our captain,*

who by this time was standing on top of the gun-pit, because we'd pulled our guns into the open, and he shouted to him, 'here they are! Hoards of them!' So I looked through my telescope sight and all of a sudden I saw the blooming Germans three hundred yards away from us. Well, we didn't have to be told! We started letting fly at them, firing at short range ... point blank over open sights.'[11]

Firing at such short range had a devastating effect on advancing infantry and Gunner Lugg's rather loose assessment of exactly how many were advancing towards them was lost in a frenzy of firing:

'There were 365 of these shrapnel bullets in one shell, and of course they splayed out all over the place. You fire at them and you can see them duck. Well, we kept firing and firing ... We fired no end of shells that day – hundreds, literally hundreds. We did a lot of damage, and we definitely slowed them down, but they were still getting nearer and nearer.'[12]

They were in fact getting so close that the two forward guns of C/83 had to be abandoned, a task easier said than done when enemy infantry are intent on taking the guns. Haybittel's primary task was to disable the guns, a process which involved removing the breech-block and sights before the enemy infantry could rush the gun-pits:

'The chaps who weren't handling the guns lay out with rifles to hold the Jerries off when we stopped firing. I was handling one of the guns, so I had to help get the breech-block out, take the No.7 sights away. Most of us managed to get back alright ... Captain Haybittel didn't go until nearly the end, because he wanted to see everyone away. We all got away except Lieutenant Patterson and three other chaps. They were on the other gun and possibly had a bit more of a struggle with their breech-block.'[13]

Pushed back into the gun-pits of the two remaining guns Haybittel realised that it was only a matter of time before they would be again overwhelmed and deployed his gunners around the perimeter with their rifles to delay their attackers. One of these men was 29-year-old Gunner Charles Stone:

'It wasn't long before the Jerries started advancing on the left of us, so we had to go back again. That's where Charlie Stone came into his own. He was a great chap, a marvellous chap, and a great friend of mine. The Germans weren't just walking towards us, you know. No! They had machine guns as they came forward. So, while we were trying to get back, old Charlie Stone lay out there, right out in front, no more than a hundred yards from the Germans, and he shot them down like a marksman.'[14]

Walter Lugg's account is corroborated by the divisional historian who described Stone's action as daring and gallant:

'He took up a position on the right flank of the two guns, and entirely unsupported, held the enemy at bay, though again and again they tried to outflank Captain Haybittel's party. Some of them managed at last to break through. Gunner Stone, regardless of the machine gun fire charged at these Germans and single-handed killed them one by one.'[15]

At 8.00pm the rear section of guns had fired over 1,800 rounds and one gun was permanently jammed. Haybittel's little band of gunners was now surrounded but incredibly he still managed to get away leaving Lieutenant Jackson and six men to cover the withdrawal, one of which was Gunner Stone. Faced with a determined enemy the gunners still managed to capture a machine gun and its team of four who were firing on the position from the rear, the irrepressible Charlie Stone chasing one reluctant German for some hundred yards before eventually taking him captive. Farndale describes their action as a 'unique and rare case of a battery acting as its own infantry and then conducting a withdrawal through an encircling enemy'.[16] Stone's subsequent award of the Victoria Cross was well deserved as was the DSO awarded to Leslie Haybittel.

* * *

Commanding the 7th Battalion Royal East Kent Regiment (7/East Kents) was Lieutenant Colonel Algernon Ransome, a regular officer who was commissioned into the Dorsetshire Regiment in December 1903. With 28 being the average age of battalion commanders in 1918, Ransome was considered to be quite an 'elderly' commanding officer at 35-years-old. Not a man to be held back, his early potential was addressed by his appointment to battalion adjutant, promotion to captain followed in 1910. By June 1915 he was a major and a little over a year later he had been awarded the Military Cross and was in command of the East Kents. Ransome was typical of his generation of professional army officers, brave, determined and 'quite willing and able to take a rifle and do a bit of stabbing himself'. Needless to say the officers and men of the 7/East Kents loved him.

On March 21 his battalion was in the 55 Brigade Forward Zone. With a frontage of 5,500 yards – running from south of Le Vert Chasseur to Lock Post, north of Travecy – it was little wonder that many in the battalion felt they were being asked to cover far too much ground with 550 officers and men. Battalion Headquarters was at Clarence Keep which was built into the side of a quarry on the D421, a position from which the great bulk of Fort Vendeuil was visible some 1,300 yards to the east along the same road. The fort was garrisoned by a mixed detachment under the command of Captain Harry Fine. Apart from the

A Company outposts – Station, Cottage and Tea Garden Posts – dug into the easterly ruins of Vendeuil village, the remaining companies of the battalion were mainly deployed in Cork and Country Redoubts on the high ground west of Vendeuil.

The ancient Fort Vendeuil had been upgraded in the late nineteenth century into the defensive system designed by French military engineer Séré de Rivières to protect the French borders with a series of defensive forts able to defend each other with their crossfire. That system was superseded long before it was completed and although the fort was disarmed in 1903 it was another nine years before it was finally decommissioned having never seen action. By 1918 Fort Vendeuil – initially designed to defend the St Quentin road and the river crossings to the east – was well and truly obsolete. Its ruins, along with those of the nearby forts of Liez and Mayot are still visible today, although all three are on private property. Now Fort Vendeuil would finally have its day and become the scene of a dogged defensive duel. Harry Fine's garrison at Vendeuil had been cobbled together with an assortment of troops:

> 'The garrison in Vendeuil Fort consisted of a platoon of the support company of the 7th Buffs, a section of Royal Engineers, 2 mortar sections, and 2 motley platoons (formed by order of Divisional HQ) which in peaceful times were employed as unskilled labourers by the REs. These consisted of men – let us be kind – who were not born soldiers. Some were old. Some were bad marchers. Some were not too bright or not too strong, or regularly in trouble. But whatever trouble they may have caused their own officers in the past, it was nothing compared to the chaos they caused the German columns trying to push down the roads nearby.'[17]

The fort was constructed with a deep moat running around its perimeter and typically thick outer walls; the main entrance with its drawbridge was located at the end of a causeway which was overlooked by the high ramparts. In normal circumstances Vendeuil village and the Oise crossings could be kept under continual observation from the ramparts. Fine was also able to keep in touch with the neighbouring Pound Post east of Poplar Wood as well as Colonel Ransome at Clarence Keep.

The early morning fog would not have come as a surprise to the British. For the past week the nights had been cold and the mornings blanketed in a thick fog rising from the river and its associated marshes and according to the defending units of 55 Brigade, greatly assisted the German attack. Enemy activity along the 55 Brigade Forward Zone quickly pierced the forward platoon posts and the survivors soon began trickling back to the security of the Fort with tales of being overwhelmed from all sides by attacking German infantry. But it had not been an easy task: the two German battalions of IR 32 reported the capturing of 'the long-stretched village of Vendeuil' in the dense fog to be a 'ghostly' experience, one which was made considerably more difficult by the British infantry machine-gun posts that continually held up their attack. It was, wrote Karl Goes, 'like chopping off the heads of a Hydra. Everywhere the British hold out to the end until the last rifle is silenced. The *Musketiere* have to fight for every ruin, every dug-out and nest, every hollow-way and copse.'[18]

At 12.30pm before the fog began to lift it became apparent that the advancing German infantry had already pierced the main defensive line and had got as far as Ronquenet Wood where the forward Guns of C Battery, 82 Artillery Brigade (C/82), were firing. From all accounts the fight was over almost before it had started, the battery commander was wounded and only a handful escaped to report to Lieutenant Colonel Austin Thorpe commanding the brigade. The battery had been under continual shell fire most of the morning and as Captain George Nichols observed:

'The Huns seemed to know their position, and had put over a regular fusillade of 4.2s and 5.9s and gas shells. The duck-board running outside the dugouts behind the guns had six direct hits, and two of the dug-outs were blown in, also No.2 gun had its off wheel smashed by a splinter with two men rather badly wounded.'[19]

The dense fog was not helping the 60-pounder guns of 138/Heavy Battery, Royal Garrison Artillery either. Dug in at the crossroads south of Remigny the battery commander, Major Harold Paris was firing blind and despite having placed Lieutenant Martin Annesley in the fort at Vendeuil to act as his forward observation officer, all communication had ceased. The fuller phone line had obviously been cut by shellfire which was confirmed by a runner from the fort who arrived at Paris's Headsquarters at 10.30am with a note from Annesley to that effect. The next time Harold Paris saw Annesley was when he arrived in a very dishevelled state with an account of his capture and escape:

'About 10 a.m. finding all communication had gone beyond hope of repair and that the enemy were reported to be in the village of Vendeuil, he [Lieutenant Annesley] determined to get out of the fort and find out what he could and rejoin the battery. No sooner had he got outside the fort with the two telephonists, than he found a party of 200 to 300 Germans all round him and was forced to be taken prisoner … They removed all his equipment and took him along with them as they advanced towards Fort Liez. They were eventually held up by machine gun fire and a firing line was formed for attack. The prisoners (about 16 in number) were left behind in a dug-out of a captured battery position with a guard of a sergeant and two men.'[20]

From Annesley's account it would appear that he had been taken prisoner and taken to the captured dug-outs of C/82, he was then escorted towards the German lines with some of the battery gunners. The party then came under fire – it is not clear from which side but in the fog it could have been British or German – and in the ensuing melee Martin Annesley and three others escaped.

> *'Lieutenant Annesley, who was one of the four, had a particularly unpleasant time, running back towards our lines being sniped at by both sides. However, by crawling along trenches and making dashes from front to front, he managed to get back to a field battery* [possibly A/82 or B/82] *and from there back to his own battery.'*[21]

About midday, the fog lifted sufficiently for the British gunners to see Fort Vendeuil and turn their guns on an enemy who were now visible. At 12.10pm Harry Fine spoke to Ransome at Clarence Keep for the last time before communication was cut, on this occasion he informed his commanding officer that Vendeuil village was now in German hands. But for Fine and his garrison the situation did not really develop until the middle of the afternoon when a large body of German infantry attempted to storm the fort from the south. Rifle and machine-gun fire from the ramparts and the 82 Artillery Brigade guns of A and B Batteries firing over open sights were persuasive enough to temporarily deter the units of IR 71 from further attack, but this was only the preliminary engagement. Clarence Keep was now under attack and appeared to Ransome to be almost surrounded, a situation which became more critical when German aircraft began to direct artillery fire onto the British positions. As far as the German infantry were concerned the fort remained a thorny problem and was succeeding in delaying the advance:

> *'But the news is bad: Fort Vendeuil has not been taken so far! In front of it II Battalion (Hauptmann von Gilsa) and parts of IR 71 (Oberstleutnant von Kornatzki) lie on the ground, waiting for the Feldartillerie to weaken the fortress in preparation for the attack. So far Fort Vendeuil remains a formidable wave-breaker. IR 71 is mixed up with parts of IR 32, IR 116 and IR 147 by now, only Leutnant Siems has managed to keep his 12th Kompanie and following the fire barrage towards the fort. Lots of scattered men join the small force until finally the outer rim of the Fort comes into sight. At the right-hand corner of the Fort a group of English have to be dealt with. A young officer of IR 32 mistakenly reports the fort already taken. Thus the men advance leaving the Fort to their left! Several English try to flee the batteries of the Fort.'*[22]

The fleeing men noted in the German account may well have been the party led by Lieutenant Annesley who would have delighted in the fact that the 82 Brigade bombardment was now being directed at the German infantry. The two 82 Brigade batteries, dug in along the Vendeuil-Remigny road, continued to fire at point-blank range with quick and accurate gun drill that took a heavy toll of the attackers.

Nevertheless, the Germans were relentlessly closing in on both batteries. Major Wilfred Dennes, commanding A Battery, was killed along with several of the battery gunners, leaving Second Lieutenant Ralph Jones to take command. Jones tried his best to organise the defence of the now useless gun pits but it was to be short-lived. The suddenness of the silence that followed in the moments the guns ran out of ammunition must have been almost deafening, but the German infantry needed only moments to exploit the A Battery difficulties and bomb the gun pits into submission.[23] There was one final moment of satisfaction for the gunners when B Battery, which was 500 yards to the south and watching the events taking place with some concern, turned their guns onto A Battery's old position and fired over 800 rounds to scatter the new occupants. By nightfall on 21 March 82 and 83 Artillery Brigades had lost thirty-one guns between them.

Back at the fort Harry Fine was now practically cut off and surrounded, his flag signals to Fort Liez requesting a counter-attack to relieve his situation were observed from Clarence Keep and, presumably by the Germans, who immediately responded with a violent thirty-minute artillery attack on the fort. At nightfall the situation remained unchanged, no further attacks were made on Clarence Keep or the fort and Country and Cork redoubts were still holding out, but Ransome was concerned about his men still in the fort. Sending out patrols to make contact with them it became plain that the enemy was holding all approaches to the south. At 12.30pm an officer arrived at the Keep with orders for all troops to be withdrawn west of the Crozat Canal, orders that Algernon Ransome refused to accept without confirmation. Verification took the form of the battalion adjutant, Captain Charles Black, cycling the two and-a-half miles to Remigny and back, only then was his reluctant commanding officer convinced that his battalion should withdraw and sent out orders to his scattered companies. It is unlikely that Harry Fine at the fort was initially aware of the withdrawal but by the time the fog lifted on 22 March it would have been quite obvious to all that he alone remained in the 55 Brigade Forward Zone. The fort held out until later that evening when having exhausted both food and ammunition the garrison surrendered.

We cannot leave the III Corps area without commenting on the actions of the 14th Division on 21 March. Under the overall command of Major General Victor Couper, the division held the line from north of Moÿ to a point west of Itancourt. In his analysis of the first day's fighting Martin Middlebrook felt that the division did not fight well: 'Its forward positions fell quickly; many men surrendered, and some hasty flights to the rear were observed.'[24] By and large this view may have some credence but there were two battalions that held out in the Forward Zone until late afternoon and their story at least is worth telling.

The Forward Zone was held by two battalions of the King's Royal Rifle Corps and the 6th Battalion Somerset Light Infantry. Behind them in the Battle Zone were the 7th Battalion Rifle Brigade, the 7th King's Royal Rifle Corps and the 5th Battalion Oxford and Buckinghamshire Light Infantry. Many of those who fought with the 14th Division believe the division had the hardest task of all the corps. 'The division was in a salient. The front held by three battalions was approximately 5,600 yards and for the defence of this sector there were three battalions of a strength of about 450 men each.'[25] Facing them were the German 103rd, 34th, 37th and 1st Bavarian Divisions.

Holding the Urvillers Wood sector of the front line was Lieutenant Colonel Charles Howard-Bury and 9/KRRC. Howard-Bury was commissioned in 1904 and posted to India where he discovered his love of high mountains, so much so that in 1905 he secretly entered Tibet without permission, an excursion that led to a rebuke from Lord Curzon, the then Viceroy of India, and one that possibly shaped the remainder of his life. For now, however, the Himalayan ranges that would come to dominate his life after the war were far from his mind as he waited for the German offensive to begin.

The front held by 9/KRRC was about 2,000 yards with outposts situated 3–400 yards apart. The battalion only had three of its depleted companies in the front line, the fourth being held in divisional reserve over two miles behind at brigade headquarters. We know that Howard-Bury was already concerned that his battalion would be wiped out in the Forward Zone, particularly as they were 'very much scattered in small groups over a wide extent of country'. His personal narrative of events begins with the opening German bombardment:

> '*By the time the bombardment had lasted two hours every telephone line from Battalion Headquarters had been broken. At 9.30am the hostile barrage gradually moved backwards, until it rested behind us. The fog was as dense as ever, we could hardly see 5 yards in any direction. At 10.00am a runner came in from C Company to say that the enemy had come over in the fog and were already on the Pechine Line (our main line of resistance in the outpost line). Immediately afterwards a runner from A Company came in to say that the Company Commander, Captain [Reginald] Singlehurst, had been killed and that the Germans had reached the St Quentin road.[26] Shortly afterwards Rifleman Blackwell dashed out into the fog and returned with a German officer, who, when he was asked what he was doing there, said he was looking for his men, who had gone on ahead.*'[27]

The German officer's maps – marked with his unit's objectives several miles behind the British Forward Zone – did little to put Howard-Bury and his men at ease. The fog was still thick and the occasional groups of Germans who 'stumbled into our trench' were quickly driven off by Lewis gun fire. At around midday the fog began to lift and it was possible to get an appreciation of what was going on around them:

'*Germans were to be seen everywhere: parties of them were to be seen hurrying along the St Quentin road, and to the south they were to be seen bringing up their artillery onto the ridge behind us. Our Lewis guns for a while had the time of their lives, and caused much confusion and delay to their artillery. At 1.00pm we fired off rockets to show we were still holding out, and had also sent a pigeon message saying that we were hard pressed, as the Boches had got into both ends of our trench, and were trying to bomb us out. In this they were not successful, as Lieutenant Mackie at one end and Lieutenant White at the other end, with a few men, managed to keep them at bay. The only effect of the rockets was to attract the attention of more Boches, who thereupon brought up all sorts of engines of war against us, flammenwerfer, trench mortars, and machine guns. The flammenwerfer was soon put out of action by rifle grenades, which were also very useful in searching out the dead ground of which there was only too much around us, where the Germans were collecting preparatory to charging.*'[28]

Although only two officers of the battalion were killed on 21 March, there is no accurate record of how many officers and men were wounded but forty-one other ranks are recorded as having lost their lives defending their posts. What is worrying is Howard-Bury's reference to the dead ground that apparently surrounded his post. If this is so then the location of some of the Forward Zone posts may well have worked against the defending garrisons. Certainly the distance between posts which, according to Howard-Bury, had no lateral communication trenches did little to assist their defence. The end came for the headquarters redoubt at 4.00pm:

'*More than half the garrison were casualties and the Lewis guns, which had done excellent work, refused to fire more than single shots. All this time the Germans had been collecting in large numbers, and, just before 4.00pm quite 500 rushed in on us suddenly from all sides, and it was all over.*'[29]

Whether this was the redoubt referred to in the German IR 30 account of the battle is uncertain but their battalion historian does describe a redoubt in Urvillers Wood which was attacked in heavy fog supported by units from the neighbouring Bavarian Division. Their attack appears to have faltered until the commanding officer, a *Major* Barth, gathered his men together and led an attack from behind the British positions after having previously taken a number of outposts, 'in little copses, reinforced with branches and wire'.

The 8th Battalion King's Royal Rifle Corps (8/KRRC) also held on until around 4.00pm, noting that the main attack appeared to come from the direction of the St Quentin road which was behind them. This certainly supports the view that many German units did not attack at ninety degrees to the British line but often attacked at an angle, which in conjunction with the fog enabled them to attack the forward positions from behind. Certainly in the 14th Division Forward Zone this tactic isolated the main defensive positions and allowed the main force to move quickly towards the Battle Zone. The 8/KRRC eventually surrendered when two German tanks appeared which were described by Major Hugh Bowen as 'larger and faster than ours':

'After a pause the tanks came on … and proceeded to trample down the wire and shoot into the trenches. We had nothing with which to beat off the tanks and, having picked up a lot of stragglers, our ammunition was getting scarce, and there were no Germans to shoot at, as they all lay low and let the tanks do the job. Under these circumstances we had no other course but to give in.'[30]

Rifleman A J Murcott makes no mention of the German tanks but remembered breaking the orderly room typewriter and burning anything that may have been of use to the enemy:

'When the Germans came quite near we all got out of the trench and the Colonel tied a white rag or towel to a stick and waved it. I can remember German officers coming in and there was much saluting and conversation.'[31]

The reputation of 8/KRRC on 21 March has been tarnished by some historians as giving up without a struggle, which from Bowen's account appears to be incorrect, the redoubt held on well into the afternoon before surrendering. Be that as it may, the Germans do not appear to have had much difficulty with overcoming the Battle Zone anywhere along the 14th Division Front and at 9.15pm orders were given for the division to withdraw to the line of the Crozat Canal.

But before we move north to look at the attack on XVIII Corps, consideration should be given to notes made by Lieutenant Colonel Julius Birch commanding 7/KRRC in the 14th Division Battle Zone. The total strength of Birch's battalion was about 500 officers and men and the front allocated to him was roughly 3,000 yards, which he tells us was 'only lightly held by small posts at necessarily long intervals, a system the policy at that time dictated'. Furthermore he makes the rather alarming observation that 'the majority of these positions or strong-points had not been completed, and in some cases they were only spit-locked, and the munitioning was only partial'. The German bombardment 'exceeded anything I had experienced before … As far as it was possible to ascertain 75 per cent of my battalion had become casualties during the six hour bombardment'. He goes on to describe his retirement:

'By 5.00pm the German line of advance was about 2 miles in our rear and we appeared to be completely cut off. The total number of men of all units with me

was about 50 other ranks and 2 officers. At fall of dusk our position began to look serious; SAA [small arms ammunition] *nearly all expended, no picks or shovels, and only iron rations; but owing to the special instructions prohibiting any retirement I was unwilling to move without orders although the German infantry had left us isolated and cut off.*[32]

With runners dispatched to divisional headquarters asking for orders they – much to Birch's amazement – returned at around midnight with orders for Birch to take command of what was left of the Battle Zone and bring all the survivors back to Jussy. He continues:

'*With no small difficulty this withdrawal was effected, as we expected every moment to be attacked by overwhelming numbers. A certain amount of grenade throwing was indulged in by the Germans but we beat them off and took a couple of prisoners … about half an hour after evacuating the position it was shelled, but the birds had flown.*'[33]

Birch's evidence is supported in a separate letter written in 1927 by his adjutant, Captain Llewellyn Davies, whose comments on the readiness of the Battle Zone underline the state of defence in the 14th Divisional sector:

'*Not only was the Rear or Green Line position more of an idea than a reality, but the actual Battle Zone was by no means in a fit state for the purposes of defence. It consisted of half dug trenches and strong points with very meagre wire … it was not a properly prepared position.*'[34]

The three battalions of KRRC did stay and fight. It could be argued that those in the Forward Zone perhaps had no choice but to fight on and although surrender early on in the day would have been the easier option, it may well have been one that Charles Howard-Bury would have had difficulty with. However, this, together with the fact that Birch and his men fought on until midnight in the Battle Zone and were prepared to remain there unless ordered otherwise, says a great deal about the men themselves and perhaps goes some way to defending the performance of the 14th Division on 21 March.

Chapter 5

Here We Fight and Here We Die

No one who has not experienced the actual moment of a critical attack can realize the primitive emotions which are stirred, or can understand how men fight when other men come to destroy them.

Lieutenant Lawrence Lumley of the 11th Hussars, at Mount Houette

The sector held by XVIII Corps ran from a line just below Selency in the north to Itancourt in the south, a distance of some nine miles held by three divisions under the overall command of Lieutenant General Sir Ivor Maxse. Major General Oliver Nugent and the 36th (Ulster) Division held the right flank with the 30th Division commanded by Major General Weir de Lancey Williams on its left. Major General Colin Mackenzie held the left flank with his 61st Division. The area was dominated by a series of ridges and valleys, many of which ran parallel to the front line, one of these in particular – the Grugies Valley – ran from the sugar factory at Grugies to the north of Urvillers and thence northwards to cross no-man's-land along the Vallée à la Maye. The dead ground of the valley was frequently used by the 36th Division battalions moving in and out of the Forward Zone positions prior to 21 March, the valley sides shielding them from observant eyes on the other side of the wire. Nevertheless, it was an advantage that could work both ways and on the morning of the attack this little valley provided the German infantry with a conduit straight into the Forward Zone.

In clear weather the Forward Zone was completely exposed to observation from the German line but the Battle Zone was masked from direct view as the ground fell away to the west as it approached the line of the Crozat Canal and the Somme. The British *Official History of the War*, commenting on the defences in the Forward Zone, makes the rather lame point that with a narrower front line to defend, the XVIII Corps Forward Zone defences were 'more fully developed than those of the III Corps'. With two principle lines of defence – a first line series of strong points backed up with what was called 'the line of resistance' and an intermediate zone of redoubts some distance behind – this would certainly appear to be the case. However, this was a view that was not shared by many regimental officers who pointed to the distance between the redoubts which one divisional historian felt 'were in no sense mutually supporting'. Captain Charles Miller and a platoon of 2/Inniskilling Fusiliers were defending one of these strong points in the 108 Brigade Forward Zone and was in some doubt as to exactly how 'strong' these strong points were:

> *'I myself was in the strong-point allotted to company headquarters. I had with me a subaltern and a full platoon. My strong-point consisted of about 150 yards of trench with one deep and very spacious dugout quite capable of holding us all and protecting us from the effects of shell fire; but a death-trap if the enemy infantry got in before we could get out of it. At each end of the trench there was a strong 'stop' with a certain amount of cover for riflemen. There was one fairly strong belt of wire running in a half-circle right round the front of the strong-point and ending about 20 yards wide of the two 'stops' at each end of the trench. Had the wire been thicker and stronger it would have been a much more formidable little place for a frontal attack. Of course by rights the wire should have been all round it.'*[1]

Frank Fox, the Inniskilling Fusiliers' historian is equally critical:

> *'The men were scattered thinly in a chain of strong points: to keep effective communication between those strong points was not possible for lack of man power. They were obviously 'forlorn hope' troops: in the case of a heavy attack they must perish.'*

We have no way of knowing, but Miller and his brother officers in 108 Brigade must have been very much aware that their right flank was the Achilles heel of the whole divisional area. The front line of the 36th Division ran roughly east – west where it rested close to Sphinx Wood at the junction with the 14th Division. From Sphinx Wood the line turned south towards Alaincourt, a change of direction that focused attention on Urvillers and the Vallée St Sauve in the 14th Divisional area. Should Urvillers be taken then the whole of the 36th Division Forward Zone would inevitably crumble, even worse was the prospect of Essigny-le-Grand falling to the attackers which would expose the division's Battle Zone. It was altogether a rather fragile situation and one that we already know became a deadly reality early on 21 March when the 14th Division was driven back.

The German infantry attack on the 36th Division began shortly after 8.30am; prior to that Father Henry Gill had noted that the enemy shellfire 'fell with an accuracy which proved that the range had been carefully taken beforehand'. According to plan, German infantry swept straight up the Grugies valley almost parallel to the Forward Zone defences, isolating the forward strong points from the main redoubts and completely destroying the concept of strength in depth in just over an hour. The German 36th Division account describes their namesake division as putting up a 'good show' and showing 'remarkable tenacity'. Jean d'Arc Redoubt, garrisoned by men of the 15/Royal Irish Rifles actually came under attack before any of the strong points did. Captain Thomas Adamson serving with the 12/Royal Irish Rifles at Le Pontchu Redoubt noted the Jean d'Arc garrison – a mile or so to his rear – was overcome at 9.30 am, leaving him with little doubt as to the intention of the German infantry:

> '*It was early apparent that the idea of the enemy was to contain the outposts meantime, and to push through all troops as far as possible and eventually to capture the outposts later. By about 11.30am after very heavy fighting the outpost line was captured.*'[2]

In the confusion of the fog many of these outposts were neutralised before they had chance to put up any sort of fight. Yet some did choose to fight on in a hopeless battle that was doomed from the outset. Charles Miller recalled the desperate moments before his tiny garrison was overwhelmed:

> '*I had two men coming at me with their bayonets, one of whom I think I shot with my revolver, while a sergeant standing behind me shot the other at point-blank range with his rifle barrel over my shoulder. But almost at the same second a German stick bomb came whistling into the trench from the parapet right into the bunch of us, and killed and wounded practically the whole lot of us – English and German alike ... Before I collapsed I tried to give the surrender signal, and hope I had succeeded thereby saving a few lives. We had done our best.*'[3]

At Le Pontchu Quarry, tucked away close to the N22, was C Company of 12/Royal Irish Rifles. Under the command of Captain Leslie Johnston, these men held out against IR 128 and the troops of *Sturmabteilung* Rohr until 3.15pm having fought gallantly for some three hours against impossible odds. As soon as the German infantry attack began Johnston took the majority of his men forward to Foucard Trench to meet the advancing enemy. Thomas Adamson remained in the redoubt but was witness to the subsequent fight. Once established in the forward strong point Johnston took stock of his surroundings and although the German bombardment had smashed up the trenches and cut great swathes in the wire the telephone line to Le Pontchu was still intact and as far as he could see in the thinning fog, the fields of fire were excellent:

> '*By the time the fog had lifted a little and owing to the excellent field of fire and the manner in which it was handled the enemy, suffering severe casualties, was driven back after three attacks. The company itself had suffered heavily. For almost an hour the enemy made no further attack, but about 12.30pm a large convoy appeared*

on the St Quentin to La Fère road. Instructions were issued that fire was not to be opened on it until it was well within range, when with two Lewis guns and rifle fire the whole convoy – both men and horses were destroyed.'[4]

By now the company was being attacked on two sides and Johnston ordered a withdrawal to Lejeune Trench down Clermont Alley, a 350 yard communication trench which linked the two systems. Closely followed by an increasingly aggressive enemy who appeared determined to bomb the Irish into submission:

'By about 1.00pm the enemy, now not willing to come over the open, made a determined attack down the trench on the left with bombs and flammenwerfer and eventually what was left of the company had to retire to the trench immediately behind Le Pontchu, there with the help of runners, cooks etc from headquarters they continued fighting ... after having done everything possible to hold up the attack and after consultation between the officers left and to save useless loss of life, it was decided to surrender the post at about 3.15pm.'[5]

After the Armistice, when the survivors had been returned from captivity and the full story of C Company became known, Johnston was awarded the Military Cross for his part in the fight but perhaps more importantly, the courage and defiance of the men he commanded was recognised by the award of two Distinguished Conduct Medals and four Military Medals. What is striking about the stand made by Johnston and the men of C Company is the determination displayed by all ranks to hold onto their positions at all costs; it was a determination that was repeated at Racecourse Redoubt a little further to the west.

The Racecourse Redoubt was dug into the railway embankment south of Grugies and garrisoned by one company of 15/Royal Irish Rifles, a garrison that included 35-year-old Second Lieutenant Edmund de Wind. In 1914 de Wind – who was born in County Down – was living in Canada and working for the Canadian Imperial Bank of Commerce in Edmonton. Like so many young men who had emigrated to the Dominions, he chose to remain in his adopted country and enlisted as a private soldier in the Queen's Own Rifles of Canada. He sailed for France with the 2nd Canadian Infantry Division in September 1915 remaining with them until 1917 after which he was commissioned into the Royal Irish Rifles. On the morning of 21 March 1918 de Wind and his men caught their first glimpse of German infantry at 9.40am. For seven hours he and a few dozen men held the position. Although he was twice wounded he refused to surrender, climbing out on to the parapet under heavy machine-gun and rifle fire on at least two occasions to clear German troops out of an adjoining trench. It was only after he was wounded a third time, and fatally, that the position fell and the survivors taken prisoner. It does appear that after de Wind had been wounded the survivors surrendered soon afterwards leaving us to consider the remark made by Lieutenant Claude Piesse that where units were under an officer who was willing to hold out until the bitter end they generally did so until that officer was killed or wounded. As far as Father Henry Gill was concerned 15/RIR had been 'sacrificed' and de Wind's award of the Victoria Cross was a poor substitute.

The dogged defence at Racecourse Redoubt was not replicated at Boadicea Redoubt despite the presence of several officers. The redoubt was the most westerly of the 36th Division's three main redoubts and occupied the high ground of the Mont des Vignes between the D67 and the D321 just south of the tiny hamlet of Giffécourt. The garrison was commanded by Lieutenant Colonel Arthur Maxwell, the 11th Baron Farnham, whose early service was with F Squadron of the North Irish Horse, a special reserve cavalry regiment that drew its officers and men principally from County Down. But like so many yeomanry cavalry regiments after 1916 the men of the North Irish Horse found themselves fighting as infantry. Farnham's first command was one of those axed under the reorganisation earlier in the year so his period of command with 2/Inniskillings had only been a matter of weeks.

There is some controversy over the surrender of Boadicea Redoubt; Martin Middlebrook provides a useful account from the history of the German IR 463 which was leading the attack made by the 238th Division.[6] For some reason the redoubt had been largely missed by the opening bombardment and the first waves of German infantry were either happy to by-pass the stronghold or completely failed to see it in the thick fog. Either way, II/IR 463 were assigned to attack the position and began bringing up artillery support. Quite how long Farnham and his men held out for is unclear, Cyril Falls in the divisional history says it was 5.50pm when three captains, seven subalterns and 241 men filed out of the redoubt after the Germans threatened to bombard the position. Apparently Farnham asked for – and was given – a document as evidence that he and the garrison had put up a good fight before they were marched off into captivity! When compared to the action at Le Pontchu and Racecourse Redoubt it does leave one wondering how events at Boadicea Redoubt could possibly be described in the divisional history as a 'rare example of cold courage'.

By evening the 36th Division had lost the whole of its Forward Zone and the majority of the troops deployed there. The Battle Zone was in a precarious state with German troops advancing through Essigny in exactly the manner which so many had predicted with the fall of the 14th Division. However, Essigny did not collapse as easily as has sometimes been suggested. The fight is vividly described by Karl Goes in an account that draws attention to the determined defence and the German casualties:

'*Essigny-le-Grand, a rubble tip transformed into an impressive redoubt by the English. Essigny is the main point of resistance within the English second line.*

Batteries east and south of the village open up, pounding the attacker [German infantry]. *But the Grenadiere* [GR 5] *move on furiously like their ancient German ancestors. II/Battalion, led by the grey haired veteran Hauptmann Raoul Faure, advances through a hail of bullets, capturing the ruins as well as a senior English officer and their reserves. Hauptmann Faure swings the rifle and shouts like a youngster, his men regard him with favour, almost love, and are prepared to follow him anywhere. By 1.15pm the Battalion stands in a trench about 250 metres south of Essigny. But the English take another stand along the railway line, supported by scattered field guns. Twice the Battalion attacks, when the beloved Hauptmann gets fatally hit in the neck by a shell splinter, his aide-de-camp, young Leutnant von Homeyer becoming fatally wounded behind him ... Around the eastern edges of Essigny, Grenadiere 5 and the Bavarians* [from 1st Bavarian Division] *throw themselves against the enemy. Shrapnel and point blank shooting of the English guns are the answer. More Bavarians lend a hand and by 3.00pm Essigny is finally taken, despite the enormous losses.'*[7]

Orders were now sent out for the 36th Division to fall back behind the St Quentin Canal, a retirement that pivoted on two Inniskilling battalions. The 9/Inniskillings were hastily rushed up out of reserve to form a defensive flank to the right of Essigny near Station Redoubt on the Essigny-Seraucourt road. Karl Goes' account again:

'*The fight rages for hours around railway embankments, ditches and station buildings. IR 175 receives support from II/Grenadiere 5 while a German howitzer battery hits its own ranks very accurately. Many veteran officers and NCOs fall due to the English lead, among them Leutnant Ewald Manche. Nevertheless Battalion Matthael succeeds in taking the station, while Battalion Jansses overwhelms the Bahnkaserne Nord* [Station Redoubt]'.[8]

While the fight for Essigny was taking place, the 1/Inniskillings under the command of Lieutenant Colonel James Crawford were required to hold onto their position near Fontaine-les-Clercs. This battalion – situated on the high ground south of Roupy – held on to their positions around Ricardo Redoubt through the night and into the next morning. Dawn brought renewed attacks as the men of A Company came under a sustained assault which they managed to contain by falling back with B Company to a line southeast of the redoubt. Here they joined C Company and, under attack again, the three companies – or at least what was left of them – fought their way back, section by section, across the Vallée du Tonnoir to the confines of the redoubt which held D Company and battalion headquarters.

Now surrounded on all sides, Crawford made the difficult decision to make a stand and fight it out, conscious that every hour he held on was an hour of delay for the enemy. The battalion historian takes up the story of the final hours of Crawford's men:

> 'He detached about 40 of the men under him to fight their way back to the rear: the rest were to see it through ...Under the rain of bomb and shell the Redoubt and its defenders were obliterated and trodden bit by bit under the foot of the enemy. But with one part of the Redoubt gone, the survivors fell back to another corner, fighting for every yard. One incident was a charge made by a force consisting of Private Bailey and Private Conway which drove out a body of enemy bombers who had got a footing within the Redoubt. Finally only one little corner of the Redoubt was left in our holding; but still the resistance continued. It must have been a relief even to the enemy ... when with nightfall the surrender came of the little handful of survivors.'[9]

The battalion had held its ground with a determination that broke a dozen assaults by the 1st Prussian Guard Division before the inevitable surrender came. They had lost over eighty men killed and those that survived and were able to stand were marched with their commanding officer into captivity.

Shielded by the Inniskillings, the remainder of the 36th Division retired west to the St Quentin Canal crossings. Shortly after midday on 21 March the 27-year-old Second Lieutenant Isaac Norman of 121/Field Company completed the destruction of the pontoon bridge and footbridge at Fontaine-les-Clercs which had already suffered somewhat from shellfire. At 10.15pm he began demolishing the group of eight assorted bridges between Le Hamel and Seraucourt while 150/Field Company and Lieutenant William Brunyate attended to the Artemps crossings further south. Shortly before midnight 107 Infantry Brigade crossed the canal using the bridges north of Seraucourt and ordered them to be destroyed behind them. No sooner than Corporal Arthur Burston had completed the job a message arrived from 108 Brigade asking that they delay the demolition as they had yet to cross the canal! Fortunately Isaac Norman was able to point them in the direction of an intact bridge before moving up the canal to demolish the main bridge at Hamel which was blown at 3.00am on 22 March.

* * *

The fourteen German divisions which von Hutier had massed against XVIII Corps had little difficulty in capturing the forward defences of the 30th and 61st Divisions. But like the Irish on the right flank, the line of redoubts put up a much more prolonged resistance and it is on the story of these redoubts which we will now focus our attention.

Just to the west of St Quentin, where the A26 Autoroute is crossed by the D930, is the l'Épine de Dallon, a small cluster of houses and farm buildings that now lie within earshot of the noise from traffic on the A26. On 21 March 1918 there was little remaining of the village and that which was still evident had been incorporated into the Épine de Dallon defences which centred on a fortified keep or redoubt situated on the crest of a small rise with good all-round fields of fire. From the redoubt the skyline of St Quentin was dominated by the badly damaged Basilique de St Quentin, a view that Brigadier General the Hon Ferdinand Stanley, commanding 89 Brigade, was not entirely taken with:

> '*The worst disadvantage of this place was that the whole of our line and most of the back areas for miles back, were overlooked from the Cathedral, the walls and the steeple of which were still standing.*'

The system of defence employed by 30th Division was to divide the sector into two brigade sub-sectors with the third brigade being held in reserve. Thus in each sub-sector one battalion held the whole brigade front line. Stanley knew that in the event of an attack there was little, if any, possibility of sending assistance:

> '*The Brigade front could not be considered anything else than a lightly held outpost line. They had a few posts out in front, about six in all, and each of these posts consisted of about six men. Behind this we had a series of other posts, and again, behind these, a couple of strong points. This absorbed two companies of the battalion. Then there was one company which was detailed for counter-attacking purposes, and the fourth, and last, company of the battalion was responsible for the garrison and up-keep of a redoubt called the Épine de Dallon. Here also was situated Battalion Headquarters.*'[10]

On 17 March the 2nd Battalion Wiltshire Regiment (2/Wiltshires) took over the front line positions, relieving the 19th Battalion King's Liverpool Regiment (19/King's). Defending the Épine de Dallon was A Company and the Battalion Headquarters under the command of Lieutenant Colonel Archibald Martin, who had taken command of the battalion on Boxing Day 1917. The outpost line was held by C and D Companies with B Company occupying a sunken road which served as a second line of outposts. This line of defence was similar to another redoubt positioned approximately one-and-a-half miles further north on Manchester Hill and defended by the 16th Battalion Manchester Regiment (16/Manchesters).

In the event of the front-line defences failing it was hoped that the two main redoubts, together with the guns of the divisional artillery putting down a barrage in the ground between them, would hold the German infantry in the Forward Zone long enough for troops in the Battle Zone to counter-attack. Clearly a realist, Martin was not over optimistic at his chances of surviving long enough to benefit from any counter-attack that might be forthcoming from the Battle

Zone. One of the last things he did before the battle opened was to ensure the officers and men who were to 'remain out of battle' were sent to the rear with Major George Rapson, the battalion's second-in-command. The selection of such a group before a battalion went into action had been standard procedure for some time, the purpose of which was to form the nucleus of the 'new' battalion if disaster should strike and the Wiltshires were reduced to a handful of survivors. After the news of who had been sent out of battle spread round the ranks, Major Walter Shepherd wrote that those who remained all knew they were up against it, were very cheerful and, 'determined to make the Hun pay heavily for any of their trenches he attacked'. Martin's last visit to his battalion's positions began as darkness fell, by the time he got back to his headquarters at Épine de Dallon in the early hours of 21 March, the German units waiting across no-man's-land were counting down the hours.

A detailed record of what actually took place in the front lines after the German bombardment began will never be possible but survivors' accounts indicate four divisions of German infantry began their attack on this sector at 10.00am. The two divisions that attacked the Wiltshires' two forward companies – C and D Companies – quickly overcame any resistance and assaulted the Wiltshires in the flanks and from behind, with B Company being overwhelmed first. A single man from C Company managed to escape and bring word to Colonel Martin at Épine de Dallon. Of the eleven officers who were in the front line posts seven were taken prisoner, two were killed in action and another died of wounds. Two still remain unaccounted for in official records.

Unable to see anything through the fog and smoke of the bombardment, the runner's arrival at Épine de Dallon must have confirmed Martin's worst fears, the redoubt was all that was left of his battalion. German infantry units had undoubtedly passed either side of the redoubt in the fog but as the fog lifted a little a large group of enemy soldiers were seen approaching from the direction of Roupy. Detailing two Lewis guns to deal with the enemy they discovered in the nick of time that all was not as it seemed:

> '*It was a party of their own cooks which they had left at the rear ... being escorted back as prisoners. The garrison at l'Épine at once rescued their cooks, who were most useful as reinforcements, and settled the escorts for ever.*'[11]

Even then it appears the small garrison was largely undiscovered until enemy troops carrying boxes of bombs and ammunition along the small valley between the redoubt and Manchester Hill stumbled into them. With the fog now dispersed the garrison opened fire with trench mortars and Lewis guns which not only scattered the carrying parties but finally signalled their position to the enemy:

'The Germans came at the redoubt in perfect order, as if on parade. The little garrison of officers and men kept the enemy at bay for a long time. They found their own defensive wire entanglement hindered their fire, and they had to stand up and shoot over the top of it ... It was on the east side, where the road cut into the redoubt, that the Germans first broke into the system. Our trenches at this point were not quite connected. The enemy bombed our men back and succeeded in getting two of their machine guns inside the circle of our defences. The Wiltshires, using the cover of some ruined buildings as cover, tried to capture one of these guns, but the Germans cut through the brickwork with such rapidity, that the scheme failed. All the time a hostile aeroplane kept flying round the Keep at a height of only about sixty feet, machine gunning our men ... When Colonel Martin had only fifty men left, all of them fighting hard though hopelessly cornered, shells from British guns started bursting in the Keep.'[12]

Probably not aware that the Wiltshires were still holding on at Épine de Dallon the artillery were firing on previously known British positions in the hope they would be damaging the enemy, not that it helped the remaining Wiltshires. Messages were sent by Martin via carrier pigeon at 12.50pm in the hope someone would receive them and inform the artillery – but there is no record of events after the messages were dispatched. Precisely which brigade of artillery was responsible is unclear but we can rule out the guns of 307 Artillery Brigade which by this time had all four of its batteries captured apart from one section of guns which got away under heavy fire. The experience of 19-year-old Second Lieutenant Gordon Stanley who was in a 307 Brigade forward observation post, was not untypical:

'When the bombardment ceased I ventured up into the narrow, shallow trench and came face to face with a Jerry who had just arrived on the edge of the trench. I was unarmed, my revolver being in my valise at the battery, so little did my CO prepare me for what might be coming! He dropped to his knee and fired at my head from about four feet. I sensed the bullet skim my helmet and saw the spurt of mud as it buried itself in the trench side a few inches from my eyes. Instinctively I ducked and, being on the top step of the staircase, skidded to the bottom ... Then there was shouting and the sound of a machine gun and, eventually, an apparently inebriated Jerry came down the staircase waving a pistol. There was nothing for it but to surrender.'[13]

The end came for the garrison at Épine de Dallon shortly after 1.00pm. Colonel Martin, a man whose language was sometimes colourful, described the final moments:

'The Huns were making a most determined bombing attack from both sides, and the Huns were shooting for all they were worth. A bomb landed and blew me into *a hole, and I woke up to realize that a bloody Hun was laughing at me in an unpleasant manner, and had an even more unpleasant bayonet. Everyone I saw near me had his hands up.'*[14]

The only officer of the garrison killed in the final rush was Captain Arthur Clayton, the battalion adjutant, still holding a bomb when he put up his hands to surrender, he was shot dead presumably because his captors thought he was about to throw it.[15] The survivors along with Archibald Martin were marched off into captivity. As to the actual time the redoubt was overwhelmed, Brigadier General Stanley thought they held out until at least 2.30pm but whatever time it was, apart from the small cadre of officers and men left out of battle, the Wiltshires – like the 12/Royal Irish Rifles at Le Pontchu – were no longer a fighting unit. The number of men wounded remains imprecise but four officers and ninety-three other ranks had been killed in action or subsequently died of their wounds and barely a handful escaped death or captivity.

The defence of Manchester Hill by the 16/Manchesters is probably one of the most well-documented of all the actions which took place on 21 March, particularly as the officer commanding the battalion, Lieutenant Colonel Wilfrith Elstob, was awarded a posthumous Victoria Cross. The 29-year-old Elstob had already been awarded the DSO and the Military Cross and was considered to be a first-class commanding officer. On the other hand, there appeared to be a vast gulf between the almost shy and retiring Edinburgh schoolmaster who enlisted in 1914 and the rather bombastic character who rose through the commissioned ranks to the command of a battalion. A vicar's son who was educated at Christ's Hospital School in Sussex, he graduated from Manchester University to embark, we are told, on a lifelong ambition of becoming a schoolmaster. But the declaration of war changed all that in 1914. The battalion historian writes glowingly of him:

'A modest idealist in times of peace, the war brought forth all the latent power of the man. He was one of those fine natures which combined in a remarkable degree of tenderness and strength, innate dignity and humility, generosity and restraint. Men instinctively trusted him.'[16]

Accepting a commission in the 1st City of Manchester Battalion in 1914, he became second-in-command to his lifelong friend and confidant, Hubert Hamilton, who commanded A Company. A strikingly tall individual, Elstob was soon given the nickname of 'Big Ben' – a name that stuck even after he took over command of the battalion October 1917.

Manchester Hill – or *Margarine Höhe* – as the Germans called it, had been taken by units of the regiment in 1917 during the German retirement to the Hindenburg Line and the fact that Elstob and 16/Manchesters were in occupation on 21 March was purely a coincidence. However, the hill was a tactical feature of some strength in a rather featureless landscape; on a clear day it commanded good fields of fire over the shallow valleys that surrounded it and the nearby Brown Quarry on the western slope provided for dug-outs and shelters. Completely wired in on all sides, the perimeter was strengthened by nine posts or strong points which together with several barricades or 'bomb stops' created an almost impregnable position.

Close to the top of the hill was a forward observation post used by the artillery and one that was familiar to Lieutenant Herbert Asquith from the nearby C/149 Battery dug in on the eastern edge of Holnon Wood:

> *'Our observation post was on the forward fringe of the Outpost Zone, on the eastern slope of Manchester Hill, and looked straight out on No Man's Land, the subalterns of our battery went to this post in rotation, and I spent many days and nights there in February, and the first three weeks of March. Looking down the hill was an excellent view of the city of St Quentin, which lay at the bottom of the slope with its Cathedral tower rising above it, as a rule, absolutely silent, with a weird and sinister appearance of complete desertion.'*[17]

Today the concrete observation post is no longer a feature of the hill but the view across to St Quentin and the Basilica remains the same. Sadly the recent intrusion across the northern slopes of the hill by the A29 Autoroute to Amiens has guaranteed the peace and solitude enjoyed by Asquith has been shattered forever. On 18 March 1918 the calm which hung over the whole of the front line would still have been apparent when 16/Manchesters took over the garrison from their sister battalion, 17/Manchesters, the storm was not about to break for another forty-eight hours.

Asquith and his fellow subalterns had no doubts as to the eventual fate of Manchester Hill and its garrison. 'It was obvious to all,' he wrote, 'that if the attack were made at St Quentin, this isolated post, strong though it was, would have little chance of surviving with the main flood of the assault rolling round it on either side.' Clearly Wilfrith Elstob shared this view, commenting as they marched up to the hill that the battalion band, which were remaining out of action, would be 'the only fellows that will come out alive'. Once in position he took great pains to impress upon all his officers and men that the redoubt was to be defended to the last man, using the now legendary phrase, 'here we fight and here we die', words which must have struck terror into the less battle-hardened youngsters in his command.

Elstob's apparent welcome of a soldier's death had been embodied in a letter he wrote to Hubert Worthington in May 1917, soon after the 30th Division's attack at Cherisy. 'I should be miserable if I were taken away from the battalion', he wrote, 'I want to be with them in the battles, and if I were taken on the battlefield I feel that I could die happy', a strangely prophetic statement that must have been on his mind when he arrived at Manchester Hill. It has to be said that while the expectation of death haunted the movement of every man and woman serving on active fronts in the Great War, very few were prepared to go as far as welcoming its arrival! Elstob's undoubted courage cannot be defined as 'hot' courage – where an individual leaps into action without thinking about consequences, as demonstrated by Lieutenant Cecil Knox on the canal at Tugny – but was perhaps a more premeditated courage defined by a desire for personal recognition.

The story of Manchester Hill begins at 7.30am when Colonel Elstob gave orders for battalion headquarters to be withdrawn from Brown Quarry to Battle Headquarters on the hill itself which comprised a dugout some 300 yards east of the quarry and mid-way between the artillery observation post and the Savy-St Quentin road. Shortly after 8.00am the bombardment became more intense after which all communication with the company posts ceased, leaving a single telephone line to brigade headquarters intact. Half-an-hour later the hostile infantry attack began on A and B Companies and the forward posts, the thick fog rendering impotent the elaborately laid fire plans that had been designed to hold back advancing infantry.

C/149 Battery at Holnon Wood had come into action almost at the same moment as the German bombardment began and began firing in response to directions given from the observation post on Manchester Hill:

'*Hundreds of heavy shells were exploding behind us in Holnon Wood; mingled with their explosions we could hear now and then the crash of a falling tree, while high above our heads huge projectiles from long-range guns passed through the sky with a metallic roar on their way to targets far behind the battlefield ... in a few minutes our signallers reported that the telephone wire to the observation post had been blown to pieces in many places within a hundred yards of our position: they went out at great risk to mend the wire, but though many attempts were made, it was found impossible to restore communication.*'[18]

Apart from the telephone line back to brigade headquarters, Manchester Hill was now cut off from the outside world and when the fog began to lift, the glint of sunshine that broke through only confirmed the enemy breakthrough was complete as German infantry units were seen advancing on either side of the redoubt. Lieutenant Asquith could see the redoubt from the top of the nearby hill:

'*On my way up Round Hill, I found that the mist was dissolving, and here we were no longer troubled by gas ... When I reached the crest, I saw that our outpost redoubt at the Brown Quarry ... was now cut off on the north and west by the German infantry: a large number of grey misty figures, easily recognisable as Germans by the shape of their helmets, stood halted on the skyline of Manchester Hill.*'[19]

The telephone line back to 90 Brigade Headquarters at least kept Elstob in touch with someone on the outside, his conversations charting the final hours of the 16/Manchesters:

'About eleven o'clock Colonel Elstob informed me that the Germans had broken through and were swarming around the redoubt. At about 2pm he said that most of his men were killed or wounded, including himself; that they were all getting deadbeat, that the Germans had got into the redoubt and hand-to-hand fighting was going on. He was still quite cheery. At 3.30pm he was spoken to on the telephone and said very few were left and that the end was nearly come. After that no answer could be got.'[20]

Elstob had been wounded three times but continued fighting alongside his men until he was killed. Private Horace Hardman was possibly one of the last to see Wilfrith Elstob alive after the German infantry had finally broken through:

'The CO ... then gave orders for all to stand up and hold the Manchester Redoubt to the last man. He then went out with his revolver, and we were firing and bringing up bombs. We managed to hold the redoubt until 3.00pm; then Jerry seemed to come from all directions. The CO's last words were, 'Here goes the gallant Sixteenth!' Then he was shot through the head. We were taken prisoners.'[21]

Although it would appear that soon after Elstob was killed, the garrison lost little time in surrendering to the inevitable, what is of interest is the conflict between the casualty figures provided in the battalion history by Westropp and those from more recent sources. Westropp reports that only 2 officers and 15 other ranks survived but a more recent appraisal suggests that of the 23 officers and 717 other ranks that were on roll – not including those who were left out of battle – only 3 officers and 78 other ranks were killed. A number of the 13 officers who were taken prisoner on 21 March would have been captured after the outposts were surrounded.

In the cold light of day the redoubt had achieved little more than many others had in similar circumstances. However, Wilfrith Elstob's award of the Victoria Cross was conferred on an officer who showed great gallantry and leadership in the face of overwhelming odds. But if the question is asked whether the stand on Manchester Hill was any more gallant than that of Harry Fine at Vendeuil or Geoffrey Lester at Triangle Post, or indeed that of Leslie Johnston and John Crosthwaite, the answer – in the opinion of this author – has to be no.

A mile north of Manchester Hill in the 182 Brigade sector was the Ellis Redoubt. The brigade was responsible for an area which ran from the southern edge of Fayet to the old Roman road running out of St Quentin towards Selency. On 21 March the 2/8th Worcestershire Regiment (2/8 Worcesters) was in the

Forward Zone with its two forward companies manning a series of posts between Roses Wood in the south and the edge of Fayet to the north, each of which was linked by a shallow communication trench. Battalion headquarters was in the Ellis Redoubt which drew its name from the officer commanding 201/Field Company, and it was the sappers of 201/Field Company that constructed the redoubt and sited it on the banks either side of the Vallée du Chemin l'Abbaye about half-a-mile east of Selency. Lieutenant Robert Petschler was one of the engineers involved:

> 'It consisted of various cunningly concealed machine guns built in deep dugouts in the sides of the banks, and the entrance to these dugouts was by means of a carefully camouflaged trench. The whole object of the machine guns was to come as a surprise and to bring close range fire on the attacking party when they least expected it ... The remainder of the redoubt consisted of trench posts mutually supporting each other and which could bring enfilade fire on an attacking party.'[22]

In addition to the fire power of B Company the redoubt also housed two trench mortars and two Vickers machine guns. Very little exists today as to what happened here but we are told the Worcesters held on until 5.30pm when their ammunition ran out and the fall of the Enghien Redoubt on their left flank had left the German infantry from IR 109 and GR 110 free to deal with them. *The Official British History* records that only one officer and six men made it back to brigade headquaters that evening.

We know far more about the circumstances leading to the fall of the Enghein Redoubt which was less than half-a-mile north of the Worcesters and situated a little to the west of the minor road – Chemin de Fayet – that runs from the D1029 from Selency to Fayet. The fortified area which contained the redoubt consisted of three trench systems in the form of a rough pentagon. On the western side Douai Trench linked with Epicure Alley – which formed the southern defensive line – while Etretat Trench completed the eastern side. In the centre was the redoubt itself, incorporating a disused quarry. Although time and progress have all contributed to an erosion of the past, the battlefield visitor will find the site of the former redoubt is only a matter of yards from Junction 10 of the A26 Autoroute and marked by a white smear across the fields. To the left a private house sits in its rectangular grounds and to the right a small stand of trees is on the approximate site of 'the cottages'.[23]

On 18 March the redoubt was garrisoned by D Company of the 2/4th Battalion, Oxford and Buckinghamshire Light Infantry (2/4 Ox and Bucks) along with the collection of cooks, signallers and runners of HQ Company. In command of the battalion was Lieutenant Colonel Harry Wetherall, an officer who was first commissioned into the Gloucestershire Regiment in 1909 and went to war as a lieutenant with the 1st Battalion in 1914. Having survived the retreat from Mons,

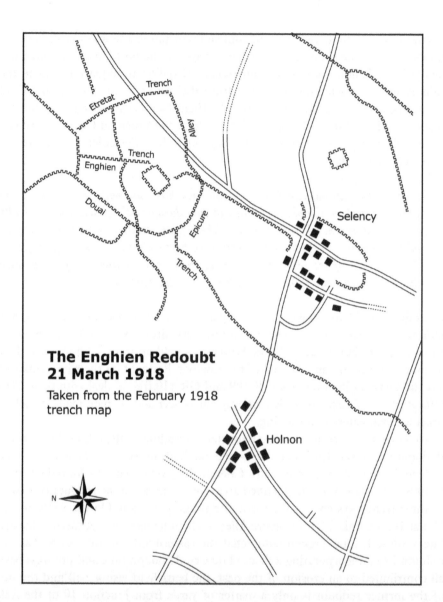

**The Enghien Redoubt
21 March 1918**

Taken from the February 1918
trench map

he fought on the Aisne and was wounded at Gheluvelt in October 1914 during the First Battle of Ypres. Rapid promotion brought him to the command of the 2/4 Battalion taking over from Robert Bellamy in May 1917.

Wetherall lost little time in making his mark on the battalion, which delighted Captain Geoffrey Rose who later wrote in the battalion history that 'his emphatic direction and enthusiasm earned early reward in the increased efficiency of all ranks'.

Shortly before the battalion went into the front line 200 reinforcements arrived from the disbanded 6th Battalion which included 23-year-old Second

Lieutenant John Cunningham and Captain George Rowbotham, both officers were posted to D Company. Once established at the Enghien Redoubt Wetherall deployed A Company to Fayet, B Company to the Dum Copse area and C Company to positions in front of Fayet along the line of the modern day D372. The 184 Brigade sector was very close to the German lines in the Fayet area, a factor that undoubtedly influenced the location of the successful raid carried out by the 2/6th Royal Warwicks from 182 Brigade on Cepy Farm on the night of 20/21 March. Fifteen prisoners were brought back from three different infantry divisions on a front usually held by one regiment, lending little doubt to the certainty that the offensive was imminent.

The Enghien story was written shortly after by Harry Wetherall while he was recovering from wounds in hospital. His account begins after the noise of the Warwicks' raid had settled down and he had been given news of the origin of the German prisoners:

'Without hearing any more I knew we were in for it. After the noise of the raid had settled down, the night was extraordinarily quiet, and it seemed impossible that a great battle was going to start in a few hours ... I slept well, and on being called at 4.00am on the 21st not a sound was to be heard, and the line reported all quiet. On going upstairs out of the dug-out, I found there was a dense ground mist and a light northwest wind. I went back to bed again and at 5.40am I was awakened by a roar from a terrific bombardment, though I could hear no shells bursting in the redoubt.'[24]

Although the extracts from Wetherall's diary of events are focused on the redoubt, they do provide an insight into the nature of the bombardment and the confusion that other units were experiencing in the dense fog. He notes that within ten minutes of the opening salvoes from the German artillery all telephone lines to his front companies were cut with the exception of the buried line linking him to 184 Brigade:

'6.00am. I go out of the dug-out and find the redoubt is full of gas, the Boches having burst their shells some distance over the redoubt and allowed the wind to blow it back on us. I order all men below, and have the gas blankets put down. Some of the men who were on sentry duty are pretty bad from its effects.

6.15am. Gas is very bad. We have orders to evacuate the redoubt if the place is badly gassed. I go out to see if this is possible, and although I know the place by heart, I have not gone 50 yards in the fog with my respirator on before I am lost. It took 15 minutes to find my way back to the dug-out and therefore I determined to stick where I am.

7.30am. We are now shelled by high explosive alone. I judge, together with a gunner officer, attached for liaison, that about three 4.2 batteries and one 5.9 battery are now shelling our quarry, a space of about 50 yards by 60.

9.20am. Very heavy shrapnel and high explosive shelling now taking place; also the noise of the bombardment of the line of resistance seems nearer. I expect they are attacking. I order all men to get ready to rush up.'[25]

Wetherall was right, the German infantry were attacking and the men of A Company at Fayet were in the path of IR 109 – the *Liebgarde* Grenadier Regiment. From the account given by *Gefreiter* Wilhelm Reinhard it appears that the initial bombardment had knocked the fight out of many of the Ox and Bucks at Fayet:

'We followed the creeping barrage quickly but, as soon as we appeared, the British threw away their weapons and surrendered. There was really no fight for Fayet. I think they were hoping for an opportunity to surrender. One of them gave me his razor. I think he wanted to thank me because he had been taken prisoner and not killed.'[26]

Whether or not anyone from A Company escaped captivity is not known but a handful from C Company did get away led by Second Lieutenant Harold Jones and CSM Francis Liddell:

'When the attacking infantry reached our trench, the fog was still very dense. A shower of stick bombs forced us to leave the trench and we climbed out onto the back to maintain a line but beyond the range of their bombs ... I saw six or seven German officers or NCOs in the open looking at a map. They were only three or four yards away so I automatically came up with the revolver I had acquired and that was the only occasion in which I can honestly say that I shot any Germans in two and a half years of front-line soldering. After that I collected together about a dozen of my men and attempted to get back to Battalion HQ in the Enghien Redoubt.'[27]

Jones and his party never reached the redoubt but did get back to brigade HQ which is probably just as well as the Enghien garrison was under attack from the Chemin de Fayt – the road that ran past the quarry – which in 1918 was a sunken road with high sides. The outlying posts had already been silenced and the main redoubt was now under threat. Wetherall's diary records a group of fifty German infantry attacking from the road of which some twenty-five were shot down:

'The rest run back into the road. The men are very steady. I asked Brigade for our last protective barrage, but only five of our 18-pounders answer.

9.50am. Captain Rowbotham reports to me that an important part of the redoubt, the sand-pit, has fallen. We organise a bombing attack, and he leads it, regaining the sand-pit, so now we hold the entire redoubt, with the exception of [the posts].

11.10am. The Boches made a big bombing attack from three sides which looks very ugly at one time, but the men fight well, and we drive them back, killing about 15.

11.30am. We are now practically surrounded, and I get an urgent message from Post 12, which is a rear post, [probably somewhere along Douai Trench] *for help, which of course I cannot give. I go down to visit them and find them very happy, a Vickers Gun having killed, I should say 60 Germans, whose bodies I can see in the fog hanging on the wire.'*[28]

At 11.45am the fog was beginning to lift which added to Wetherall's concern as to what might take place once the German infantry had the advantage of clearer visibility. If the artillery at Holnon could put down a barrage on Selency village where he suspected German infantry to be massing, it might disperse the attack, but first he had to be sure there was any artillery left to provide that support. Typically Wetherall decided to make the reconnaissance himself particularly as he felt John Cunningham 'was doing so well'. There his diary of the redoubt ends as he is shortly afterwards captured at Holnon and despite making his escape, only regained the safety of British lines at 10.00pm that evening.

John Cunningham was acting adjutant and had been commissioned into the regiment in August 1916. An account of the action written by Captain Walter Moberly makes it is clear that Cunningham was the senior officer in command of the redoubt at the time of its capture and was responsible for the resistance made by the garrison in its last hours. Sadly there is little detail recorded of the remaining three hours in which the redoubt held out apart from conversations held between Cunningham and Brigade Major Harold Howitt at 184 Brigade Headquarters. Shortly after Wetherall had left for Holnon the tiny quarry was surrounded and German infantry began firing into the garrison from the quarry sides. Holding out until about 5.00pm Cunningham's final message to brigade was to seek permission to withdraw:

'The last message I received was "we are surrounded now, Sir, what are we to do?" It was an agonizing position, so I rang the divisional commander and, as the whole front had collapsed, I was told to give them permission to cut their way out if they could. It was five o'clock before I was able to get back to them, and after that I heard no more'.[29]

With permission granted the remnants of the garrison attempted to escape, John Cunningham was wounded and captured but a handful were reported to have got away to the Battle Zone a mile to the rear. Cunningham's award of the DSO was gazetted in January 1920 after his return to England. The casualty figures for the battalion vary depending which source is used, however a figure somewhere between 86 and 100 officers and men killed on 21 March is not far short of the truth. The battalion like so many others had practically ceased to exist as a fighting unit and as Walter Moberley wrote in April 1918, 'I am afraid the battalion is completely smashed up. We always knew that whatever battalion happened to be in the front at the time of the German assault was bound to be done-in.'

The last redoubt in the 61st Divisional sector was at Fresnoy-le-Petit on the D57 which runs northeast from Fayet. The redoubt was held by the 1/5th Gordon Highlanders and constructed in and around the crossroads in the centre of the village, a fortified position which included the south western corner of Marronniers Wood. Battalion Headquarters and the counter-attack company were just to the west of the village while the right and left front companies held the forward trenches either side of Gricourt. The Gordons were commanded by Lieutenant Colonel Maxwell McTaggart who was appointed in June 1915 having previously served with the 5th Royal Irish Lancers. McTaggart arrived after the fighting around Ypres in May 1915 with a newly-won DSO ribbon on his chest. Lieutenant Colonel W N Nicholson met him soon after he joined the battalion, which was then serving with 183 Brigade, 51st (Highland) Division:

'*He came to us from the 5th Lancers to command the 5th Gordons, a battalion that needed a leader, and he proved up to the hilt the value of a good Regular officer. The change in his unit in a short time was extraordinary; they caught his enthusiasm, stuck out their chests and rightly regarded themselves as a very fine body of men. How pernickety the little man was about the set of his kilt, the size of his Glengarry; I fancy he had never worn either before in his life. He might have posed for the Gallic Cock; a most gallant little man; all blood and thunder.*'[30]

As to exactly what happened on the morning of 21 March we can only assume it was similar to that of the other redoubts, no account of the battle by McTaggart or any other man who fought that morning that has so far come to light. Captain Thomas Davie, the battalion medical officer, is in little doubt the attack caught the battalion by surprise:

'*The first warning of the imminence of a German attack was the gas shell bombardment at about a quarter to five in the morning. As regards the actual attack later on, no knowledge of this was forthcoming from the various company headquarters owing probably to damage to the cables; but also to the fact that the enemy had made a lateral approach under cover of the heavy mist; and the first knowledge of this was a rapid enfilade fire on Battalion Headquarters.*'[31]

When it became obvious the battalion had been overrun, Davie made his escape from the battalion aid post with two men and eventually caught up with what was left of the battalion near Marteville where he found a few men of A Company that had been collected together by Regimental Sergeant Major Park.[32] Falls in his history of the regiment has only this to say:

> 'There is little that can be said of the fate of the 5th Gordons except that they were overrun and thereafter existed only as a handful of survivors … At 12.20pm the 183rd Brigade headquarters received a message from the commanding officer, Lieutenant Colonel M F McTaggart, that his redoubt was surrounded and that he feared he would be unable to hold out for long … The number of survivors who managed to get back to brigade headquarters was not more than thirty.'[33]

McTaggart and his second-in-command, Major Charles Robertson, were taken prisoner at the redoubt and were later joined by another twelve officers. As to the number of other ranks, we know that at least thirty-three were killed but the number of wounded remains imprecise; however, we can be sure that the fiery McTaggart and his men in the redoubt put up a stubborn resistance before the end came around 1.30pm.

Chapter 6

The Forlorn Hope

Lance Corporal Sayer showed throughout the utmost contempt for danger and the enemy – he inspired everyone by his conduct, and by his actions undoubtedly enabled my post to hold out as long as it did for nearly two hours, that is until just before the mist rose about 12 noon.

Lieutenant Claude Piesse at Shepherd's Copse

The XIX Corps sector was contained by the two river valleys, the Omignon in the south and that of the Cologne to the north which joined the Somme at Péronne. To defend the five miles of front line Lieutenant General Herbert Watts had two infantry divisions; Major General Arthur Daly commanded the 24th Division and Major General Neil Malcolm the 66th. The undulating nature of the XIX sector was both suited for defensive action and, as it turned out, offensive action, the same valleys on which the British had constructed their defences served to provide cover for the assaulting German infantry under the cloak of dense fog.

The British defences in the south of the sector, where no man's land was at its widest, were less well developed than that of the north. In the southern two thirds the Forward Zone took the form of isolated posts which were designed to be supported by machine-gun nests. This differed from the north of the sector where the narrower no man's land was faced by a more substantial three-line trench system. The Battle Zone took the form of a front line with four strongly defended areas: Vadancourt, Le Verguier, Jeancourt and Templeux le Guérard.

Bordering the 61st Division on the right flank were the swampy reaches of the River Omignon, a wide river valley which neatly divided the two battalions in the Forward Zone. Battalion rotation on 18 March had placed the 8th Battalion Royal West Kents (8/RWK) north of the river and the 1st Battalion North Staffordshire Regiment (1/North Staffs) to the south. A trestle bridge between Vadancourt and Maissemy – where the North Staffs had their headquarters – and another similar construction at Bihecourt were the only crossing points across the river valley. The Omignon valley was also the boundary between two German Armies – von Hutier's Eighteenth and von der Marwitz's Second; thus north of the river the first waves of the German 208th and 4th Guard Divisions were poised to attack the left of the British 24th Division, while to the south, the 113th Division's objectives would bring them up against the North Staffs and Lieutenant Colonel Maxwell McTaggart's 1/5 Gordon Highlanders around Fresnoy-le-Petit.

The Staffs established their HQ at the Essling Redoubt which was dug into a slope on the D735 running south from Maissemy towards the St Quentin road. Arriving in the line three days previously the battalion was dismayed to be told they were to defend a sector from Gricourt to Pontruet. Alarm bells began ringing when the forward defences were found to be in a poor state as most of the work had been concentrated on the Essling Redoubt. Although Major General Daly felt the battalion had done all it could to improve the defences, he was 'not at all happy about them'. The French had done little to strengthen the position and the defence depended on interlocking machine-gun fire. 'I remember telling the OC [Lieutenant Colonel Vyvyan Pope] that it looked as if his battalion were liable to be overrun at an early stage.' Presumably Pope kept the divisional commander's opinion to himself!

Fortunately progress across the river, where 8/RWK had established its headquarters on a ridge of high ground amongst the ruins of Vadancourt Château, was further advanced. In command of the battalion was Lieutenant Colonel Herbert Wenyon, a former private soldier whose leadership qualities were recognised with his promotion to second lieutenant in October 1915. Command of a company soon followed as did the award of the DSO in 1917. Promotion to lieutenant colonel and command of the West Kents came a mere three months later. In addition to Headquarters Company and Colonel Wenyon, the redoubt defences held the men of A and C Companies who manned the numerous posts around the ruins of the château. It was unquestionably a strongly fortified position, commanding good fields of fire and with wide views across the valley that formed no man's land.

From Vadancourt the old Roman road – known as Watling Street – ran northeast towards Riqueval and the St Quentin Canal. Approximately half-a-mile along Watling Street – now the D33 – lies Cooker's Quarry, which formed part of the sector held by the 3rd Rifle Brigade (3/RB), running from Ascension Farm in the north to the line of Watling Street in the south. Commanding the Rifle Brigade was Lieutenant Colonel Edward Kewley who, after deploying B Company to the outpost line, established battalion headquarters in Caubrières Wood. A and D Companies were in reserve at Vadancourt and C Company were at Cooker's Quarry.

The opening bombardment on XIX Corps was as devastating and continuous as it was further south and, as Lieutenant Colonel Pope, commanding the

North Staffs, had expected, all communication with his forward companies was immediately severed leaving him little option but to employ runners to reach his outpost line. Pope's personal account unfortunately sheds no light on the action in the redoubt itself:

> 'The visibility was now about twenty yards but provided my flanks were secure, I thought we could give a good account of ourselves. On the left flank there was a gap between headquarters and C Company, but I had posted a machine gun to cover that and the ground between was open. On the right was a dangerous re-entrant, but the Argylls would see to that. I walked round the line and told the men what to expect. All the shelling of our trench had now ceased and the men were generally cool and confident. When I reached our right, however, I found nobody had seen anything of the Argylls.'[1]

Pope's concern was the re-entrant on his right flank which, if compromised would result in the battalion being outflanked and the Argyll and Sutherland Highlanders were an essential part of this defence:

> 'I told [Captain William Stamer, Battalion Adjutant] I was going to find the Argylls ... Stamer did not view this suggestion with any great favour and asked me whether they were to hold on to the last if attacked. 'I shall be back long before that can happen,' I replied, 'but if things do go wrong I don't want you to uselessly throw away the men's lives.'[2]

Pope did not get far before he heard firing coming from the direction of the redoubt. In trying to regain his headquarters he blundered into a small group of German infantry; opening fire with his rifle he hit the leading soldier but was wounded himself by the second man whose shot shattered his elbow. Pope was now out of the frame as far as the fighting was concerned but fortunately managed to reach a dressing station before he passed out. As for the Staffs they did hold out until they were overrun and we are told as few as thirty NCOs and men managed to escape.

German infantry were now advancing up the road from Maissemy towards Vadancourt and Wenyon gave the order for the bridges over the Omignon to be blown. Lieutenant Arthur Fairbourn and his section of 103/Field Company Sappers duly obliged, blowing both bridges before heading to Vermand where three more crossing points had been prepared for demolition. Fairbourn's work had provided some protection to the West Kent's right flank but as visibility improved German infantry were seen in occupation of the ridge in front of Vadancourt. Confirmation that Mareval and Pontru Trenches had been taken arrived with several wounded men from B Company who came into the battalion dressing station. An account written after the war by the company commander, Captain Charles Allworth provided a little more detail:

> 'During the bombardment ... I decided to go up and visit the forward platoons; my runner accompanied me. We had left the trench and proceeded about 200 yards, when two Germans appeared out of the mist, one was a wounded man and the other a medical orderly or a stretcher bearer ... this was our first indication that the enemy had attacked. The enemy had occupied Pontru village and all the foremost positions. About 8.30am they attacked our line (Pontru and Mareval Trench). The wire in front of the trench had been untouched by the bombardment and owing to our Lewis gun and rifle fire they failed to get through it. The enemy then brought up a machine gun on the flank bridge across the Omignon, this was put out of action at once by our right Lewis gun. They then brought up another gun and owing to a jam in our Lewis gun, put our team out of action. A number of the enemy came down the banks of the stream and occupied the right of Pontru Trench. We attempted to bomb them out, but they got round in the rear of the trench, and we had a rather exciting retreat down the trench to Company Headquarters, where we established a block.'[3]

German infantry were also advancing down the road from Bellenglise which provided Allworth and his men with plenty of targets to shoot at, at the same moment a machine gun from Cooker's Quarry also opened up on the advancing infantry which, had the West Kent's not run out of ammunition, would have caused even greater damage than it did. At this, with discretion being the greater part of valour, Allworth ordered what was left of B Company to retire. 'We then, with fixed bayonets, got out of the trench and attempted to get back to the battalion's main positions, but we ran into large numbers of Germans and were overpowered.' Taken prisoner with his men, Allworth had the opportunity to take a little more notice of what was going on around him. 'The effrontery of the enemy was astounding. He was marking out the line of his advance with white flags, and far in the rear the forward movement of battalions with full transport could be seen in all directions.' But with the swampy ground of the Omignon forcing the assaulting infantry to use Watling Street, C Company of the 3/Rifle Brigade at Cooker's Quarry now stood in their way.

The situation was now critical. Units of the German 113th Division were advancing through Maissemy towards Vermand and in the process had outflanked the West Kents who were holding on at Vadancourt on the north bank of the Omignon. Unless the Rifle Brigade could remain intact on the left flank, Vadencourt would become untenable and the West Kents would be in serious trouble. Even so it was a situation that could have only one outcome, the question facing Major General Daly was straightforward: just how long could these two battalions hold back the two German Guard Divisions facing them? With the inevitability of retreat in mind he ordered Lieutenant Fairbourn and his sappers to blow the bridges at Vermand and Captain Archibald Thorburn of 259/Field Company to destroy the two trestle bridges at Caulaincourt.

The Rifle Brigade positions had suffered considerably from enemy shellfire, particularly as the forward posts had not been completed and many of the trenches were too shallow. Lieutenant Colonel Kewley's account pulled no punches. 'This line was a peculiarly bad line consisting of a system of carriage drives (ie very broad trenches only a few feet deep which were no protection from any sort of fire.' Kewley's thinking was along the same lines as his divisional commander:

> '*On our northern or left flank the Queen's* [Royal West Surrey Regiment] *were putting up a great fight and were holding their own. On our southern flank the enemy appeared to be gaining ground. Our artillery had by now brought a fire on the portion of trench by Dean Copse which the enemy were holding ... At the same time the situation was black; there was that nasty gap in the centre, reinforcements did not arrive, the right flank had a very unpleasant appearance and it was doubtful how long Cooker's Quarry could hold out. It became a race for time, if we could stick it till dark something might be done.*'4

Despite a truly magnificent defence the Cooker's garrison fell just before dark but by holding out as long as they did enemy movement along Watling Street was severely disrupted. An earlier message from the quarry saying they were completely surrounded had made Colonel Kewley very much aware of the precarious nature of C Company's position and it was no surprise when, at 7.00pm, a runner arrived with a message from Captain Thomas Fenner to the effect that the quarry had fallen and Fenner and his garrison had retired to Vadancourt. Thus, as darkness fell it was touch and go as to who would arrive first, the Germans or reinforcements. Fortunately it was the latter and new positions were organised on a line running from Bihecourt to just west of Caubrières Wood to Le Verguier.

Now in danger of being completely outflanked and surrounded himself, Lieutenant Colonel Wenyon gave orders for his battalion to retire:

> '*At 8.30pm it was decided that we would make an attempt to withdraw under the cover of darkness to the Brown Line at Bihecourt, some 600 yards behind. This was no easy matter ... a strong rearguard was organised, and took up positions on the threatened flank* [right flank]. *Lieutenant* [Ernest] *Goulden, Second Lieutenant Pfeuffar and Second Lieutenant Tiley, with a number of men with four Lewis guns formed the guard, and they set up a powerful demonstration of fire for nearly an hour ... Four Vickers guns and teams also remained behind under the command of Second Lieutenant Peachy of the 24th Divisional Machine Gun Battalion. The*

rearguard got back about 10.00pm and thanks to their work, we achieved almost a miracle in getting back without a single casualty.[5]

Senior officer casualties in the division had been relatively high on 21 March. Apart from Colonel Pope of the Staffs, 38-year-old Lieutenant Colonel Lawrence, commanding the 9th Battalion East Surrey Regiment (9/East Surreys) had been killed in the afternoon near Villecholles. Moving swiftly to restore some resemblance of order to the line, Daly placed Lieutenant Colonel Wenyon in command of forces north of the Omignon and Colonel Rowland Anderson, who had arrived with units of the 1st Cavalry Division as reinforcements, found himself commanding forces south of the river.

Anderson established his headquarters first at Villecholles and then on the mound in the centre of Vermand. Under no illusion as to the seriousness of his position he gave orders for the line which ran in front of Villecholes to Mount Houette Wood to be strengthened. Beyond the wood the line was continued by the 61st Division. The wood was held by C Squadron, 11th Hussars and some of the 9/East Surreys, a little to the west of the wood B Squadron 11th Hussars linked up with the East Surreys on the Villecholles-Maissemy road. To the south of the wood and running up a slope, lay the defences of Spooner Redoubt which was held by a collection of units which included some East Surreys, Hussars and the 1/8th Battalion Argyll and Sutherland Highlanders from 183 Brigade, one company of whom occupied a forward position on front of the redoubt. It may well have been from this position that Second Lieutenant John Buchan won his Victoria Cross: refusing calls for surrender he was last seen surrounded by the enemy but still fighting. Sadly the award was posthumous as Buchan died of his wounds the next day.[6] Although the redoubt was protected by wire on all sides, the trenches were by no means completed and at two feet deep offered little protection from shell and bullet.

The morning of 22 March was similar to the previous day; a dense mist covered the ground concealing any movements the enemy might be making. The first indication of the impending attack came as German gunners began searching for the position with high explosive, during which time a company of the 19th Entrenching Battalion arrived to reinforce the line with Lieutenant Eugene Rivière. The shelling, which continued for an hour or so, fortunately lacked accuracy and very few landed in the trenches. But Spooner Redoubt soon came under attack:

'Looking up I saw in the fog a small group of men, about six in number, come up to the wire and lie down in front of it. 'Don't shoot!' I yelled, thinking that it might be the company of Argylls trying to come back. At that moment one of the group stood up and I saw it was a Boche; he was an enormous man wearing a steel helmet; from his belt he drew out a bomb, pulled the string, flung it into the wire

and fell back dead. Our men, without waiting for further orders had opened fire, the bomber and his section were riddled with bullets and lay writhing on the ground. And then rising up from the earth, they had crawled up unobserved in the long grass, appeared hundreds upon hundreds of Boches, all making for the wire, some throwing bombs, and others trying to cut it with nippers. With a roar our machine guns and Hotchkiss guns opened fire, and the men yelling, cursing and swearing jumped onto the parapet and shot for their lives. The enemy were swept down like grass under a scythe, but there were always more to take their places and they too met the same fate. Nothing that moved was allowed to live.[7]

Three attacks were dealt with in a similar fashion by the men at Spooner Redoubt during which Major Robert Moir, commanding the Argylls was reported to have walked up and down the redoubt encouraging his men, 'his magnificent leadership was an inspiring example to all the troops in this part of the line' wrote Lumley. The situation was not improved by an all round shortage of ammunition and a classic situation of friendly fire. British gunners, perhaps alarmed at the reports from stragglers that the Germans had overrun Spooner Redoubt, opened fire on the redoubt with considerably more accuracy than the German barrage had managed. Lawrence Lumley was horrified, 'I came upon a trench only about two foot deep: it was full of men from every kind of unit and many were wounded.' In one of those awful accidents of war the position was under artillery fire from both sides, one shell actually passed underneath Captain Luke White's arm as he was leaning against the entrance to a dug-out, fortunately it was a dud! Lumley was wounded soon after, although he is loyal enough not to blame the British gunners.

At 11.40pm the hand of fate dealt the men at Spooner Redoubt and Mount Houette Wood a lifeline. Under the impression they were going to have to fight it out until the last man they now received orders from Anderson to retire. Retirement under fire is always a hazardous operation but in this case it was doubly so. German infantry were closing in on both flanks and although they had been largely beaten off on the eastern side they were still within 200 yards of the line. It was a recipe for chaos. Given that the line was manned by remnants of units which included East Surreys, Sherwood Foresters, Argylls and 11/ Hussars, some of which were without their officers and senior NCOs, it was little wonder that once retirement was seen to be taking place, everyone wanted to go at the same time. Lumley is convinced that 'the order to retire had reached the left of the 61st Division about the same time as that of the 24th Division', which he felt was partly responsible for the confusion.

Fortunately good sense prevailed. Captain White ordered the Hussars to stand fast and engage the enemy who were by this time bringing up machine guns and pouring a deadly fire down on the crowd of men who were heading for the gap in the Spooner Redoubt wire. Discipline had vanished in the panic to reach safety and escape the German machine guns. But then, as Lawrence Lumley watched, order was restored:

'Whether one man or several were responsible, is not known. What is certain is that as he came calmly through the gap in the wire, the hoarse voice of Major Moir of the Argyll and Sutherland Highlanders was heard shouting, 'Stand fast – the Argylls'. Other officers took up the cry. In a moment the scene changed. Instead of a crown of disorganised fugitives, the slope became dotted with small groups of men who had collected round their officers; they formed into ranks and even when shells ploughed through them they took extended order as if on parade and lay down and fired at the enemy ... For the few who witnessed this scene it was a sight so dramatic in its sudden change and so reassuring as to remain one of the most striking memories of the war.'[8]

Despite being wounded, Lawrence Lumley managed to escape capture, thanks to the efforts of Sergeant William Turner. Captain White and the 11th Hussars retired along the southern bank of the river to Villeveque where they joined 183 Brigade.

* * *

When the 8/Queen's relieved the 1st Battalion Royal Fusiliers in the Le Verguier sector on 18 March 1918, their commanding officer was 32-year-old Lieutenant Colonel Hugh Peirs. A graduate of New College, Oxford and a solicitor in civilian life, Peirs was typical of the professional class who in 1914 answered the call of duty, placed their former lives on hold and took up the mantle of soldiering. By the end of 1917 his courage and leadership on the battlefield had been rewarded with promotion to major and the award of a DSO and bar, further acknowledgment came on 3 March with the long overdue command of a battalion. The 8/Queen's were at Montecourt when Peirs took command which left precious little time for training before the inevitable move back to the front line. Fortune dictated the Queen's were to occupy the Forward Zone.

The Queen's positions were dictated to a large extent by the shallow valley which ran from Le Verguier to Villeret, command of the valley would severely disrupt any potential threat by attacking infantry. Accordingly C Company took up commanding positions in and around Shepherd's Copse and A Company held the posts around Graham Post. These posts would be directly in the path of any attack. Shepherd's Copse stands on a bend of the D57, just east of the Bois du Roi and on the eastern edge of the Vallée à Facon. It was here at Shepherd's Post that Lieutenant Claude Piesse was in command of C Company headquarters. A little further to the east the remainder of C Company occupied the forward posts which went under the names of Goat, Sheep, Lamb and Ewe Posts. Each of these posts was connected by a communication trench which formed a junction at Shepherd's Post.

On the opposite flank and holding the more isolated posts around and south of Grand Priel Farm was A Company. These posts, some of which assumed names such as Ding, Dong, Dick and Jim, were unconnected and in the swirling fog of the morning of 21 March those A Company men occupying these posts must have felt as if they were on another planet altogether.

Although shelling of Le Verguier had commenced before the attacks on the outposts began, the German assault on the village defences did not begin until well after midday. The only possible explanation for such a delay is the hold-up at Shepherd's Copse. Hugh Peirs was not slow to recognise the tactical importance of his forward companies and the effect their action had on his own positions around Le Verguier:

> '*I think our ability to defend the place* [Le Verguier] *during the 21st March was very largely due to the officers and men in the forward posts who, though surrounded, were undefeated for many hours, by which time we could see to shoot.*'[9]

The defence of Shepherd's Copse and the subsequent award of the Victoria Cross to 38-year-old Lance Corporal John Sayer have only recently received the recognition it deserved. Incredibly the history of the regiment fails to mention the action and it was only through the tireless efforts of Claude Piesse and Hugh Peirs that Sayer's bravery was eventually recognised. There is little doubt that the action of the men in the Queen's two forward companies significantly delayed the German assault from the northeast and it is only through Claude Piesse's account of the fight at Shepherd's Copse that we are able to grasp the precarious and desperate nature of the action as the main thrust of the enemy assault came along the Vallée à Facon. Clearly unhappy with the physical positioning of his post, Piesse was in command of the C Company advanced outposts:

> '*At 4.30am the enemy started a very severe bombardment with high explosive and shrapnel, which lasted until 10.00am. At this hour L/C Sayer in charge of a small party was returning to Coy* [Company] *HQ and had just reached the post when the enemy attacked simultaneously from both sides. Thick mist prevented visibility at more than thirty yards. L/C Sayer at once seized the junction of two communication trenches about 20 yards southeast from my post: a position which commanded the approach from the east – this position had been previously noted by me, but having a permanent garrison of only 4 men and 1 NCO, I was unable to make arrangements to occupy it. L/C Sayer held this position for nearly two hours against all attacks of the much stronger enemy, defending it by bayonet and rifle with almost incredible bravery. One German was bayoneted in the trench and died at his feet. Later, on several occasions, by his constant resolute attitude and ability to use his rifle and*

bayonet, he single handed caused the breakdown of several attacks on the trench. I personally saw him kill several of the enemy and when the fight was over and I was being taken back as a wounded prisoner, I made note that about this place there were six dead Germans, who I most certainly believe were killed by L/C Sayer.'[10]

John Sayer was a married man with six children when he enlisted in July 1916 and by the time he fought his last battle at Shepherd's Copse he was, by the standards of the day, a relatively experienced soldier, having been in France since December 1916. He would of course have had no idea that his actions and those around him would have such a marked effect on the defence of Le Verguier. Even Hugh Peirs would not be in possession of the full facts until after the war when he and Claude Piesse were able to piece the whole story of the day together, a story that Piesse tells us ended not with surrender but with his tiny garrison being overpowered:

'Three quarters of the garrison were killed, the enemy finally rushed the post, 5 wounded men being made prisoner, one of whom was L/C Sayer; at the time unconscious from a bad wound which necessitated the amputation of a leg and a short time after caused his death at Le Cateau.'[11]

Piesse later wrote that he 'was out before the end, but the Red Cross stretcher bearer told me he was the only man standing when the enemy finally got into the trench.'

With the forward companies gone, the attack focused on Le Verguier which by now had become a salient projecting into enemy-held territory as the battalions on either side retired in the face of heavy attacks. Peirs estimated that the enemy was 'well past Villeret and well towards Jeancourt by 2.00pm'. Late in the afternoon the village again came under a sustained attack, this time from three sides which the beleaguered Queen's held off very successfully with rifle and Lewis gun fire. At 7.00pm, having failed to enter the village, the enemy infantry deferred to the artillery which kept up a bombardment through most of the night. At 9.30am on 22 March, with the village under a determined assault, Peirs, this time using the fog to his own advantage, ordered a retirement. It was a decision that he had grappled with since the previous day:

'Speaking for myself I had considerable doubts at Le Verguier in ordering a retirement. We were in a fog and nearly surrounded and incidentally, quite defenceless and it weighed considerably with me whether I might get out with the two companies I still had and save them for another day or wait and chance my luck. I chose the former alternative, but I very much doubt whether I should have done so had I been a regular soldier with my career dependent on my obeying orders.'[12]

Piers had made the correct choice and only one man was wounded in the hand as the remnants of the battalion withdrew.

On the 66th Division frontage the first waves of the German 25th and 208th Divisions soon broke through the Forward Zone from Grand Priel Woods in the south to Templeux le Guérard in the Cologne valley. The initial German attack quickly cut through the Forward Zone posts, the 4th Battalion East Lancashires – dug in in front of Hargicourt – were dealt with swiftly by an attack which took them in both flanks while the 2/8th Lancashire Fusiliers, to the north of Hargicourt, received similar treatment. By 10.30am, with the fog lifting, the German infantry were on the forward edge of the Battle Zone. Half-an-hour later they broke into the Battle Zone at Brosse Wood – the junction of the 24th and 66th Divisions. Here the advance was checked temporarily by a company of 2/7 Manchesters. Interestingly, Captain Richard Bond, the 199 Brigade Major, recalls a conversation that took place on 20 March between Brigadier General Guy Williams and divisional headquarters that highlighted the difficulties experienced by commanders in the front line in communicating with divisional staff. The brigadier – in the light of the warning of an imminent enemy attack – apparently wanted to bring the 2/7 Manchesters forward to their battle positions; his request was refused. In the event the battalion was faced with 'a five-hour move in gas masks under an intense bombardment before reaching its position in the line'. Bond remains convinced that had the reserve battalions been brought up the night before the attack 'we should have put up a better show ... and given more support to the 17th Brigade in Le Verguier'.[13]

Major Neil Baillie-Hamilton of the 2/7th recalled it was necessary to leave the roads and valleys and move along the spurs using a map and compass. Gas masks had to be worn during the whole march except for a rest of a minute now and again when the Medical Officer said they could be removed for a breather. Baillie-Hamilton established Headquarters Company with one rifle company under the command of Captain John Brown just north of Brosse Woods:

'About 1.00pm the attack dwindled and aeroplanes showed our position by dropping lights over it, this was followed by 10 minutes intense shelling and the attack was renewed. Communication with Brigade and Division could not be obtained so at 3.00pm the Fuller Phone was broken up. At 4.00pm pigeons were dispatched to say we hoped to hang on till night and then withdraw under cover of darkness. At 5.00pm Captain Brown who had been keeping the enemy off with bombs for hours was killed. Shortly afterwards the supply of bombs was finished. Soon after 5.00pm the only Lewis gun still working jammed.'[14]

With stocks of ammunition practically exhausted and 70 per cent casualties amongst the garrison, Baillie-Hamilton surrendered: 'I walked out and informed the enemy that we surrendered.' As to the fate of the other companies, we can only assume they were overwhelmed in the fog, as no survivors' reports have come to light to date.

Holding on a little to the north around Fervague Farm, the 2/6 Manchesters remained in position for several hours until forced back at 1.00pm by *Flammenwerfer* attacks. Fighting with the Manchesters, Private Charles Martin recalled the final moments before he was taken prisoner:

> '*I saw, a little distance away, a sergeant and some men climb out of the trench with their hands up. I tried to escape along the trench but the way through was blocked by dead bodies … when I turned in the opposite direction, I saw two German soldiers approaching, spraying the trench ahead with liquid fire. One held the nozzle and the other had the cylinder on his back.*'[15]

Twelve officers and 150 other ranks was all that remained of the battalion as they fell back to Carpeza Copse. Here, under the command of Major John Whitworth, they held on doggedly until 2.00pm on 22 March before finally falling back to Hebescourt. Captain Gilbert Fox, the battalion adjutant, remembered the enemy machine-gun fire at Carpeza Copse being particularly heavy:

> '*And under cover of this he* [the Germans] *made several attacks on the copse, but we eventually managed to hold the same until reinforced by a detachment of dismounted cavalry, about 6.00pm. Throughout the day touch was lost with the unit on our right and repeated efforts failed to connect up. However, by means of B Company (in reserve at Hervilly Wood) being sent up to fill a gap, our left flank was secured. Casualties were heavy, but after dusk, with our reinforcements, we consolidated the position. Contact with troops on our right flank was found impossible, though several efforts were made. During the early morning* [22 March] *touch was lost with B Company and a gap was created on the frontage occupied by this company, thus leaving us as an isolated post.*'[16]

The retirement was made under cover of the fog, Gilbert Fox's reference to bouts of hand-to-hand fighting with groups of Germans 'who had come through the gap on our right and also on our left' providing the only clue to the desperate nature of the withdrawal. John Whitworth received the DSO for his command of the battalion at Carpeza Copse.

It was not quite a disaster along this front as the Battle Zone was still for the most part intact but it was only a matter of time before sustained pressure, between Hargicourt and the left-hand divisional boundary along the Cologne valley, broke the front defences of the Battle Zone. The quarries northeast of Templeux le Guérard had been isolated early on in the morning with German infantry apparently satisfied with keeping the garrison under a heavy barrage of machine-gun fire while passing on either side, intent on taking the more important Templeux le Guérard village itself. The quarries stood on the southern edge of the Cologne valley and were held by two-and-a-half companies of 2/7 Lancashire Fusiliers and two companies of 1/5 Border Regiment. Machine-gun fire from the Lempire ridge at 10.45am was the first indication Captain Oswin Feetham had that the Forward Zone had been pierced:

'Apart from desultory shelling and sniping afterwards we were left alone until later in the day, although we could see German troops passing down the valley opposite Ronssoy Woods and the valley running from Hargicourt. About 1 o'clock from the top of the slag heap we watched the Germans attack Fervaque Farm ... Our battalion dressing station in Templeux le Guérard was taken about 1pm and the MO compelled to attend German wounded.'[17]

Feetham was in command of the two companies of 5/Borderers and although they kept up a rapid fire on the advancing German infantry which he notes was 'most excellent shooting', they were conscious that the hoards of enemy now pouring over the crest from Hargicourt on the way to Templeux village had practically cut off any chance of escape:

'At 3pm the Germans brought up some heavy minenwerfers which completely destroyed our battle positions, and at the same time, they effected an entrance in the north end of the quarry tunnels. About five o'clock we surrendered. Approximately 60 men being available out of a total garrison of 450'.[18]

Oswin Feetham may well have been the officer mentioned by Karl Goes as *Leutnant* Möller and the men of 7th Kompanie from IR 31 finally overcame British resistance in the Hargicourt quarries:

'Out of nowhere 30 English and their officer stand right in front of them. A short conversation in the face of imminent captivity ends with an urgent remark by the Leutnant: 'The quarry's garrison is doomed. The Germans are already in Templeux, way behind your back sir!' The English officer pulls a wry face, he and his men lay down their weapons, other parties following the example, the resistance in the quarry fades away.'[19]

The attack now centred on Templeux le Guérard. The battle positions allocated to the 2/6 Lancashire Fusiliers were a line of trenches to the north of the Roisel-Templeux road, a position they immediately moved to when the bombardment began. 'The fog began to thicken and get worse as we neared the ridge,' recalled the battalion adjutant, Captain Leslie Robinson, a situation which was not improved by the occasional German shell that burst along the road. The fog was so dense in places that one of the Headquarters Company runners, Private

William Harrop, felt it necessary to grope his way to the line maintaining touch by 'each man holding onto the bayonet scabbard of the man in front'. It was not the best of circumstances in which to go into battle. But despite the adverse weather conditions and being on the receiving end of enemy shelling, three companies of the battalion were in position at 6.00am. The German bombardment would have been less effective had the German gunners not had their exact co-ordinates and the trenches themselves been dug a little deeper. One direct hit took out most of the headquarters signallers and blew the signalling officer and the commanding officer 'a considerable distance.'

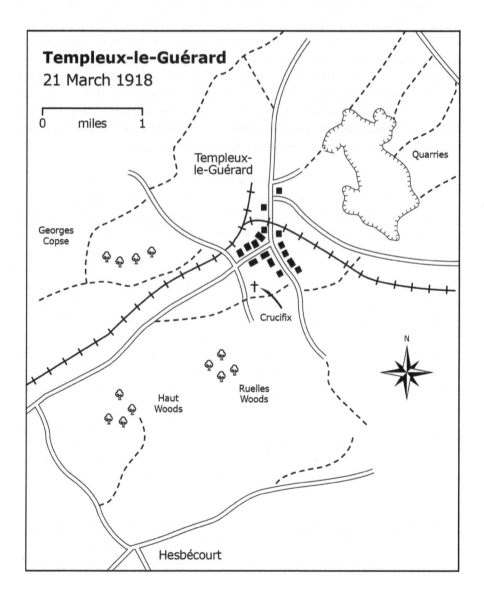

Once the fog began to lift, the steady stream of casualties coming down the road from Templeux and the sight of German infantry and gunners on the ridge beyond the quarries meant one thing only: the Forward Zone had 'gone' and the 2/6th would soon be joining the fight. But as Robinson pointed out, what was more worrying was the obvious enemy advance taking place on the left flank. 'We could see the enemy advancing in quite large numbers, almost between ourselves and Épehy; the division on our left [16th Irish Division] had gone too.' If Major William Cuncliffe's observation of enemy troops at Grand Priel Wood at 10.30am was at all accurate they were already outflanked.

Cuncliffe's observation point was the top of the Templeux Quarry ridge where he and his gunners had managed to get B Battery, 330 Artillery Brigade (B/330) to new positions. In full view of the enemy, the B/330 gunners maintained a steady shrapnel fire on the advancing troops of the 113th Reserve Division who continued to 'work away to our left all morning'. Cuncliffe sited four of his 18-pounders in the bank at a position known as Brosse II and detached one section 200 yards to his left. Despite the fact that this allowed a very effective crossfire to be maintained Cuncliffe must have realized he had very little chance of getting away once the German attack focused on his battery :

> 'The position was 400 to 600 yards behind the Red Line [Battle Zone] and it is difficult to for me to see how the position could have been maintained even if the Red Line had held. As to the Red Line itself, despite what has been written to the contrary, this was not dug to more than 12 inches in depth on my front and in some places only the sods were removed.'[20]

That their fire was effective is evident from the testimony of Major William Wike who watched in admiration from the Fusiliers' trenches as 'a complete German battalion was annihilated by its fire'. Cuncliffe merely noting the battery 'shelled a battalion passing through Hargicourt and did enormous damage'. The battery fought to the last, keeping the enemy at bay with Lewis gun fire before their gun pits were rushed at 6.00pm and the survivors taken prisoner. Cuncliffe was later awarded the Military Cross but in the opinion of Major Wike, 'the fight he put up was worthy of a greater honour'.[21]

The Fusiliers' counter-attack got underway shortly after midday on the 21st with B and D Companies advancing under the command of Major Wike to the western edge of Templeux. Robinson's account makes it ominously clear that, in his opinion, the battalion was unlikely to survive in the face of the oncoming assault:

> 'The attack was across a perfectly open plain, and had the enemy machine guns been properly sited we should have suffered very heavily. By 2.00pm we were established in the village of Templeux, but in a very bad position, as our communications from

the front line were overlooked by the enemy on the high ground beyond the village, and both our flanks were in the air ... we tried to get in touch with our flanks, but all efforts failed: there was no one on our flanks to get in touch with. It became very obvious that in the event of any further advance on the part of the Boche our position, or that of our forward companies, would be untenable.[22]

In actual fact the counter-attack did not clear the whole of the village and the Fusiliers were gradually forced out of the village buildings until they took up a line on the outskirts. The brunt of the fighting in Templeux village was carried out by a battalion of IR 31, Karl Goes reporting that 'at certain times the artilleries of both sides fire right into the heavily disputed village. Rifle fire cracks out of caves and whole clusters of houses become the focal point of severe combat.' Not that the Fusiliers gave ground willingly, the men of IR 116 reported vicious fighting on the southern edge of Templeux and a counter attack by the British that isolated and 'annihilated' one of their companies.

The Fusiliers' advance had been watched by the men of A Company from their trench line east of the road running into the village. The company was on detached duty and under the orders of the officer commanding the village defences and at the time had no idea the attack they were witnessing was being carried forward by their own battalion. Small parties of enemy troops were still making use of the high ground and passing through Georges Copse on the right flank, and despite the best endeavours of the battalion, the enemy drove a wedge down through the centre of the village, preventing A Company from getting in touch with the remainder of the battalion and forcing D Company to take up positions close to the crucifix at the crossroads 200 yards south of the village. Here they linked up with A Company who had also retired in the face of heavy flanking fire whilst B and C Companies were on the western side of the Roisel-Templeux road. The battalion was now together again, albeit along a wide front and in very trying circumstances.

Just before dark, aware of the precarious position of the two forward companies, Robinson requested permission from brigade headquarters to withdraw to their previous battle positions. This was refused, the reply making it quite clear they were not to withdraw 'one inch but do the best we could where we were'. Robinson was unimpressed, remarking that 'if there were any divisional reserves they failed to put in an appearance, except a few cyclists, cavalry and other stout fellows'.

During the night of 21/22 March Captain Lyell Lee, who was in command of A Company, reported attacks by strong enemy fighting patrols which did not deter the more important task of bringing up much needed rations and replenishing the depleted stocks of ammunition with that collected from the dead and wounded. Nightfall had in effect rendered the village as a temporary no-man's-land as patrols from both sides probed each other's defences. As dawn broke – with a similar fog that had cloaked the German advance the previous day – the Fusiliers were greeted by heavy gas shelling after which the first German infantry units began putting in an appearance. Those that blundered up against the wire were quickly dealt with but it soon became obvious that the Germans, aided no doubt by the dense fog, were streaming past them on both flanks. A momentary lifting of the fog confirmed they were surrounded and although they could maintain their position while stocks of ammunition lasted, it was obvious to Robinson that they 'could do no good by remaining where we were'.

Eventually German infantry, possibly from the 6th Division, moved in to take the position. The last moments of the 2/6th came as battalion headquarters was surrounded and captured. In the confusion of battle only two officers managed to avoid capture, the battalion medical officer Captain John Dingley and Second Lieutenant John Sutherland. 'Doc' Dingley's recollection of ghostly figures looming around the entrance to his dug-out prompted him to make a hasty exit through the other entrance as a fusillade of shots followed him up the steps; fortunately the fog provided enough cover for his rapid retreat to the defensive post that Sutherland had set up east of Roisel. Sadly, John Sutherland was killed shortly afterwards. The 27-year-old from Tarves in Aberdeenshire who arrived in France just before Christmas 1916 as a private soldier in the Gordon Highlanders, was posted missing believed killed. Lieutenant Colonel Thomas Biddolph was taken prisoner along with Lee, Robinson, Wike and the surviving ranks of the battalion. Lee was shot through the leg and brought down, a mishap he feels resulted in his capture 'by the Germans who appeared to be countless'.

Definite casualty numbers are difficult to ascertain but at Templeux le Guérard Communal Cemetery five other ranks and Second Lieutenant James Bell from A Company can be found, while eight more other ranks have been laid to rest at the nearby Templeux le Guérard British Cemetery. Commemorated on the Pozières Memorial are thirty-three other ranks and three officers, including John Sutherland and Captain James Cameron who commanded D Company, all of whom were killed on 21/22 March or died of wounds over the next day or so. As for the number of wounded we can only assume it must have been high. Captain Lee noted that of the nine officers in A and D companies on the morning of 21 March only three were left by dusk and by 7.00am the next day this had been reduced to a single officer. Of those who managed to get away, Private William Harrop remembered the brigade commander, Brigadier General Oswald Borrett, being present at roll call and visibly upset by so few men of the battalion answering to their names.

Chapter 7

Ronssoy and Épehy

A retreat was the one possibility that had never occurred to us, and, unfortunately, it involved a kind of manoeuvring in which we are unversed, in spite of our experience. For the time being the enemy has turned the tables in a manner in which it is difficult to realize, so great is the contrast with what would have been possible at any time during last year.

Lieutenant Colonel Rowland Fielding – 6th Battalion Connaught Rangers.

The VII Corps Forward Zone was relatively narrow and consisted of a continuous trench line along the eight mile front interspersed with strong points, machine-gun emplacements and switch lines. The Battle Zone – in places only 1,500 yards behind the Forward Zone – consisted of a single trench line along the front and rear with the villages of Ronssoy, Lempire and Épehy organized into strongly defended areas. The sector, under the command of Lieutenant General Sir Walter Congreve VC, was defended by three divisions: the 16th (Irish) Division, the 21st Division and the 9th (Scottish) Division. Facing them across the wire were ten divisions from the German XXIII and XIII Corps.

The Forward Zone along the 16th Division's sector collapsed very quickly and this may well have been due to the large number of battalions deployed in manning the front line. On 14 March Hubert Gough visited the 16th Division's headquarters to discuss Major General Aymatt Hull's objections to this overly large deployment. The 16th Division was relatively new to Gough's Fifth Army, having been transferred from the Third Army only three months previously. Major General Hull was even more of a new boy; his command began on 10 February after Major General William Hickie was invalided home on sick leave. Hull wanted only three battalions in the Forward Zone, a notion that was clearly alien to Gough's preoccupation with a strongly defended front line. In overruling his divisional commander Gough demonstrated a distressing lack of understanding of the concept of defence in depth and in this particular case consigned the Irish battalions in the Forward Zone to virtual annihilation. It is patently unfair to write off the 16th Division on 21 March as lacking in fight; their forward battalions took the full force of the German bombardment and suffered the highest number of men killed on the first day of the assault in the whole of the Fifth Army. Had Gough listened to General Hull's objections the story may have been different. As it was, German infantry, having overcome the forward defences, were soon advancing along the Cologne valley towards Ronssoy which was under attack as early as 9.30am. It was these troops that Captain Leslie Robinson of the Lancashire Fusiliers had seen as his battalion was moving up towards Templeux le Guérard.

Apart from the over manning of the Forward Zone, the 16th Divisional staff felt very strongly that the whole sector suffered as a result of being in a salient:

> '*Owing to our salient position and the general trend of the corps boundary,* [between 16th Division and XIX Corps] *an enemy attack delivered at right angles to the front line on either side of the corps boundary must, if successful, drive straight up against the right flank of our Battle Zone, and then, if successful, tend to roll up our whole line from the right.*'[1]

This is exactly what happened of course, and was why the experience of Captain Arthur Patman of the 7th Battalion Royal Irish Rifles, was probably very similar to that of other regimental officers of battalions in the Forward Zone. Having only rejoined the battalion from Bassè Boulogne the evening before the attack commenced, he was, as he dryly remarked, a prisoner of war by 1.00pm the next day! His battalion was on the extreme right of the 16th Divisional sector, practically all the outposts were annihilated by the opening bombardment and the company defensive posts were ignored by the advancing troops until the second wave arrived. Patman says that 12 men including himself managed to get away after their company post was attacked but not one managed to reach British lines. 'All our rear areas appeared to be in German hands.' Patman's assessment was distressingly correct: Ronssoy village, for example, which stood on rising ground, had been entered from behind by German infantry using the valleys to the north and south of the village, which according to another observer was encircled and entered by noon on 21 March.[2]

All of which left the 2nd Battalion Royal Irish Regiment (2/Royal Irish) in a rather isolated position to the east of Lempire where they had been since 20 March. Commanding the Royal Irish was 28-year-old Lieutenant Colonel John Scott, a regular officer who had been commissioned in September 1910. War and the rapid promotion it produced, had boosted Scott's career; in 1917 he rose from captain to lieutenant colonel in three months, taking command of the battalion in August of that year. The 2/Royal Irish was a fighting battalion with a long pedigree of stubborn resistance. In August 1914 under the command of Major Stratford St Leger, the battalion had fought a classic four-stage rearguard action over the Bois la Haut at Mons, giving ground reluctantly and inflicting heavy casualties on the pursuing enemy in what was probably the most outstanding feat of its kind of the entire retreat. Almost four years later at Lempire the battalion found itself in a similar position, except the line of retirement was not so clear cut.

23-year-old Lieutenant John Terry was in command of B Company when the battalion took over the front line and its forward posts. Terry's headquarters was at Kew Lane, a position he and his men were not at all familiar with:

> *'We were severely handicapped in the opening stages of the battle owing to the fact that we took over a new portion of the front line which was strange to us, as the relief was not carried out until nightfall and was not completed until after midnight. B Company had not a very sound knowledge of the geographical conditions in their immediate vicinity and it was only when the fog cleared about 1.00pm on March 21st that we were able to survey our surroundings which were, by then, in the enemy's hands.'*[3]

Terry's reserved assessment of his situation does not hide the feeling of helplessness he and his men must have felt in this unfamiliar sector of the front line. Making the best of the situation Terry was anxious to know if the enemy's wire had been cut in preparation for an attack, a fear that was confirmed by a reconnaissance patrol, large gaps had been cut in the enemy's wire, clearly the long expected attack was imminent. Leaving Second Lieutenant Norman Abbot in command of the post, Terry's final task was to visit his company outposts and give last-minute instructions:

> *'I left the last outpost at about 4.30am and the bombardment commenced whilst I was making my way back across country to B Company headquarters, accompanied by my runner, Lance Corporal O'Brian MM. Gas shells were used pretty freely upon the forward defences and we had to don our box respirators and owing to the smoke and gas shells we had great difficulty in finding Kew Lane.'*[4]

At 9.30am the barrage ceased and Colonel Scott had moved the Headquarters Company and two platoons of D Company into Rose Trench where soon after they were engaged on their right flank – which was approximately the time that John Terry and his men first came into contact with German infantry. At this point in the battle it must have been quite clear to all concerned that the Forward Zone was now almost completely cut off but the Royal Irish kept on fighting, so much so that at 11.00am B Company was still sending out fighting patrols and captured a German medical corps team which was brought back for interrogation. Terry writes that when they were found to be in the possession of stick grenades and automatics 'they were very severely dealt with'. Quite what was meant by that is anyone's guess! But soon after this Kew Lane was subjected to several serious assaults and the enemy brought up several small howitzers and trench mortars, by which time Terry writes, the Royal Irish were in 'desperate straights'.

Back at Rose Trench the enemy attack was being directed from both ends, the battalion war diary recording that at 1.30pm the enemy broke through on the left forcing the survivors to retire to Irish Trench on the northern outskirts of Ronssoy, 'the trench was deserted when we got there, the remainder of the village had been in German hands for some time'. At 2.15pm the Germans began bombing the northern end of Irish Trench and positioned a machine gun at the southern end. 'We immediately charged the machine gun which the [Germans] left on seeing us make a determined effort.' Fifteen minutes later the order was given to retire on St Emilie but as the war diary gloomily confirms, 'very few succeeded in reaching St Emilie, probably 3 officers and 15 other ranks'.[5]

No one from B Company managed to get away. With ammunition running out and runners failing to return from battalion headquarters, Terry was left with very little choice:

> '*Eventually the garrison was reduced to a dozen or so unwounded and ammunition became so scarce that 2/Lt Abbott and I decided that the only alternatives were either to surrender or to try and fight our way back to our own lines. We decided upon the latter course and the men received their instructions accordingly. The Germans by this time had penetrated our post and before we had gone fifty yards they turned machine guns upon us with such good effect that there were only 3 or 4 left unwounded. 2/Lt Abbott was shot through the knee and I dropped into a shell hole beside him. The Germans threw a few hand grenades at us and I received a bayonet wound in the thigh before they considered us hors-de-combat.*'[6]

It had been a courageous rearguard action but the casualties were frighteningly high. Although only Lieutenant Colonel Scott and three other ranks are recorded as killed in action by the war diary, sixteen officers were posted as missing in action along with 499 other ranks, many of whom were taken prisoner. However the CWGC database lists 154 Royal Irish soldiers and five officers who were killed on 21 March, the majority of whom are commemorated on the Pozières Memorial. At what point in the battle John Scott was killed is not mentioned in the war diary but he is one of the very few who have a headstone, he can be found at the Unicorn Cemetery, Vendhuile.

The fall of Ronssoy not only put the gun lines in the shallow valley of St Emilie under immediate threat but provided access to Épehy from the south along the ridge of high ground which ran south from Ronssoy Wood to Templeux Woods – known as the Raperie Switch line. Divisional staff officers were of the opinion that enemy units had occupied the Raperie Switch by 12.20pm which was before the Ronssoy posts had finally fallen, adding weight to the notion that enemy infantry had evidently worked their way onto the ridge from the Cologne valley north of Templeux le Guérard. The answer to why the 16th Division had not deployed troops on this high ground – which was so vital to the integrity of the right flank – probably lies in the overall lack of reserves, a problem exacerbated no doubt by the number of battalions placed in the Forward Zone.

Two battalions from 47 Brigade had been held in reserve and these were now ordered up to counter-attack. The 6/Connaught Rangers were in the reserve trenches at Villers-Faucon when Lieutenant Colonel Rowland Fielding received orders at 12.25pm to move forward. Using the narrow gauge railway line to approach St Emilie, the battalion incurred several casualties from enemy shelling which at this point in the day was still relatively heavy. Establishing a temporary headquarters in the railway cutting 'opposite a building known as the Crystal Palace', Fielding reported to Brigadier General Phillip Leveson-Gower, commanding 49 Infantry Brigade. Gower's orders to Fielding were to attack Ronssoy to the north of the St Emilie road immediately in co-operation with the 1st Battalion Munster Fusiliers (1/Munsters) who were to attack south of the road. Whatever Fielding's private thoughts may have been about the folly of this attack he most likely kept them to himself at this stage, but as he usually did, he unburdened himself after the event in a letter to his wife, Edith:

'As we reached the firing line the trench was being heavily and effectively shelled. A few hours before it had been a reserve trench – almost our rearmost line of defence; so far behind, in fact, that it was only partly dug. There were considerable gaps; and, as there was no communication trench leading up to it, the only approach was across the open ... We found it occupied by a few living stragglers – remnants of the garrisons of the forward positions, and strewn with the bodies of the dead who had already fallen to the enemy's shell fire. Among the severely wounded there lay one of my company commanders [Captain] *(Denys Wickham) – an admirable officer who weathered two years of the worst of the war.'*[7]

Rowland Fielding's description of the carnage that was inflicted on his beloved battalion before the attack began paints a vivid picture of men under shell fire, detail that he excluded from the war diary account and only revealed in letters to Edith:

'As the companies assembled for the counter-attack the hostile shelling seemed to increase, and, more than once there was a direct hit upon a bay, killing or wounding every man in it. A whizz bang skimmed the parapet and hit the parados where I was standing, splashing my face with earth with such a smack that for a moment I thought my cheek was shot away ... As I recovered, a recently joined subaltern came to me and reported that [Lieutenant Fenton] *Cummins – second in command*

of his company – and several men with him had just been killed by a shell, and the men on either side were shaken; which was indeed scarcely to be wondered at, seeing that many of them were experiencing their baptism of fire. I told him I was afraid he would have to carry on just the same, and I must say that the plucky and unhesitating manner in which this boy turned back to his job was admirable.[8]

Keeping B Company in reserve the battalion attacked at 3.45pm with two companies – A Company on the left and D Company on the right- with C Company in support. Both attacking companies reached the sunken road which borders the western edge of Ronssoy Wood but of the 1/Munsters on the right there was no sign. But as C Company moved forward they could see what initially was thought to be the Munsters, but which turned out to be German infantry, lining the ridge to the right:

[Captain Conolly] *Norman immediately engaged the enemy, forming a defensive flank along the Ronssoy-St Emilie road, but soon fell, wounded in three places. Lieutenant [Arthur] Russell then took command but fell almost immediately, mortally wounded. Simultaneously, the only other officer with the company – McTiernan – was mortally wounded, and the greater part of the company having in this short time also become casualties, the remainder were forced to fall back upon the trench they had started from, together with the few that remained of the two attacking companies, who had suffered equally, the commander of one – Captain [Thomas] Crofton – having been killed leading his men forwards, while the commander of the other – Lieutenant [Alfred] Ribbons, who had succeeded Wickham – was made prisoner.*[9]

The two tanks that had been allocated to this attack also failed to materialize and apparently proceeded independently: both of them, Fielding tells us, were knocked out. The Connaughts' attack stood no chance of success in the face of violent German shelling and the Munsters' failure to cover the right flank doomed Fielding's men from the outset, reducing the battalion to 'the Headquarters Company and thirty-four stragglers'. At 5.15pm Fielding was at St Emilie reporting to Leveson-Gower:

'He was apologetic and explained his orders for this operation should have been cancelled: they had, he said, been cancelled in the case of the Munster fusiliers, but he had been unable to communicate with me. Then he added: 'I hope you will not think hardly of me.' There was no answer to this – at least no civil answer I could see for his having failed to communicate with me; nor, having failed, could I excuse him for having cancelled his orders to the Royal Munster Fusiliers to counter-attack, knowing that we were counting upon their co-operation.'[10]

Fielding's war was far from over and we will come across the Connaught Rangers again later. But before we look more closely at the action around Malassise Farm by the 2nd Battalion Royal Munster Fusiliers (2/Munsters), the story surrounding a young subaltern from 94 Brigade RFA is worthy of mention. There were numerous stories of gunners abandoning the infantry to their fate – no doubt embroidered considerably as they were passed on from soldier to soldier – all of which did little to improve the image of the artilleryman to the disgruntled and retreating infantryman. However, retirement and the subsequent breakdown of communication left many gunners almost completely isolated, circumstances no better illustrated than by the frustration experienced by the brigade major of VII Corps heavy artillery who reported all communication broken by 10.00am on 21 March and that 'the first intimation we had of any infantry action was when our own [infantry] retired through the battery positions'. Undoubtedly there were untold numbers of gunners who performed single acts of bravery in the face of the enemy that went unrecorded or even unnoticed. One exception was Second Lieutenant Gordon Chapman of 94 Brigade RFA.

Born in Sheffield in 1897, Chapman had moved to South Africa with his parents as a child and had first served with the South African Medical Corps in German South West Africa in 1915 and then Egypt before attending an Officer Cadet Unit in Britain. Commissioned into the RFA in February 1917 and in France by the following October, on 21 March 1918 Chapman found himself in command of a single 18-pounder and posted from the 21st Divisional sector to the neighbouring 16th Division with orders to fire across the length of the 21st Divisional front. When the 16th Division withdrew in the direction of St Emilie, Chapman and his gun crew maintained their position and protected the right flank of the 21st Division until about 1.00pm when their ammunition ran out. The gun was then run back to the waiting limber by hand while Gordon Chapman and his remaining gunners held up the enemy with rifle and Lewis gun fire until the gun and its crew were able to escape. Three days later this same officer accidently found himself on the outskirts of Péronne before he discovered the town had been occupied by the enemy. 'Chapman unlimbered in the road', wrote his brigade commander, 'browned the Germans in the streets, and limbered up and returned to his battery, passing through the British front line some two miles further back.' Chapman's DSO was gazetted in September 1918.[11]

* * *

The battlefield southeast of Épehy – including Malassise Farm – remains today very much as it was on 21 March 1918. The farm is still in the same position northeast of the crossroads formed by the Chemin des Charbonniers – which runs northeast along the shallow valley known in 1918 as Deelish Valley- and the D58. To the north lies Tetard Wood, a mere 350 yards from the communal cemetery on the south eastern edge of Épehy. One of the two original railway lines still runs from St Emilie, along the eastern edge of Épehy and Peizières crossing the D24 as it heads north skirting Vaucelette Farm towards Gouzeaucourt.

The 2/Munsters – a battalion that had already written itself into legend in late August 1914 with its epic last stand at Etreux, just 37 kilometres due east – moved into battle positions on the night of 21/22 March. The battalion's main axis of defence ran from Malassise Farm to Tetard Wood along a trench line known as Ridge Reserve North with two strong points – M and U Posts – some 200 yards to the east along Room Trench which was manned by two platoons from B and C Companies. In the railway cutting to the west was battalion headquarters and one platoon of C Company. A Company were in reserve at the crossroads southwest of the farm. Ridge Reserve North was garrisoned by D Company and the remaining platoons from B and C Companies. Major Marcus Hartigan, second-in-command of the battalion up until the evacuation of Lieutenant Colonel Ireland, had no illusions as to the role the reserve company were to perform. They were 'in reality a support to the company garrisoning Malassise Farm, and had instructions that in the event of the enemy attacking the farm … it was to counter-attack without further orders'.[12]

Marcus Hartigan was 40-years-old by the time he was transferred to the Munsters from the Royal Dublin Fusiliers and already had a noteworthy career and a DSO behind him. Wounded in the Boer War he fought in South West Africa at the onset of the Great War, raising and commanding the well-known Hartigan's Horse before moving to the Western Front. Hartigan wrote two accounts of the battle; the first was smuggled out from Holtzminden POW Camp and another, which he wrote in 1927, was composed in response to the War Office Historical Department's request for information regarding the battalion's action. His account appears to be more accurate than that of the regimental history which fails to mention the contribution of Lieutenants Kidd and Whelan altogether.

Although Hartigan is unsure of the exact time the farm came under attack, he thinks it was at about 9.00am, the support company had already gone forward from the crossroads when Hartigan received the first report from the farm that the company commander, Lieutenant Patrick Cahill, had been killed. For Hartigan the alarm bells were already ringing:

'At the same time it was observed that the 2nd Royal Dublin Fusiliers whose sector was the Catelet Valley were retiring and that the enemy had occupied their positions in the Forward Zone, getting into their trenches under cover of the fog and bayoneting the men before they could realize they were the enemy. The situation at about 9.30am was: The two companies engaged at Malassise Farm were lost, if there were any survivors from the support company they must have joined the 2nd Dublins. Later that day while a prisoner in the hands of the enemy, then occupying

Malassise Farm, I was complimented by a German major upon the splendid fight that Lieutenant [William] *Kidd and his company had put up in the farm.'*[13]

According to the Munsters' war diary, Malassise Farm was assaulted from behind as the Dublin Fusiliers fell back, leaving the right flank open to attack by units from RIR 262. Here reports differ a little as to exactly where the Dublins were and at what time. An account written by Captain Geoffrey Peirson, a staff officer with the 48 Brigade Advanced Headquarters at Épehy, is quite certain the attack upon the Dublin Fusiliers began between 8.00am and 9.00am and that the Munsters' outposts in Room Trench were still holding out at that time. Hartigan tells us in his account that the Dublins were falling back by 9.00am – presumably from their forward outpost positions – and by 9.30am Malassise Farm was lost. This places the remnants of the Dublin Fusiliers a little to the west of the railway line somewhere in the triangle of ground framed by the D24 and D58. But whatever the case, we do know that the retirement by the Dublin Fusiliers spelt the end for the garrison at Malassise Farm and put the focus firmly on C Company at the northern end of Ridge Reserve Trench and Tetard Wood.[14]

At 10.00am Lieutenant Colonel Herbert Ireland was badly wounded and Hartigan assumed command, moving battalion headquarters from the railway cutting to a new position 500 yards southwest of Épehy. With enemy infantry closing around them the Munsters were in no mood to give ground:

'One of the features of the fight in this sector during the day was the fine leadership of Lieutenant [Harry]*Whelan who organized and held the posts in Tetard Wood and his magnificent example of daring and initiative was responsible for a most determined resistance which cost the enemy dear for every foot of ground he gained. About noon Lieutenant Whelan – under orders – withdrew what remained of his company, less than a platoon, to a post on the southern edge of the ruins of Épehy where he continued the fight.'*[15]

The war diary adds more detail:

'Rifle and MG fire from Ridge Reserve prevented the enemy from moving artillery up the Malassise road and every attempt up to 4.00pm resulted in the horses and drivers being shot down and this effective fire was maintained in spite of the repeated attacks on our right flank ... by 4.40pm the enemy assault troops had pressed Lieutenant Whelan back into the last two or three bays in Tetard Wood from where he side-stepped into the trench at the head of the Catelet Valley.'[16]

There is little doubt that this spirited defence assisted the Leicesters – who were holding the ruins of Épehy – in retaining the integrity of their right flank. Hartigan was captured at about 6.00pm en route from Tetard Wood to Épehy and although the situation was desperate the defences at Épehy and Peizières were still holding out – just.

When day broke on 22 March, unlike the conditions on many other sectors, there was not a trace of fog anywhere and from his position on the edge of Épehy, Harry Whelan was able to overlook a section of road up which the enemy were attempting to bring artillery:

> *'So effective was this fire of the Munsters on this spot that the road became impassable being literally blocked with the dead bodies of the gun teams. About noon on the 22nd, having fired every round of ammunition Whelan buried his revolver and surrendered.'*[17]

Many survivors of the battalion were captured at Épehy. Whelan was badly wounded but at what point is not clear and his wounds were so severe that he died three weeks later on 11 April whilst a prisoner at Kassel. As is often the case from such a ferocious and prolonged stand, casualties were heavy; the majority of the officers and men killed in action over the two days of the fighting are commemorated on the Pozières Memorial. The others are scattered between Épehy Wood Farm Cemetery, Roisel Communal Cemetery, Tincourt New British Cemetery, St Emilie Valley Cemetery and Templeux le Guérard British Cemetery. Harry Whelan is buried at Niederzwehren Cemetery at Kassel. Lieutenant Colonel Ireland died of his wounds at Rouen on 28 March and is buried in the Military Cemetery at St Sever.

* * *

The 21st Divisional southern boundary ran roughly north of Capron Copse before crossing the D58 north of Malassise Farm to skirt the edge of Épehy village. The Forward Zone here lacked depth, particularly in the sector north of Peizières where the ground between the two zones was in some places as little as 200 yards in depth. The front line of the Battle Zone ran along the ridge from Ronssoy to the twin villages of Épehy and Peizières, before it joined the 9th Division sector just north of Chapel Hill. The German battle plan had already identified Épehy as a potential 'trouble spot' and the two divisions detailed for this sector were under no illusions as to the difficulty of the task that awaited them:

> *'However, high above the plain, providing a perfect 360 degree view, the English have built a remarkable fortress, four square kilometers of trench systems riddled with MG nests and concrete dug-outs: Épehy! The fight for this fortress won't be easy, that much is clear to Generalleutnant von Schüßler [ID 183], bound to attack frontally, as well as to Generalmajor Landauer [ID 79], who is to proceed south of the village via Malassise Farm.'*[18]

From a purely defensive point of view Chapel Hill should have been part of the 9th Division sector as the loss of this unassuming bump of ground would seriously compromise the South African Brigade which held the ground to its north. We will return to Chapel Hill in Chapter 8. The 21st Division comprised of 110, 62 and 64 Infantry Brigades and was commanded by Major General David 'Soarer' Campbell, a cavalryman who had led the 9th Lancers into action at Audregnies south of Mons when they charged the German gun line on 24 August 1914. On that day the regiment had suffered heavily against German machine-gun and shrapnel fire in an action that was redeemed to some extent two weeks later at Moncel when he again led his regiment in the first lance against lance cavalry action of the war. From command of 6 Cavalry Brigade in November 1914 he was promoted to command the 21st Division in May 1916. His nickname came from the name of the horse on which he rode to victory in the Grand National in 1896.

The 110 Infantry Brigade – known as the Leicester Brigade – was under new command, Brigadier General Hanway Cumming only arriving at Saulcourt to take up his new post on 18 March. His brigade sector ran from the southern extremity of Épehy along the railway cutting to the slopes below Vaucelette Farm

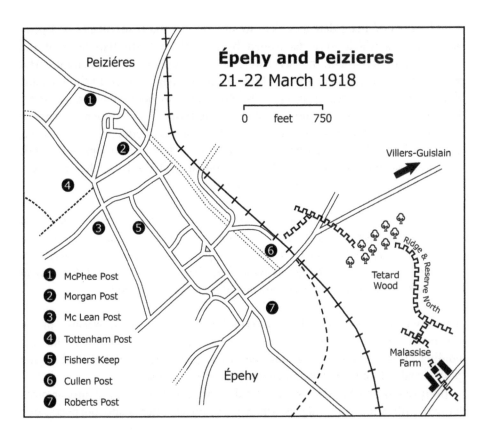

Peiziéres

Épehy and Peizieres
21-22 March 1918

0   feet   750

Villers-Guislain

Ridge & Reserve North

Tetard
Wood

Malassise
Farm

❶ McPhee Post
❷ Morgan Post
❸ Mc Lean Post
❹ Tottenham Post
❺ Fishers Keep
❻ Cullen Post
❼ Roberts Post

Épehy

which was held by units of 62 Brigade. The principle weakness of the Forward Zone centred upon the three re-entrant valleys which ran down from the ridge to the German front line. These valleys – Linnet, Thrush and Fourteen Willows Road – were obvious lines of attack and quickly identified as such by Cumming who had very little time to assess the effectiveness of his defences.

On 21 March Cumming was woken by the crash of the opening bombardment. 'It came down like a thunderclap on all parts of the line, even as far back as Brigade Headquarters, and left no doubt in any one's mind from its depth and intensity that this meant business.' To Lieutenant David Kelly, the 110 Brigade Intelligence Officer, the opening barrage sounded like the propellers of a passing ship, he lost little time finding shelter:

> *'In another second I was in the sunken road outside my cupola and could have no doubt that "the day" had come. Our whole area, and all the areas to the north and south, were being flooded with high explosive and shrapnel shells, the former falling in serried ranks, with concentrated fire on all roads and trenches in front of us, while an incessant stream of shells whistled over our heads to the transport routes and camps, including the ruined village of Saulcourt behind us.'*[19]

The Leicesters' main defences were in and around the twin villages of Épehy and Peizières which were garrisoned by the 7th and 8th Battalions of the Leicestershire Regiment. In reserve were two companies of the 6th Battalion who were at Saulcourt. Fortunately the bulk of the front-line troops in the Forward Zone had been withdrawn to the Battle Zone an hour before dawn as planned, leaving only scattered outlook or observation posts. This eminently sensible decision – presumably taken by Campbell – not only reduced casualties but contrasted sharply with that which was taken when deploying troops in the 16th Divisional sector further south. The consequences of the latter decision were observed by Lance Corporal Sydney North:

> *'Looking to our right, we could see Jerry troops steadily making their way into territory we had been told was held by the 16th Division. About half a mile to our right, we could see the Germans moving forward in single file and many were already well behind us. It was not yet midday. Jerry was moving as if there was no opposition and we reckoned we were in real trouble on the flank.'*[20]

The observation posts were soon overrun but not before giving warning of the advancing enemy. Second Lieutenant Albert Farey of 7/Leicesters who was holding Plane Trench in the Linnet valley had just enough time to send off the SOS signal before he was wounded and captured at 9.30am.

Both Épehy and Peizières were defended by a series of strong points or posts located within the twin villages which were, for all intents and purposes, one continuous development. However, as Hanway Cumming remarks in his account of the battle, they were both garrisoned separately and very strongly defended:

[They] *were well wired and disposed for mutual support of one another. The position was further strengthened by a strong machine-gun defence from the rear and flanks and a converging artillery barrage so arranged as to sweep the valleys at irregular intervals as they formed obvious forming up places for attacking troops; and it is quite possible that this bore good fruit, as the frontal attacks on Épehy and Peizières did not develop to any extent for some considerable period.*[21]

The 7/Leicesters at Peizières were commanded by Lieutenant Colonel Guy Sawyer, a regular officer who had begun his career with the Royal Berkshire Regiment. Sawyer deployed D Company amongst the four strong points in his end of the village and pushed A and B Companies out to the east of the village, keeping C Company in reserve. Épehy was similarly garrisoned by 8/Leicesters and under the command of 32-year-old Lieutenant Colonel Archibald Utterson, a man who, like Sawyer, was a regular officer. Utterson's headquarters was at Fishers Keep on the Rue Neuve which was one of six similar strong points dotted around the village, supporting the battalion in the village were two companies of 6/Leicesters.

At Peizières Lieutenant Cyril Scarfe, commanding C Company, also had two Mark IV tanks to call upon to support his men should a counter-attack be deemed necessary. The company was positioned in what Scarfe refers to as a 'shallow trench in the rear of Peizières' where for some time he and his men were forced to wear gas masks while the gas 'appeared to cling to the mist as there was no breeze to disperse it'. At around 10.00am enemy troops broke into the Peizières defences after attacking McFee Post in the north of the village capturing six men and getting into the nearby railway cutting. Scarfe and his company were ordered up to remedy the situation which was done surprisingly quickly:

'*The two tanks got away first and met with practically no opposition as the raid or incursion was not one of great strength. Similarly each platoon of my company reached its objective without serious fighting, passing through Peizières and occupying the position in extended line along the top of the railway cutting.*'[22]

Scarfe presumably had a good view of the road bridge which crossed the railway line northeast of the village, accounting for his assertion the enemy incursion into Peizières and the temporary capture of McFee Post was down to the sappers failing to destroy the road bridge. 'It was understood that the RE were instructed to do this but whatever the cause the bridge was left intact.' The attack that captured McFee Post was also directed at Vaucelette Farm. Situated in the valley between Chapel Hill to the north and Peizières to the south the farm guarded the approaches to Railton and Heudicourt. Captain Lionel Borthwick was of the opinion that 'the Germans penetrated our front along Andrew Street (the road from Villers-Guislain to Peizières) and then marched outward. One party attacking and capturing Vaucelette Farm from the south and another penetrating into Peizières.'

Borthwick was at Tottenham Post for most of the two–day German assault on Épehy and was under no illusions as to the critical nature of Vaucelette Farm, holding as it did a vital position in the 21st Division's main line of resistance. He cites the thick fog on the morning of 21 March as one of the principle factors in the early capture of Vaucelette Farm, a fog, he writes, that rendered direct shooting impossible. 'In one case to my personal knowledge, a machine gun post of 4 guns on the southern end of Vaucelette Farm was overrun without a shot being fired.'[23] The farm was garrisoned by men of the 12/13 Northumberland Fusiliers and the first word 62 Brigade received from the Fusiliers was at 7.30am reporting everything was OK on their front except a breakdown in communication with their right company. This must have been the first indication that the farm was under attack as by 11.15am the 62 Brigade war diary tells us that 'the enemy were in Vaucelette Farm'.

The exact nature of what happened at the farm still remains uncertain. One company of Northumberland Fusiliers was deployed in and around the farm but after communication with battalion headquarters was lost at 7.30am nothing more was heard. However, at 10.00am the first report arrived at the neighbouring 1/Lincolnshire headquarters in Birchwood Copse to the effect that the Germans had broken through the line between Andrews Street and Vaucelette Farm:

> *'A few minutes later, through the fog, we saw their leading infantry surround and actually lead away as prisoners the commanding officer and the personnel ... whose headquarters in a sunken road were about two hundred yards from our own battalion headquarters.'*[24]

There was only one senior officer taken prisoner in the vicinity of the farm and that was Major George White who was commanding the Fusiliers in the absence of Lieutenant Colonel Howlett who was on leave. The sunken road referred to was probably at the western end of 'Leith Walk' where the road crosses the railway line – a mere 100 yards southwest of Vaucelette Farm. Major White remembers a considerable number of German infantry in the sector but only becoming apparent when the fog began to lift. His account recorded the fierce hand-to-hand fighting that took place in the final moments before they were overwhelmed:

> *'Parties* [of Germans] *came from the right rear of the battalion, these were dealt with by the details of battalion headquarters, few of my men remained unwounded.*

Later, parties of the enemy were seen advancing from the front line and it was obvious that their attack had succeeded. Both the Adjutant and myself, with the remains of the details were in the trench, we were both using rifles and whilst firing at the oncoming wave, were attacked from the rear right by men who had come forward, one of these proceeded to attack us with a shovel and another pulled the string of a stick-bomb and threw it between McKinnon [adjutant] *and myself.*[25]

White tells us that the grenade failed to explode and a German officer appeared waving his pistol and ordering his men to stop. By this time the battalion was completely surrounded and 'further resistance was impossible'. The German officer who accepted White's surrender – obviously a keen boater – asked White how long he thought it would be before he would be able to use the river at Boulter's lock at Maidenhead. White does not record the content of his answer!

Captain John McKinnon, the Northumberland Fusiliers adjutant, and White were taken prisoner along with Captain Ernest Griffin – the medical officer attached to the battalion. Griffin was already the recipient of the Military Cross when his award of the DSO came in November 1917 for establishing his forward dressing station under shellfire and remaining out in the open for some 36 hours to bring in all the wounded. It is unlikely his conduct under fire was any different on this foggy March morning. There is a postscript to the Vaucelette Farm episode which suggests that the Farm held out longer than has been suggested. A patrol of 11/Royal Scots sent out to 'clear up the situation on the right penetrated almost to Vaucelette. He [Lieutenant Alexander Kennedy] reported that some of our troops, 21st Division, were still holding out there – gallant fellows.' Exactly what time this was is unknown but Brigadier General Croft (27 Brigade) describes the encounter as later in the day.[26]

With Vaucelette Farm and the Peizières ridge now in enemy hands, the neighbouring 9th Division had good cause to feel nervous, particularly as the right flank of the 21st Division had also given way. The enemy penetration from Vaucelette Farm had formed a salient in the line around Épehy and Peizières and although the attacking Germans must have suffered enormous casualties in this pocket they were still intent on taking Revelon Farm. On the right flank the German advance towards St Emilie soon began to compromise the Épehy defences to the south, a situation that was temporarily stabilized by two companies of 6/Leicesters, which had hitherto been kept in reserve, being brought up to form a defensive flank pivoting on the southern edge of Épehy. The insecure position that 110 Brigade was in was already quite clear to Lieutenant Colonel William Stewart and his men as they moved into position.

As for A and C Companies of 6/Leicesters, which were deployed in Épehy, they were under the command of 31-year-old Captain Archibald McLay and Lieutenant Ellis Lane-Roberts with headquarters at Cullen Post, an observation point directly behind the cemetery, on the Rue Louis Georges. They and their men had been standing to ever since the first German shell had fallen earlier that morning, Lane recalling that the gas had been thick and heavy forcing them to put on the hated box respirators, but adding that 'after falling down a few times and colliding with walls etc we took them off again'. From their vantage point at Cullen Post the battle for Ridge Reserve North and Tetard Wood had little chance of going unnoticed and it was probably to Cullen Post that Whelan and his Munsters retired that evening, although Roberts makes no mention of this. By nightfall the survivors of 6/Leicesters were still in place along the north eastern edge of the village – 8/Leicesters had withdrawn to Prince Reserve Trench where their Lewis gun and rifle fire had successfully repelled several further attacks.

At 7.00pm David Kelly was directed by Brigadier General Cumming to visit all three battalions and collect reports on the situation facing them:

'The whole area had been transformed during the day, the green weedy fields were everywhere torn up with fresh shell holes, and the air was reeking with gas in many places. As I started out the enemy artillery resumed their fire with fresh vigour to stop possible supplies or reinforcements coming up under cover of darkness, and part of the way down the road to the 7th Battalion I had to run hard. The Battalion Headquarters had been shelled out of their new dugout, and were sitting in a slit about a hundred yards away. Having seen the Colonel, I went on to Peizières, visiting our posts on the way, and hugging the walls of the main street which was being swept by occasional bullets, indicating the enemy were working round our right flank through the 16th Division. Arrived at Fishers Keep, the headquarters of the 8th Battalion ... Tierens, the medical officer of the 6th Battalion came in and told us his aid-post in the south end of the village was in German hands, and that he had been taken prisoner, but released by his captors when they saw his Red Cross armband.'[27]

At 9.30pm Kelly and Tierens left Fishers Keep to find the 6/Leicesters who were somewhere in the fields behind Épehy. It was a journey that took an hour-and-a-half through a maelstrom of shellfire that was made all the more frightening by the darkness that surrounded them:

'Colonel Stewart's report of the situation was gloomy. The whole of our right flank appeared to be in the air, and the great Épehy to St Emilie road was infested with enemy patrols. The 6th Battalion had too few men to form a defensive flank, for they had lost heavily from shell fire and the process was still going on. The dug-out was full of wounded, some terribly mutilated. About midnight I took my leave of Colonel Stewart, who had always been a very good friend, for the last time. He was shot down in front of his headquarters a few hours later.'[28]

Martin Middlebrook concludes that the situation at Épehy was unusual in that the fog lifted relatively early in the day which he feels may well have been the reason why German units failed to encircle the position. They had already been confused by finding the empty forward positions which, together with well-directed artillery fire from three British batteries, had brought the German divisions frustratingly to a halt, despite the penetration on the right flank by the 9th Bavarian Reserve Division. The German account underlines their frustration over the inability to crack the Épehy stronghold:

> '*Landauer's 79th Reserve Division couldn't manage to take the bulwark from the south. On its right wing Battalion Kühne of RIR 261 clings to the outer defence of Épehy, two of its companies had attacked regardless of losses to open a breach, supported by Leutnant der Reserve Leman and his crack Stormtroops of Lübbener Jäger [Jäger Battalion 3], which carries an Infanterie-Geschütz-Batterie and another forward battery along. Fierce hand-to-hand fights leave two Züge [platoons] of Kompanie Nadolni almost annihilated. Only a few Jäger survive the day unscathed and many Kanoniere are being ripped to pieces at their guns ... Battalion Kühne of RIR 261 tries again and again in vain to gain the high-lying main English position. The division's left regiment, RIR 263, led by Oberstleutnant von Behr somehow manages to reach the railway line south of Épehy but has to withdraw due to a hail of our own artillery shells.*'[29]

The next day German gunners lost no time bringing yet another bombardment down on the Leicesters in their salient, but no infantry attack developed until 8.15am when Corporal Douglas Bacon was somewhat alarmed by a simultaneous German attack on the southern end of Épehy and on 6/Leicesters on the opposite flank:

> '*Fierce fighting ensued, but the result was the isolation and capture of the southern groups on our flank. This heavy fighting continued until 9.00 am, the attack from the Épehy-St Emilie road growing stronger and more determined. The 6th and 8th Leicesters were ordered to withdraw to the northwest and take up a position pivoting on Capron Copse to the edge of Épehy on the Saulcourt road. Lieutenant Colonel Stewart DSO was killed just prior to this withdrawal.*'[30]

The early morning bombardment and subsequent infiltration by enemy units into the ruined outskirts of Épehy forced Lieutenant Scarfe and his company back to the shelter of Tottenham Post in the north eastern corner of Peizières. On arrival he found the only officer badly wounded and a dwindling garrison of 7/Leicesters made up from survivors of C and D Companies:

> '[The men] *were suffering from a combination of machine gun fire from both land and low flying aeroplanes, bombardments by shells of many calibres, sniping and*

trench mortar bombardment from under cover of a ruined building in Peizières. So accurate and severe was the trench mortar shelling that a corporal and two other ranks volunteered to form a bombing party and raid that particular gun.'[31]

The bombing party succeeded in silencing the mortar but Scarfe never saw the men again. Shortly afterwards the two front companies were ordered to withdraw but no orders reached Scarfe at Tottenham Post. He described the circumstances that finally prompted him to order his men to retire at 3.30pm:

> 'I decided to cover the retirement of these two companies for as long as possible. Only the exhaustion of all our ammunition and bombs (even the dead were stripped of their cartridge clips) caused the final evacuation of Tottenham Post by the survivors of the garrison. A subaltern, the Company Sergeant Majors of C and D Companies and about twelve other ranks, besides myself, finally withdrew.'[32]

Their attempt to reach the battalion was hopeless from the start, the group soon ran into the enemy who were by now 'almost everywhere'. But at least Scarfe and his men were captured intact and not shot down as were many of the retiring Leicesters.

Lieutenant Lane-Roberts was facing a similar difficulty at Cullen Post. While the remnants of 8/Leicesters were still holding out in front of his post he felt unable to withdraw but as soon as they began to move through the ruins of the village Lane-Roberts decided to chance his luck and ordered his men to follow:

> 'With the 8th having retired to the left I decided to make a dash for it. I started off and expecting Germans to be in the trench ahead, bombed my way down. Lieutenant Thirlby, who was with me, brought up the rear. The Germans were closing in on us now and we had not gone very far when they jumped in the trench in between us and completely surrounded us on top.'[33]

Lane-Roberts fortunately survived those critical moments after surrender but after his capture he writes how, fearing the worst, he asked permission to go and find Stewart Thirlby who had not been with the party when they were captured. Permission refused, Roberts was marched away to Le Cateau and imprisonment.

Cumming's orders for his battalions to retire were sent out at 11.00am while he and his headquarters staff moved to Longavesne to await the arrival of the brigade. The retirement from Épehy was a challenge in itself which, despite the almost complete encirclement by the enemy, was carried out through the one remaining gap that was left. Inevitably the orders failed to reach some units, certainly neither of David Kelly's two orderlies made it back to Longavesne:

> *'Rearguards fought obstinately in Épehy to cover the retreat; Captain McLay of the 6th Battalion, one of our best company commanders, was killed there, and I heard the streets were full of German dead. In the Brown Line, by which I had come to the Quarry, the miscellaneous garrison were mostly cut off through ignorance of the general retirement, and our brigade headquarter cook and mess-waiter were taken prisoner while Captain* [Arthur] *Lawson who commanded our light trench-mortar battery was killed.'*[34]

Lieutenant Colonel Utterson and his garrison at Fishers Keep had found themselves surrounded long before the order to retire was received – if indeed it ever reached Fishers Keep – and fought on until surrender became the only sensible option. He and some sixteen other officers joined Ellis Lane-Roberts and Cyril Scarfe in captivity. Exactly how many NCOs and men were taken prisoner is unclear but at roll call on the evening of 22 March, 31 officers and 1,200 men were missing from the brigade.

Those who managed to retire from Peizières may well have heard the two explosions that came from the direction of the bridges to the northeast of the village. These were the same bridges that Lieutenant Cyril Scarfe rather angrily referred to after the enemy incursion into Peizières and the temporary capture of McFee Post on the previous day. With orders to remain at his post until instructed otherwise, a sapper from 126/Field Company continued to repair the leads throughout the two days of 21 and 22 March until the arrival of Captain James Vanner at 12.15pm. Remaining at his post in such trying circumstances was an act of courage that the 21-year old James Vanner would have understood completely. Vanner's service with the battalion began just after the attack on Bazentin-le-Petit in the early hours of 14 July 1916 when 7/Leicesters lost over half of its number and 18 officers. Promotion came easily to men like James Vanner, particularly if they managed to stay alive and ten months later he was in command of A Company with the rank of captain and the ribbon of the MC on his chest. If he and the sapper were to avoid capture there was very little time left in which to escape the enemy who were already on the road bridge. The citation for Vanner's DSO records his 'conspicuous gallantry and devotion to duty' whilst in command of two companies during the withdrawal from Épehy and blocking the railway cutting by the demolition of two bridges 'while the enemy were crossing'. Both men escaped.

For a week previous to 21 March, A and B Companies of the 1st Battalion East Yorkshire Regiment (1/East Yorks) had manned battle positions a mile east of the village of Saulcourt. From 4.00am on 22 March the village was subjected to a heavy bombardment of gas which forced the East Yorkshiremen to wear gas respirators for the next seven hours. As the Leicesters fell back from Épehy and passed through the East Yorkshire lines, these two companies remained in position repulsing several attacks. By 1.45pm A Company had lost all its officers and only two remained with B Company – Lieutenant Charles MacMahon and Second Lieutenant Nelson Gasson. The order to withdraw which arrived some fifteen minutes later was quickly followed by counter orders to attack east of the village towards Chauffeur's Wood. Faced with a heavy infantry attack and with a large proportion of his men dead or wounded around him, Charles MacMahon could have been forgiven if he had ignored such an order and simply retired, but judging from the spasmodic firing ahead of him there was still a token resistance taking place south of Chauffeur's Wood. The counter-attack went ahead and the sunken road was occupied:

> *'A machine gun officer of the 64th Brigade was still in position in this sunken road although devoid of personnel he, with great bravery, still manipulated his gun with the help of a couple of men from B Company. At 4.00pm the enemy made a determined attack on both flanks and enveloped this composite company. However every man stood his ground and the final scene was the company commander* [MacMahon] *indulging in a duel with a German officer, the latter brought to the ground with a nasty wound in his thigh and the former with a wound in his arm and taken prisoner.'*[35]

Nelson Glasson was also taken prisoner along with a handful of the surviving men although it is unlikely that many would have shared the sentiments expressed by MacMahon that it had been 'one of the many glorious fights' that took place that day.

Brigadier Cumming's short tenure of 110 Brigade had been a dramatic one and as the remnants fell back in the face of the German advance David Kelly was aware that 'we were now back on the edge of the old Somme Battlefield, utterly deserted since April 1917. All around stretched the old wilderness of shell holes, mostly overgrown with grass.' [36]

Top left: Sir Douglas Haig, Commander-in-Chief of British forces on the Western Front.

Top right: General Oskar von Hutier, commanding the German Eighteenth Army.

Centre left: David Lloyd George, the British Prime Minister 1916-1922.

Centre right: Erich Friedrich Ludendorff.

Bottom left: Hubert de la Poer Gough, commanding the British Fifth Army.

The present day site of 'Main Keep'at Luzerne Quarry where Lieutenant Colonel Richardson commanding 2/2 Londons held on until just after midday on 21 March.

German soldiers in the ruins of Fort Vendeuil shortly after its capture.

The ruins of Fort Vendeuil are still in evidence today although they are on private property and very much overgrown.

The woods mark the probable site of the 'Main Keep' at Travecy garrisoned by Captain Maurice Harper and A Company of 2/2 Londons.

Lieutenant Colonel 'Kit' Bushell who won the Victoria Cross on 23 March at Bois Halot. He was killed four months later.

Gunner Charlie Stone of 83 Brigade RFA won the Victoria Cross on 21 March for his gallantry in defending his battery position and covering its withdrawal.

Captain Maurice Harper who commanded A Company 2/2 Londons at Travecy.

Lieutenant Cecil Knox of 150/Field Company was awarded the Victoria Cross for his actions at Tugny on 23 March.

The September 1918 casualties buried in Gauche Wood Cemetery serve as a stark reminder that the wood was fought over again six months after Captain Garnet Green and B Company of 2/South African Regiment defended it so tenaciously on 21 March. In the distance is Villers–Guislain.

Lieutenant Colonel Frank Heal, commanding 1/South African Regiment, killed at Marières Wood on 24 March.

Rudolph Binding, the German officer who spoke to Brigadier Frederick Dawson after the South Africans had surrendered their positions at Marières Wood.

The observation tower at Morgan Post still remains on the outskirts of Peizières close to the Villers-Guislain road and 500 yards southeast of the former site of McPhee Post.

Brigadier General Hanway Cumming, commanding 110 (Leicester) Brigade at Épehy on 21/22 March. Hanway had only taken command of the brigade two days before the offensive and had little time in which to familiarize himself with the Épehy defences.

Top left: Major Frank 'Cully' Roberts who won the Victoria Cross at Pargny on the night of 23 March and Lieutenant Alfred Herring **(top right)** who won his cross on the Crozat Canal on 22/23 March. Both men survived the war.

Bottom left: Lieutenant Edmund de Wind won his Victoria Cross on 21 March serving with 15/Royal Irish Rifles at Racecourse Redoubt and Lieutenant Colonel Wilfrith Elstob **(bottom right)** was awarded his Victoria Cross on the same day serving with 16/Manchesters at Manchester Hill Redoubt. Both awards were made posthumously.

Manchester Hill as it is today. The trees mark the site of Brown Quarry.

The view of St Quentin and the Basilique that Brigadier General Ferdinand Stanley complained overlooked the British line and most of the back areas for miles beyond.

The ruins of St Quentin and the Basilique taken in 1918 after hostilities had ended.

The historic meeting room in the Mairie at Doullens where Foch was confirmed as supreme commander on the Western Front on 26 March 1918.

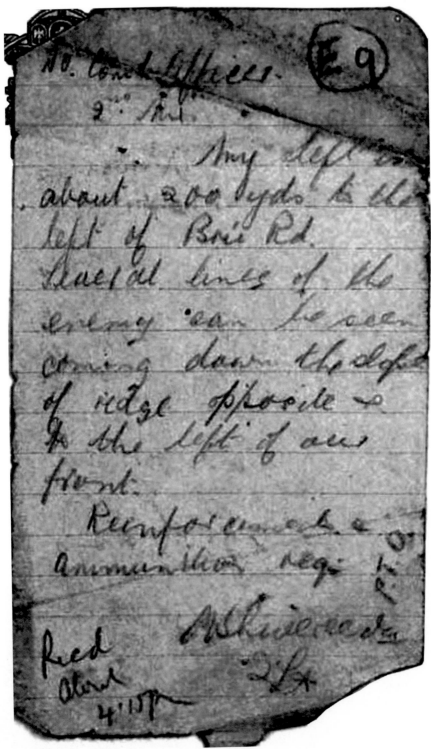

The final communication sent by Second Lieutenant Alexander Liversedge to battalion headquarters on 25 March. Liversedge was in command of the remnants of B Company, 2/Middlesex at Brie. He was killed in action later in the day.

Lieutenant Colonel Rowland Fielding commanding 6/Connaught Rangers. Fielding was highly critical of Brigadier Phillip Leveson-Gower for failing to cancel the Connaughts' attack on 21 March.

Lance Corporal John Sayer of 8/Queen's won a posthumous Victoria Cross at Shepherd's Copse on 21 March.

Lieutenant Thomas Ginger the 4/Yorkshires' Signals Officer who won the Military Cross at Brie on 23 March.

Corporal John Davies of 11/South Lancashires who won the Victoria Cross at Eppeville on 24 March.

The site of the former road bridge at Pargny which was destroyed on 23 March by Lieutenant George Baylay of 1/Field Squadron. He was killed almost immediately afterwards.

Captain Maurice Toye of 2/Middlesex who commanded C Company at Eterpigny on 25 March. The citation for his award of the Victoria Cross refers to two further occasions when he displayed conspicuous gallantry, but the action at Eterpigny was the most outstanding.

Lieutenant Colonel Maxwell McTaggart commanding officer of 1/5 Gordon Highlanders at the Fresnoy Redoubt.

Lieutenant Claude Piesse who was in command at Shepherd's Copse on 21 March.

Lieutenant Colonel Herbert Wenyon was placed in command of all forces north of the River Omignon on 21 March.

Jack Seely (standing on the right) commanded the Canadian Cavalry Brigade at Moreuil Wood. He is seen here with Winston Churchill who was present at the 9th Division Headquarters on 21 March when the opening bombardment began.

The railway embankment south of Jussy which was defended on 23 March by a scratch force commanded by Julius Birch. Birch's headquarters was at the level crossing marked by the raised traffic barriers.

The forest house occupied by Willy Lange and the IR 27 machine gunners on 23 March. The nearby section of the forest road running north from the D35 was lined by 10/Essex before they fell back to Rouez Farm.

Gordon Flowerdew was killed leading his squadron of Lord Strathcona's Horse at Moreuil Wood and awarded a posthumous Victoria Cross after his death on 31 March 1918.

Captain George Howson (front row, centre) who fought with 11/Hampshires at Doingt and founded the British Legion Poppy Factory after the war. He is pictured with (back row left to right) Bill Adams, Arthur Phillips and Jack Pallatt with Fred Williams (left) and Bert Harkinson (right) sitting on the front row. All of these men were disabled to some extent during the war and were the first employees to work with Howson at the factory.

The Crozat Canal south of Jussy, close to the former site of the Montagne Bridge defended by Alfred Herring. Herring's VC was one of three awarded for gallantry on 23 March.

The entrance to the Pozières Memorial northeast of Albert commemorating nearly 15,000 casualties who were killed between 21 March and 7 August 1918.

Chapter 8

Jocks and Springboks

The whole countryside was grey with moving Boches, like lice on a trench sodden kilt.

Brigadier General William Croft

The sector held by the 9th (Scottish) Division is characterised by its undulating nature and rolling downs, which, in 1918 was dotted with the ruins of numerous villages. To the east and west of Gouzeaucourt lay several low ridges which joined together at Chapel Hill, a little to the west of Chapel Crossing. The British front line ran along the Quentin Ridge to the Quentin Redoubt – just south of the D16 – before it swung northwest to Fifteen Ravine which was not only the boundary between the 9th and 47th Divisions but that between the Fifth and Third Armies. Temporarily in command of the 'Jocks and Springboks' was Brigadier General Henry Tudor.

The sector was organized into the three standard zones of defence which on 21 March was held on the left by 26 Infantry Brigade and on the right by the South African Brigade, with the three battalions of 27 Brigade in reserve. The brigade was also in touch with 140 Brigade on the extreme right of the Third Army. Brigadier General William Croft, commanding 27 Brigade was one of many senior officers who shared concerns over the army boundary being on the left flank of the division. Croft knew from experience that 'joints are always weak, however good the material may be which is used for the soldering; and that joint was to be the cause of the gravest anxiety to us'.

He had good reason to be anxious. The 9th Division was on the southern edge of the Flesquières Salient and stood in the path of the four divisions of Georg von der Marwitz's Second Army whose task it was to drive into the shoulders of the salient from the south in conjunction with Otto von Below's Seventeenth Army which would carry out a similar manoeuvre from the north before linking up with the Second Army behind Flesquières and advancing on Bapaume. Divisional officers knew full well that should the 47th Division on their left be compelled to pull back, the direction of their retirement would be to the northwest while any retirement by the 9th Division would be to the southwest. But there was perhaps a greater danger that lay with the intended direction of von der Marwitz's Second Army advance. If all went according to plan Ludendorff expected to take the Flesquières Salient without a frontal infantry assault thus neutralizing the three divisions of V Corps and in so doing force a capitulation. If the 9th Division was required to retire – as indeed it did – then its line of retirement would be directly across the path of the German advance.

The 21 March opened with an 'ear splitting noise', wrote Captain John Ewing, 'and our lines were robed in smoke and flame'. In the Forward Zone the bombardment – particularly on the 26 Brigade front – was not exceptional but the back areas of Dessart Wood, Heudecourt and Sorel-le-Grand were heavily shelled, including as far back as Nurlu where Tudor had his headquarters. Also at Nurlu on that morning was the Minister of Munitions, Winston Churchill – who had famously commanded 6/Royal Scots Fusiliers at Ploegsteert in 1916 – and was spending the night with his old division when he was woken by the bombardment:

> *'And then, exactly as a pianist runs his hands across the keyboard from treble to bass, there rose in less than one minute the most tremendous cannonade I shall ever hear … It swept round us in a wide curve of red leaping flame stretching to the north far along the front of the Third Army, as well as of the Fifth Army on the south, and quite unending in either direction … the enormous explosions of the shells upon our trenches seemed almost to touch each other, with hardly an interval in space or time …The weight and intensity of the bombardment surpassed anything which anyone had ever known before.'*[1]

Churchill, had he realized it at the time, was caught in one of a myriad of specific targets the German fire plan had identified as communication and command centres. Croft remembered 'a real fat Bertha of a Percy made excellent shooting all the time we were in the neighbourhood, landing one right on the Expeditionary Force Canteen'. These 'Purring Percies' as he called them, were accompanied by quantities of gas which forced them to 'keep their gas masks on for hours'. Gas was also a feature of the bombardment on the Third Army in the Flesquières Salient and although they would not be subject to any direct infantry assault on 21 March they were certainly on the receiving end of the opening barrage which served admirably to mask German intentions. In fact north of Gouzeaucourt there appeared to be very little enemy infantry activity at all Lieutenant Colonel John Ritson, commanding 12/Royal Scots on the south side of Dessart Wood, reported his battalion did nothing on 21 March but were unable to get in touch 'in any way with the 26 Highland Brigade' on his right or the Third Army to the north.

At 9.53am news that German infantry were advancing on Gauche Wood and the Quentin Ridge announced the beginning of the infantry assault. The main attack fell on the South African Brigade commanded by Brigadier General Frederick Dawson and holding some 2,000 yards of line which included the strong point of Gauche Wood. Of the three German first-line divisions attacking between Gouzeaucourt and Épehy, it was ID 107 that would bear the brunt of the fighting in and around Gauche Wood:

> '*Out of Gauche Wood heavy rifle fire meets the attacking Division Havenstein* [ID 107]. *South Africans, the well-known 'Springböcke' hold the defence with their in-built tenacity. They are ordered to hold the line up to the last man. Havenstein's Division is to veer in towards Gouzeaucourt thus protecting Maur's Württembergers* [ID 27] *at the flank on their way to take both Vaucelette and Révélon Farms. Even before reaching the jump-off point English shells have caused havoc among the marching columns and the train. The Stoßbatterie* [advanced battery] *is smashed, the group of men and material shuffled in a shellhole is pounded for hours. Only one gun can be saved and is brought single-handed to the front by Oberleutnant Giebeler, Leutnant Frohnhäuser and Unteroffizier Landau alone!*'[2]

Gauche Wood was held by B Company of the 2nd South African Regiment (2/ South Africans) under the command of 29-year-old Captain Garnet Green who was alerted to the German infantry attack when Number 1 Platoon came under fire. The platoon was positioned at the junction of Gauche Alley and Chapel Trench, one of three strong points in the wood, a fourth post was positioned in the open ground to the north of Chapel Alley on the southwest side of the wood where, on a clear day, it was possible to see across the valley to Vaucelette Farm.

The irony of fighting in another wood would not have been lost on Garnet Green and his South Africans. Having fought the Germans in South West Africa in 1914 he arrived on the Western Front in time to fight on the Somme in the carnage of Delville Wood. At midnight on 14 July 1916 the South African Brigade had entered Delville Wood with 121 officers and 3,032 men, six days later only 142 officers and men were present at the relief and of these, Garnet Green was one of only three officers to leave the wood alive. His award of the Military Cross for his part in the action was gazetted shortly before a second award in 1917 which added a bar to his purple and white ribbon.

Today if you walk along the Chemin du Bois from the western edge of Villers-Guislain, Gauche Wood soon comes into view as the ground rises gently ahead of you. Where the track divides the left fork will take you to Gauche Wood Cemetery while the right heads towards the north eastern corner of the wood. It was these two tracks that the attacking German infantry would have taken on 21 March. Under cover of the thick fog the Germans were able to gradually infiltrate the wood managing to get between the outposts north of the wood along the shallow valley to the south of Quentin Redoubt and enter along Somme Alley. Like all fighting in dense wooded areas, the combat is confused and intense for the men of both sides:

> 'In a dense mist loaded with toxic fumes the combat around Gauche Wood and the trenches just south of it rages. Major Buchholz [RIR 227] throws two Battalions into the bubbling cauldron. Neither man nor [tree] trunk is distinguishable from each other. Previously written orders are worthless, who can carry them out in this pandemonium? Communication cables are ripped apart, Very Lights are disappearing in the mist, tracer bullets smothered in the screen of fog, radio intercepts providing no more than babble in both German and English, carrier pigeons and messenger dogs are useless, even dispatch runners are always on the move.'[3]

Eventually the two South African posts at the eastern edge of the wood were surrounded. The small garrisons under the command of Lieutenants Thomas Bancroft and Second Lieutenant Meller Beviss were eventually overpowered with Beviss and a mere handful of men managing to find their way back to company headquarters.[4]

Meanwhile Garnet Green, with the enemy closing in on three sides of the wood, gradually withdrew his diminishing company south towards Gun Post, contesting the ground every inch of the way:

> 'The hostile troops at first exposed themselves recklessly and as they were within some 50 yards of Captain Green's men, the latter caused then exceedingly high casualties, especially in officers, with the fire of their Lewis guns and rifles. So heavy were their losses that they did not attempt to advance beyond the eastern edge of the wood but commenced to dig in there.'[5]

At 11.30am the South Africans had relinquished the whole of Gauche Wood but still retained 50 yards of Chapel Trench and were in touch with the 1st Battalion Lincolnshire Regiment (1/Lincolns) who were to the south of Chapel Alley. It had been a desperate fighting withdrawal through the wood, one which had reduced his company of 130 to about 40 effective fighting men. And it was not over yet. With the fog now lifting, Green's precarious situation at Gauche Wood enabled Brigadier General Dawson to direct the fire of all the artillery at his disposal on the wood – which together with a sustained rifle and Lewis gun fire from the 1st South African Regiment in Quentin Redoubt forced the enemy to go to ground. Throughout the remainder of the day both sides held their positions despite several attempts by groups of the enemy to bomb their way down Chapel Trench.

Up until 11.00am on 21 March reports arriving at Tudor's headquarters suggested the division – apart from the loss of Gauche Wood – was holding its own. On the right the Lincolns still held Cavalry Trench to the east and south east of Chapel Hill and to the north the 47th Division in the Third Army sector was not under any infantry attack. However, all was to change with the news that the enemy were concentrating in large numbers southwest of Vaucelette Farm with the intention of pressing home their attack on Chapel Hill and the nearby Chapel Crossing. This was Brigadier Dawson's recurring nightmare:

> *'This hill overlooked the whole of the trench system known as the Yellow Line and its possession was therefore of vital importance to the defence. A company of the 2/ South Africans reserved for counter-attack purposes was therefore sent out to the trenches on the north slope of the hill … With the enemy in possession of Chapel Hill the situation of the two advanced battalions was most critical and the SA Brigade was ordered to assume responsibility for the defence of Chapel Hill.'*[6]

The 2/South Africans met the German Guard Fusiliers on the northern slope of the hill and were beaten back leaving Captain Harry Bunce and A Company of the South African Scottish – who presumably had advanced from the south western side – to take the hill.

The control of Chapel Hill together with Revelon Farm and Railton provided the divisional flank with some security and maintained a tenuous link with the 21st Division. But, as is often the case in the confusion of battle, the 'attack' by the South African Scottish on Chapel Hill is mired in controversy. The action was described by Lieutenant Colonel Bertie Fisher, who was commanding 1/ Lincolns, a little differently to the account in the South African Brigade War Diary. Fisher is quite clear that 'the 1st Lincolns and attached troops were *relieved* on Chapel Hill during the night of 21/22nd by the South African Scottish, 'the relief being completed by 8.00am on 22nd'. No mention of a counter-attack by the South Africans! He is also most emphatic that 'at no time throughout the day were Chapel Hill and Chapel Crossing lost by the 1st Lincolns', and concluded by adding, 'the enemy made no impression on the front of 62 Brigade'. It is a view that is supported by Brigadier General George Gater, the officer commanding 62 Brigade, who wrote in 1927 that he had 'formed the impression that justice is hardly done to the 1st Lincolns who were the battalion in the line on the left of my brigade front. It was really the action of their commanding officer which saved Chapel Hill on that day.'[7]

Fisher's account makes it clear that the Lincolns successfully held off the German attack, citing the number of graves of the Guard Fusilier Regiment situated between Chapel Hill and Vaucelette Farm – discovered in September 1918 – as ample proof of the resistance his battalion encountered. So was Dawson allowing his concern to override an accurate assessment of the situation on Chapel Hill? The answer probably lies somewhere between the two accounts. The temptation is to ignore the effect of the extreme pressures of the burden of command in battle and forget that communication between brigades – let alone between divisions – was practically non-existent on 21 March. Dawson was reacting to patchy information in a rapidly changing battlefield scenario and, as any soldier will testify, in that situation it is better to be safe than sorry.

* * *

Fast forward now to the events of 23 March. Tudor's orders to withdraw on 22 March were precipitated by events further north in the Third Army sector and by the 21st Division retirement on the right. The attack on the Third Army is beyond the scope of this book but the retirement of the 47th Division and the subsequent delay in evacuating the Flesquières Salient impacted directly on the movements of Tudor's 9th Division. Congreve had little doubt as to who was to blame for the widening gap between his left flank and the 47th Division:

> '*In my opinion, the real cause of the constant gaps between V and VII Corps was due in the first instance to the retention of the Cambrai* [Flesquières] *Salient, from which the V Corps never recovered. Its retirement was forever northwest instead of being southwest, as ordered to conform to the dividing line of the two armies, which ran southwest. The result was a perpetual extension to the north by 9th Division which thereby became weak everywhere.*'[8]

Congreve's view was loudly supported by the 9th Division and Lieutenant Colonel Thomas Mudie, who insisted that it was the retirement of Byng's V Corps that forced the retirement of the 9th Division and not 'the other way about'.

But gap or no gap, behind the scenes Hubert Gough was still reeling from the intensity of the first day's onslaught. After dinner he spoke to Lieutenant General Sir Herbert Lawrence on the telephone. Lawrence was Chief of the General Staff and a former banker who had been in post since January 1918. Gough was clearly worried and had every right to be so:

> '*I then went on to express very considerable anxiety for the next and following days. The Germans would certainly continue to push their attack on the next day, Friday, and it would undoubtedly continue with unabated fury for many days. Could our tired and attenuated line maintain the struggle without support? That was the question and it was a grave one. Lawrence did not seem to grasp the seriousness of the situation; he thought that 'the Germans would not come on again the next day after the severe losses they had suffered'. He thought they "would be busy clearing the battlefield and collecting their wounded".*'[9]

Lawrence's prediction proved to be entirely without substance and clearly annoyed Gough considerably, confirming his belief that GHQ did not fully grasp the seriousness of the situation facing the Fifth Army. It may also have been the beginning of the blame culture that finally sealed Gough's fate five days later. At 6.30pm on 22 March Gough visited Byng at his Albert headquarters to discuss the essential nature of keeping the two wings of their respective armies in touch, a move that was reinforced that evening by an order from GHQ to Third Army headquarters to maintain touch with the 9th Division – even if it ultimately meant withdrawing west towards the Tortille River.

The 9th Division retirement sealed the fate of one company of 11/Scots Fusiliers at Revelon Farm – which received no order to retire – and that of Captain Garnet Green and the remainder of his B Company, who were by this time in a quarry to the east of Heudicourt. For Green there was no chance of withdrawal and he and his men 'died fighting to the last' as the remaining men of the South African Brigade dug in along the Nurlu-Péronne line – the so-called Green Line – in the early hours of 23 March.

Although nominally in reserve, the South African Brigade was on the right flank of 27 Brigade and in touch with units of 21st Division but the German assault on the Green Line made no allowances for the casualties of the previous two days. The Green Line was hardly an impressive line of defence as 19-year-old Private Alex Jamieson, serving with the 11/Royal Scots in 27 Brigade, discovered. Initially he thought the partly-dug trenches were intended as tank traps:

'They were twice the width of a normal trench – about twelve feet wide – and they had no fire steps. That was the first moment I was frightened, really frightened, because the orders came along, "This position must be held at all costs until the last man." … Everybody was thinking, how on earth can we hold this position? It's impossible!'[10]

It was fortunate they didn't. The fog that greeted the dawn of 23 March also heralded the attempt by von der Marwitz to drive a wedge between the Fifth and Third Armies and marked the first change of strategy by Ludendorff. Persuaded by the massive extent of the retreat of the BEF westwards he ordered von Below to swing around Arras from the west and von der Marwitz to advance on both sides of the Somme towards a line running between Miraumont on the north bank and Lihons to the south.

At 4.30pm Tudor arrived at Dawson's headquarters; the situation looked depressingly bleak. Despite the Third Army's 99 Brigade being drafted in to plug some of the gap, Tudor's division was holding an impossibly long front of 6,000 yards in trying desperately to man an increasingly widening gap which had opened up along the Army boundary. It was a gap which von der Marwitz lost little time in exploiting. The attack that afternoon against 99 Brigade and Brigadier General John Kennedy's 26 Brigade had penetrated between Kennedy's Highlanders and Croft's 27 Brigade, forcing 99 Brigade back to Rocquigny and Le Transloy and leaving Kennedy's brigade – critically low on ammunition – in great danger of envelopment.

In the circumstances Congreve had little choice but to retire across the Canal du Nord, making it quite clear to Tudor that the line west of Moislains – running from Government Farm down to the Cléry road junction – must be held at all costs and regained if necessary by counter-attack. In Épinette Wood 6/KOSB were already under attack which was, wrote Croft, touch and go for a short time:

> '*He* [the Germans] *attacked on that weak right flank and Smyth with his Borderers had all he could do to hang on. Luckily a number of South Africans were in the wood, and these, led by an officer riding a grey horse – I never found out who it was – made a gallant counter-attack which relieved the situation. The South Africans, be it noted, were past masters in the gentle art of counter-attacking in those black days.*'[11]

The KOSB, led by their one-armed commanding officer Lieutenant Colonel Gerald Smyth, and fighting every inch of the way, withdrew company by company down the slope to the Canal du Nord covered by Captain William Cockburn and A Company whose rearguard action did much to prevent a destructive and bloody fighting retreat. Croft writes glowingly of Cockburn, describing him as 'a splendid company commander', who handled his 'rearguard like a book and so enabled his battalion to get across the canal in safety'.

Cockburn's commanding officer, Gerald Smyth, began the war as a lieutenant of engineers with 17/Field Company and lost his left arm in September 1914 whilst rescuing a wounded man of his section, winning his first DSO. Appointed to command the battalion in October 1916, he was described by the battalion historian as 'a one-armed Irish warrior of dauntless courage and one of the outstanding figures in this battalion of Borderers'. A hugely popular but demanding commanding officer, Smyth was immensely proud of his Borderers and did not take kindly to being harried by the seemingly endless ranks of German infantry. Once across the canal the battalion took refuge in the Bois St Pierre Vaast where darkness provided some temporary relief. However Smyth was intent on hitting back at his enemy:

> '*As darkness came on the Germans pressed on in hoards … It was then that the fertile mind of Smyth bethought him to make a reconnaissance in force with A and B Companies northwards between the Bois St Pierre Vaast and the Bois des Vaux. In the dark the Germans were found en-masse and fired at with machine gun with good effect as they debouched from the Bois des Vaux.*'[12]

The KOSB counter-attack caught the enemy in an unguarded moment. Unfortunately during the encounter Gerald Smyth was wounded for a fifth time but the situation had been stabilized for the moment and the battalion withdrew unmolested to the south of Rancourt.

Meanwhile the remaining brigades had also completed their withdrawal crossing the canal where possible by bridge or, in the case of the Black Watch of 26 Brigade, swimming across, before retiring to a position east of Sailly-Saillisel. When John Ritson reached the canal he found a partly-demolished bridge that was only possible to cross via one broken span:

> '*In fact we only managed to get across by sacrificing about half a company who took up position on the German side of the canal – somewhere in the vicinity of Riverside Wood – because I can distinctly remember moving some men who were taking cover behind brush-wood heaps to better positions. This enabled the majority of the battalion to cross the river and we took up our positions on the eastern edge of Vaux Woods.*'[13]

The South Africans, now reduced to 500 officers and men, took up positions on the ridge of high ground to the west of Bouchavesnes close to the northern end of Marières Wood. They were in position by 3.00am and to Dawson's relief they had linked up with friendly units on both flanks:

> '*In the course of the night, touch was obtained with the left brigade of the 21st Division which had retired and advanced again joining up with the right of the South African Brigade. The left flank was in touch with the KOSB, but the company which it was in touch with did not know the whereabouts of the remainder of the brigade.*'[14]

The South Africans were tenacious fighters and seemed destined to be forever associated with patches of shell-blasted woodland. Now perhaps their finest moment was upon them as they prepared to fight near Marières Wood. Dawson lost no time in making Tudor's orders clear to his two battalion commanders:

> '*Lieutenant Colonels Heal and Christian commanding the 1st and 2nd South African Infantry Regiments – the remnants of the 4th were attached to the 2nd – were seen by the Brigadier and told that the position had to be held at all costs. It was pointed out to them what this expression meant and they were told that, without orders, the brigade would not retire, whatever the troops on the flanks might do.*'[15]

Second Lieutenant Geoffrey Lawrence described the orders a little more lucidly:

> '*Major Ormiston came up and gave the officers our orders. He said you are now the rearguard to the whole of this front and you are to hold the line. You will fight to the last man and the last round. There will be no surrender or retreat, all forward*

troops of ours retiring will be stopped on this line, if necessary, with your revolvers and you will shoot any man who refuses to stand.'[16]

Lawrence accepted the orders with a quiet dignity but later wrote that it was difficult to 'describe the feeling that came over me,' particularly when he realized this ridge was 'to be our final sacrifice'. Like many in his position, it was the acceptance of the inevitable that enabled him to carry on.

As the cold light of dawn broke on the Bouchavesnes Ridge the troops on the right of the South Africans – 62 Brigade – reported Cléry to be in the hands of the enemy and were about to make a further retirement. Despite the patchy morning fog Geoffrey Lawrence could see the troops on his right streaming back and noted the 'bursting shells falling everywhere, dumps of ammunition going up and burning food supplies emitting great clouds of black smoke'. A glint of controversy over the apparent KOSB withdrawal on the left flank surfaced in 1927 in a letter written by Major Ormiston. His assertion that the KOSB let them down was unmistakable: 'I suppose you know', he wrote, 'the KOSB left our left flank in the air on the 24th at Marières Wood'.[17] After Gerald Smyth had been wounded at the Bois des Vaux, Major Ambrose Innes-Browne assumed command as the battalion fell back to Maricourt. Whether they left the South Africans to their fate is debatable but they were hard pressed all the way back to Combles where Croft tells us, 'we held them for some time, fighting from ridge to ridge in perfect co-operation with our gunners'.

At Marières Wood Dawson described the brigade positions as 'having one good trench and one or two bad ones'. The ground of the ridge sloped down towards the east and then rose again to another ridge about 1,000 yards from the front line. It was as good a place as any to make a stand but 'all ranks had been three nights without sleep and were in a state of exhaustion from their physical exertions and the strain of the previous days. There was no road through the position and communication with division was by runner only.'

An hour later at 9.00am German gunners opened fire from some abandoned trenches on the ridge east of the South African defences, a bombardment that was replied to by British batteries, presumably from the 21st Division, which unfortunately appeared to be targeted on the South African trenches rather than the enemy's. Providentially there were no casualties apart from a rather hurried evacuation by brigade headquarters to a safer location! As the bombardment died away the infantry attack began:

'The hostile infantry advanced over the ridge to the east and took up a line some 750 yards from the positions. They did not however, attempt to approach closer, evidently recognising that an advance across the valley would be attended by heavy losses. An attack from the south was also held up. An hour or so later a very heavy attack was made on the left front and flank from the north east. By means of setting

fire to the grass, using the smoke as a screen and a very skilful combination of fire and movement, the enemy gradually worked his way to between 100 and 200 yards of the front line. For some hours, however, all attempts to approach nearer were frustrated.[18]

With little chance of being re-supplied with ammunition the brigade withheld their fire until the enemy were within 400 yards and even then every man fired carefully, making sure each round was on target. All firing at longer ranges was left to the Lewis gunners:

'Soon after the commencement of the attack, the enemy attempted to bring up a field gun into action at a range of 1,000 yards. The gun was wheeled forward by hand, but a Lewis gunner of the 1st South African Infantry, acting under orders of Major Ormiston knocked out the personnel before the gun could be fired. Some hours later the enemy made another attempt and on this occasion a gun was brought forward by its team at a gallop. The fire of the same Lewis gunner was, however, too accurate, the team got out of hand, overturned the gun, men and horses going down in a struggling mass. This greatly cheered our men.'[19]

The Lewis gunner, according to Lawrence, was Private Jeffries, 'a member of my old C Company'. By 2.00pm the ammunition shortage was becoming critical. The equipment of the dead was scoured for live ammunition and every spare round was collected from other casualties:

'By 2 pm. we were completely surrounded and the enemy had opened fire from the west of our position as well as from the east and south. Some snipers on the west side were also very troublesome. I saw numbers of the enemy on the north side also, within 200 yards of my brigade HQ, and sent Lieutenant [Arthur] Cooper with some 20 men to take up a position about 200 yards to the north of brigade HQ in shell holes from which they could more effectively bring fire to bear on the enemy. They did excellent work, their behaviour being beyond all praise; their casualties were, however, heavy, frequent reinforcements having to be sent to them. Lieutenant Cooper, I regret to say, was killed.'[20]

An hour later the enemy on the north side began to retire which, apart from providing the South Africans with an excellent target, raised hopes that units of the promised 35th Division were counter-attacking towards them. Hope was raised even further when the German gunners put down a heavy barrage to the west. But it was not to be. The seriousness of their situation was underlined by Lieutenant Colonel Ewan Christian who reported to Dawson that he was afraid 'we could not hold out much longer'. Casualties were high and the position was only held by isolated groups of men:

'I had no further hope of relief, but thought it possible we might hold on till dark and then fight our way back. At 4.30pm however, the enemy came into sight to the east northeast of brigade headquarters carrying out the final stage of the attack, in great strength and thick formation. From personal observation and subsequent investigation the number of our effectives at that time was approximately 100, scattered over a large area. Had we had ammunition we could have stopped the attack, but under existing circumstances we could only fire a few scattered shots, and the few remaining groups were taken by the enemy as he got up to them. I believe that no one got away. The final rush was carried out by three battalions of fresh troops.'[21]

Dawson's men held onto their ridge for seven hours and delayed the enemy advance to the extent that the road from Bouchavesnes was blocked by a continuous line of transport and guns. The CWGC database lists 238 men and nine officers killed on 24 March. The list included the 23-year-old Meller Beviss, Lieutenant Colonel Frank Heal, commanding 1/South African Infantry and 36-year-old Major Frank Cochran, the Australian Brigade Major who settled in South Africa after the Boer War.

Amongst those who were marched into captivity with Brigadier General Dawson was Second Lieutenant William Faulds who had won the Victoria Cross at Delville Wood. To that he would soon be able to add the ribbon of the Military Cross for his actions during the retreat to Marières Wood. Watching the survivors filing out towards Bouchavesnes was *Leutnant* Rudolph Binding; his chance meeting with Frederick Dawson remained etched on his mind for some time afterwards:

'Out from the lines of our advancing infantry, which I was following, appeared an English General accompanied by a single officer. He was an extraordinary sight. About thirty-five years old, excellently – one can almost say wonderfully – dressed and equipped, he looked as if he had just stepped out of a Turkish bath in Jermyn Street. Brushed and shaved, with his short khaki overcoat on his arm, in breeches of the best cut and magnificent high laced boots such as only the English boot makers make to order, he came to meet me easily and without the slightest embarrassment. The sight of all this English cloth and leather made me more conscious than ever of the shortcomings of my own outfit ... By way of being polite I said with intention, 'you have given us a lot of trouble; you stuck it for a long time,' to which he replied, 'Trouble! Why, we have been running for four days and four nights!'[22]

Running they may have been but the 15 mile retreat of Dawson's South Africans since their first encounter at Gauche Wood had been contested every inch of the way. The officer with Dawson was Lieutenant Colonel Christian, the only surviving commanding officer left with the brigade. Christian, like Dawson, may well have pondered the necessity of their stand during their months in captivity which followed, although both men undoubtedly knew that once the battle had begun that morning their position precluded any withdrawal. All too often in the preceding days units were on the receiving end of orders to 'remain until the last man and the last round'. Such orders tend to have an elasticity that unit commanders can interpret as necessary. In this case, however, Dawson believed that he had little 'option but to remain until the end'. His diary betrayed his strict adherence to duty: 'Far better to go down fighting against heavy odds than it should be said we failed to carry out our orders.'

Chapter 9

The Crozat Canal

The fog began to lift, and a party of the enemy, consisting of one officer and about thirty men, were seen advancing along the road towards the level crossing, but were wiped out by fire from two Hotchkiss guns at about 100 yards.

Lieutenant Colonel Julias Birch, 7/KRRC at Jussy

W e now need to return to the III Corps sector to the point where the surviving units were ordered to fall back across the Crozat Canal. On 21 March Lieutenant General Butler was one of the first corps commanders to receive a visit by Gough, who found him 'a little anxious'. Under the circumstances Butler's palpable anxiety was understandable. The 14th Division had been driven back on to the rear of its Battle Zone and in so doing had exposed the left flank of the 18th Division, while the 58th Division's Forward and Battle Zones around La Fère had been overwhelmed. To his credit Butler had foreseen a likely retirement across the canal and had already ordered much of his remaining artillery to be withdrawn to the west bank where it could support the inevitable retirement of the infantry later that night. Gough's visit simply served to rubber stamp a decision that had already been taken. Butler issued his orders for the retirement to the canal at 7.25pm and by the time those orders had filtered down from divisions to their constituent battalions it was 9.00pm before movement was underway.

The Crozat Canal was some forty feet wide and unfordable and as such presented a much needed defensive line behind which to regroup. The defence of the canal line was not only important in stemming the German advance but was also vital in respect of maintaining a secure front with the French to enable their reinforcements to arrive unmolested. However, little time or effort had been put into securing the west bank of the canal as a defensive line and apart from some spitlocked trenches, the canal line had been largely ignored. As far as the demolition of bridges was concerned the sheer number must have been a cause for concern in itself! On the 58th Division's sector alone there were fourteen road and several footbridges that crossed the canal, while on the front of the neighbouring 18th Division, there were six road bridges and numerous footbridges between Liez and Menessis. From Menessis to Jussy in the 14th Division's area there were seven road bridges and a further five that were the responsibility of the French. In the event German troops also used the canal locks to cross the canal at Liez, which, in order to preserve the depth of water in the waterway, had not been destroyed.

We last left the Londons on the morning of 22 March – now a composite force under the command of Lieutenant Colonel William Dann – dug in along the Vouël Line, extending south from the twin hills of the Butte de Vouël to the Chauny-Tergniers road, and attacking enemy infantry crossed the canal using the remains of the main road bridge between Tergnier and Fargnieres. Although the bridges had been blown by 303/Field Company, it was to the eternal frustration of RE officers that infantry commanders continued with the assumption that demolition would automatically scatter bridge structures and leave nothing behind. With larger structures such as rail and major road bridges, demolition would collapse a bridge sufficiently to prevent the crossing of transport and artillery but often leave enough of the structure for determined infantry to clamber across, a scenario only too well illustrated in the assertions of Captain Clive Grimwade, the 4/Londons' historian who pointed to demolition charges not exploding and 'one or two bridges ... not ... entirely demolished after our withdrawal'. Only the bridges constructed of wood could be destroyed completely and no one wished to be reminded of the warning voiced by Lieutenant Colonel Arthur Walker, CRE to XIX Corps, that bridge demolition alone would have a limited effect on an advancing enemy. In the event the ability of German infantry to cross the canal using the debris from 'demolished' bridges ultimately led to the loss of the canal line.

Once across the canal German infantry extended northwards and pushed 8/Londons back from the canal onto the Vouël Line, a position that became critical by mid-morning of 23 March after two battalions of the French 125th Regiment were thrown back from the canal and the 18th Division was forced back towards Villequier-Aumont – an encounter we will return to later.

As 173 Brigade withdrew to a new line east of Viry-Noureuil it was almost immediately compromised by the German penetration of Frières Wood to the north. For Brigadier General Rivers Worgan, commanding the brigade, the likelihood of being cut off from the 18th Division on his left was fast becoming a reality but in the meantime he had the defence of Chauny to worry about.

With what must have been tinged with a hint of desperation, Worgan ordered Major Albert Grover of 2/4 Londons to organize all the available personnel for the defence of the town. Albert Grover and Lieutenant Colonel Dann had previously served together in the Bedfordshire Regiment and quite naturally when Dann took over command of 2/4 Londons he wanted his second-in-command to be an individual he knew and trusted. If anyone could hold Chauny it was Grover:

> 'With remarkable skill and despatch Major Grover collected a heterogeneous force
> of clerks, cooks, officers' servants, transport drivers – anyone who could hold a rifle
> – and by dusk reported himself in position on the eastern outskirts of Chauny with a
> force of ten officers and 270 other ranks at his command. Of these two officers and
> fifty-four other ranks were of the 2/4 Londons.'[1]

Grover's Force – as it became known – was one of the first of the 'scarecrow armies'; units assembled from every available officer and man and pushed into the line as a last gasp defence. In many cases the men involved had not used a rifle in anger for some considerable time but desperate times called for desperate measures and anyone wearing khaki was required to fight. And fight they did! Little has been written of the Chauny episode but we do know that Grover's Force came under attack at 11.00am on 24 March after a French outpost on the canal had been overwhelmed in the morning mist, announcing to Grover that units of enemy infantry were working their way round the southern edge of Chauny along the canal.

By this time brigade headquarters had been moved back to Abbécourt but the enemy incursion to the south of Chauny – unmistakably an attempt to drive a wedge between Chauny and the Condren bridgehead – prompted a further withdrawal that was rendered even more imperative by the rapid German advance towards Guiscard and Noyon. The Londons' regimental chaplain thought Saturday 23 March to be an 'exciting day' as he observed the retirement west of Chauny:

> 'The road behind Chauny was chock-a-block with civilians, British transport and
> other evidences of war. I met Garraway, our Brigade Staff Captain, and asked
> him what the orders were. He said, "we go back to Noyon, but the Germans have
> broken through on our left, and their cavalry will be in Noyon before us." We both
> agreed it looked as though we were caught.'[2]

In the meantime Grover's Force was fighting it out along the canal and in the streets of Chauny. The men took up positions covering the eastern exits to the town from the St Quentin Canal to a point north of the Chauny -Vitry Noureuil road. On their right, straddling the canal and the Oise, was the 18/Entrenching Battalion – previously the 12/Middlesex – which had been disbanded in January 1918 but was now back on the front line as a fighting unit. It would have been elements of this battalion who were defending the trestle bridge over the Oise at Chauny when German infantry began crossing using the debris which was still largely above the waterline. It was only the efforts of Major William Tamlyn of 504/Field Company, who, in the face of the enemy, set fire to the wooden structure that prevented the enemy from crossing *en masse*.

In Chauny Grover's Force was coming under increasing pressure from German units:

> '*For several hours Grover's details ... maintained their fight, but in the afternoon the withdrawal began in accordance with the orders already issued. Under Grover's command the mixed force was skilfully withdrawn, fighting a stubborn rearguard action, to a prepared position about 1,000 yards east of Abbécourt.*'[3]

At some point during this withdrawal Albert Grover was badly wounded and command of the force fell to Captain Samuel Askham. By 4.40pm Abbécourt had been evacuated and the very tired remnant of 173 Brigade eventually crossed the Oise at Manicamp, blowing the bridges behind them and setting fire to the RE Dump at Chauny. Grover survived his wounds to take over command of 2/4 Londons in June 1918. His award of the DSO was gazetted in July 1918, the citation highlighting his organisation of stragglers 'into a fighting force to enable him to hold an important line, which was subsequently repeatedly and unsuccessfully attacked ... Finally, when severely wounded he continued to direct operations from a stretcher, refusing to be evacuated until he had explained the situation to another senior officer.'[4]

William Dann's diary entry for 24 March told the story of the final days of 173 Brigade: 'The remnants of the 2/2nd, 3rd, 2/4th and 8th Londons, which I had been commanding, were withdrawn across the Oise at Manicamp and went out of action to be reformed into one battalion.'

Extending the British line north from Vouël were units of the 18th Division. The 7/Queen's Royal West Surreys were in position in the shallow valley to the north of the Butte de Vouël – approximately along the line of the present-day D1 – with the remainder of 55 Brigade at the Bois de Frières, close to les Francs Bois Farm. 3 Cavalry Brigade and the 12th Entrenching Battalion – now under the orders of Major General Lee – held the line of the canal from Quessy to Menessis, while 54 Brigade was holding the line from the north of Menessis to the eastern edge of Jussy.

At 10.00pm on 22 March command of Cator's 58th Division passed to the French 6th Army which immediately despatched two battalions of the French 125th Regiment of Infantry to counter-attack and regain the line of the canal in the neighbourhood of Tergnier, an attack in which 55 Brigade was asked to cooperate. The French reinforcements were certainly needed but whether they would delay the increasing numbers of German infantry now across the canal remained to be seen

In the early hours of 23 March a conference of senior officers from 55 Brigade convened in a forester's hut to the west of the Bois de Frières where it was agreed that two companies of 7/Queen's would support the French infantry in taking the high ground west of Quessy at le Sart and from there regain the Crozat Canal line. Commanding 7/Queen's was Lieutenant Colonel Christopher 'Kit' Bushell, a Special Reserve officer who had marched with his battalion during the retreat from Mons in 1914 and had been wounded on the Aisne on 14 September of that year. Rising through the ranks of the battalion from company commander to commanding officer, he had already been awarded the DSO and twice mentioned in despatches. Captain George Nichols, the Adjutant of 82 Artillery Brigade remembered meeting Bushell on 19 March, shortly after he had taken command of the Queen's:

> *'Tall, properly handsome, with his crisp curling hair and his chin that was firm but not markedly so; eyes that were reflective rather than compelling; earnest to a point of absorbed seriousness – we did right to note him well. He was destined to win great glory in the vortex of flame and smoke and agony and panic into which we were to be swept within the next thirty-six hours.'[5]*

Present at the meeting with Kit Bushell were Lieutenant Colonel Algernon Ransome of 7/Buffs and Lieutenant Colonel Minet of the 18th Machine Gun Corps. What their private thoughts were concerning the likely success of the attack remain unrecorded but the arrival of the French infantry at 6.00am with only thirty-five rounds of ammunition per man did not bode well. Further doubts must have arisen when it became apparent the French infantry commanders had no knowledge of the terrain over which they were to attack, terrain which was shrouded by the thick morning fog. Captain James Snell, the Queen's Adjutant, was of the opinion that:

> *'The attack of the French was doomed from the outset. The enemy was in great strength and had only been kept in check by the tremendous efforts on the part of the 7/Buffs and Queen's, together with the magnificent assistance from the NCOs of the 7th Cavalry Brigade who kept their machine guns in action for hours without ceasing, a part of 7/Queen's being employed in filling their belts.'[6]*

As the fog began to lift George Nichols could see 'the Boche swarming over the canal':

> *'The Bosche outnumbered us by at least four to one. I walked between two rows of British and French infantry lying ready in their shallow, newly-dug trenches. They looked grave and thoughtful; some of them had removed their tunics. I remember noting that of four hundred men I passed not one was talking to his neighbour.'[7]*

Nevertheless, preceded by an hour-long artillery bombardment, the attack went ahead. Initially, the counter-attack made good progress despite the heavy German machine-gun fire, but the German recovery was swift and, handicapped by limited ammunition, the French attack began to waver. James Snell was with B Company:

> '*The French gallantly advanced towards the enemy, but were seriously shaken when their commanding officer was one of the first to fall. The enemy met the advance with a barrage of machine gun fire of an intensity which I had never before witnessed, signifying their tremendous numerical superiority. Our allies tried several times to advance and then withdrew followed by the enemy. Our field of fire was so affected that it was with much difficulty that the enemy advance was again held.*'[8]

Around 10.00am Bushell took command of the French left flank as well as the two companies of 7/Queen's, his presence rallying the troops and keeping the line steady but at the same time making himself a target for enemy snipers. It wasn't long before a glancing ricochet hit him in the head, but again and again he rallied his troops, walking up and down in front of them, encouraging them to fresh efforts. 'Not until he had assured himself that his positions were intact,' wrote Nichols, 'did he go back to Rouez to report to General Wood.' Even then he returned to the firing line where 'he visited every portion of the line, both English and Allied, in face of terrific machine-gun and rifle fire, exhorting the troops to remain where they were and to kill the enemy'. The conduct of the 30-year-old former barrister had been exemplary; Christopher Bushell's award of the Victoria Cross was published in the *London Gazette* in May 1918.

The Queen's war diary entry for 23 March records one officer killed, five wounded and a further ten missing. Amongst the NCOs and men 16 are known to be killed, 66 were wounded and a further 141 recorded missing at roll call that evening. A comparison of the 1918 casualty figures with the present day CWGC database provides the more accurate figures as: four officers killed, four wounded and six taken prisoner. Of the 141 missing NCOs and men we now know 62 were killed, 66 were wounded and the remainder taken prisoner.

As for Christopher Bushell, with his head swathed in bandages, he remained upright long enough to see his men fall back in an orderly fashion towards Frières-Faillouel, aided no doubt by the guns of 82 Artillery Brigade which were firing continuously from their position south of the Bois Halot. As the mist cleared it was obvious that the Germans had worked their way through the Bois Halot and were heading directly towards Rouez Farm. Here Bushell's men joined the defensive line running through the Bois de Frières which held the enemy temporarily, but events at Chauny and further north at Jussy rendered the line impossible to hold forcing yet another retirement to Villequier-Aumont where French troops took over the line and 55 Brigade were withdrawn to Bethancourt.

The 10/Essex crossed the Crozat Canal at 11.00pm on 21 March using the bridge just north of the main lock at Liez and marched to Frières-Faillouel where they spent the night in the open before moving to Rouez Farm the next day. On the morning of 23 March it must have been obvious to the 28-year-old Major Alfred Tween, commanding the Essex, that the Anglo-French counter-attack on the far side of Frières Wood had been unsuccessful, particularly when streams of French infantry began passing through the battalion:

> 'Presently the crackling of rifle and machine gun fire obliterated the sound of tramping feet. A French liaison officer, feverishly gesticulating, and asking for the General, bore on us the truth that the enemy were in the wood, and only a few hundred yards away. Orders were rushed on company commanders and in a twinkling companies filed out into the wood. There was barely enough time to get a line flung out along the road to Frières when the advancing hoards were upon us.'[9]

The Essex were now lining the forest road running north–south through the wood with their right flank on the junction with the Tergnier-Rouez road, it was 3.00pm.

Advancing towards them with IR 27 was 38-year-old *Hauptmann* Willy Lange from Frankfurt. Together with IR 75, IR 27 had been part of the second wave troops advancing from La Fère with the 211th Infantry Division mopping up the countless British positions that had been left isolated in the fog. On 23 March Willy's battalion was ordered to meet the advancing threat of approaching French reinforcements and found himself, along with IR 75, heading through the wood towards the forest road and the men of the 10/Essex. Captain Randolph Chell watched the German infantry advance out of the wood before giving the order for his company to open fire:

> 'The Essex rifles scorched through them like jets of fire. New lines sprang up, and were mown down again until one almost sickened of the slaughter. There were at least three battalions of the enemy, (sic) and again and again the waves were crippled and sent back.'[10]

But it was not all one-sided. On the edge of the wood was a gamekeeper's cottage which was quickly occupied by German IR 27 machine gunners who brought a heavy destructive fire down on the nearby D Company positions:

> 'At the [cottage] eight to ten heavy machine guns raved incessantly ... The well behind the lodge was in constant use to refill the thirst of the steaming guns. One of ours climbed right onto the road to get a better view. Bullets buzzed through the air and smacked without pause against the walls and trees ... although all platoon leaders dropped out one after another, me and my company commanders almost emerged unscathed. I received but two minor scratches, nevertheless everybody got shots through his overcoat or gas mask at least.'[11]

With both flanks threatened the Essex began to withdraw through the wood towards Rouez Farm:

> *'It was at this stage that Lieutenant* [Arthur] *Gallie refused to withdraw, and ordering his platoon to go back with the rest of the company he continued to fight on with only his servant to help him. Finally he ordered his servant to go back and was last seen still fighting.'*[12]

It was in the vicinity of the farm that enemy troops were seen to be about to take the ridge of high ground on the right flank. Tween immediately recognised this was the critical point in the battle: should the high ground fall then the Essex positions would become untenable:

> *'All the rifles were in the line holding the Germans back in the wood, so Major Tween decided there was nothing for it but to attack with Battalion Headquarters – just a handful of pioneers, signallers, runners and even sanitary men. He led the attack himself running out in front shouting the men on. Alas, Tween himself was mortally wounded and died a little later – but they hoofed the Germans out and took the position.'*[13]

As inconsequential as this clash appears to be at first glance, Brigadier General Harold Higginson would have been alert to the reality of the situation, and as Chell himself remarked, 'it was pregnant with consequences'. Every moment gained by the Essex at the vital junction with the French was crucial in preventing von Hutier from driving a wedge between the two armies. As the Essex battalion history takes pains to remind us, this was not just a British battle. Even though the 9th French *Cuirassiers à Pied* that were fighting alongside the Essex were still short of ammunition, 'the French armoured cars dashed up and down in acrobatic fashion, pouring out bullets in streams, and effectively assisting in holding up the enemy'.

At about 6.00pm the order was given to withdraw, the Essex – now under the command of Major Herbert Innocent – pulled back through the narrow exit corridor behind them to the Chauny road where they reformed. Many felt it had been something of a miracle that the battalion had managed to escape being surrounded; a situation they certainly would have found themselves in had they remained for much longer.

Casualty figures for the day's fighting added a further two officers and thirty-two NCOs and men to those who had already lost their lives since the offensive began. In addition to Major Tween who died of his wounds, Captain Robert Binney and Second Lieutenant Norman Hight had both been killed. Second Lieutenant John Amps – who had only been with the battalion for three weeks – was captured along with Lieutenant Arthur Gallie who had courageously remained behind fighting after the initial withdrawal from the Frières road. As for the numbers wounded, the war diary is not specific, but during the first five days of the March offensive eight officers were wounded together with 155 other ranks.

* * *

North of Mennessis the canal continues on its north westerly sweep towards Jussy, passing under the site of the former Montagne Bridge and the broad-gauge railway bridge before it dog-legs around the northern edge of the town. The Montagne Bridge crossed the canal near la Montague Farm while the larger railway bridge – some 700 yards further west – carried the railway from Montescourt to meet the railway triangle formed at the junction with the line from Tergnier to Ham. In addition to the road bridge at Jussy and some 16 foot bridges, there were two light railway bridges to the west. While the majority of bridges were destroyed after III Corps units had crossed the canal, in the confusion as to which engineers – British or French – were responsible for demolishing the three railway bridges, these were left intact. Sappers from 89/Field Company were sent to deal with the bridges west of Jussy but to the south the Montagne Bridge was still intact and passable, as was the broad-gauge railway bridge. Although the railway bridge had been prepared for demolition by French engineers, Lieutenant Moore and his sappers found it abandoned when they arrived. Firing the French charges a single span of the bridge remained intact and Moore's attempts to cut the girder with guncotton failed leaving the bridge still negotiable on foot. This was bad enough but with no explosive available for the Montagne Bridge the scene was set for another rearguard action that would end with the award of a Victoria Cross.

As with the line of the canal further south, had it been properly prepared as a defensive position it might just have held long enough for the retreating III Corps to regroup behind it and form an effective opposition. As it was, the rearguard action here was piecemeal and not entirely helped by the failure to destroy the two bridges to the south of Jussy, a detail noted with some dismay by Captain Henry Brookling, commanding a company of 11/Royal Fusiliers. 'The bridges were entirely intact and the substantial railway bridge crossing the canal just south of Jussy was only partially displaced and was passable by troops on foot.'[14]

Captain John Batten-Pooll, commanding C Squadron of the 5th Royal Irish Lancers, was part of the dismounted cavalry defending the canal to the west of Jussy. His squadron was responsible for the defence of three of the bridges. 'I had no alternative but to allot one troop to each bridge,' he wrote. But the fact he was cut off from some of his men by infantry units that appeared to be wedged in between him and his regimental headquarters prevented a combined action by the regiment and played havoc with communication. 'The same must have been true of the infantry.' His observations on the state of the canal defences are interesting:

> *'When the regiment took up positions to defend the various bridges it was found that a partially dug system of trenches existed. These, however, were some 200 to 300 yards to the south of the canal, which ran between embankments, and wire entanglements had been constructed on the southern bank. For a defence of the line of the canal the siting of these works was quite useless and positions had to be occupied on the banks itself. The wire entanglements seriously interfered with those positions and were dismantled as far as possible in the time available.'*[15]

On the morning of 22 March the canal line south of Jussy was held by the 7th Battalion Bedfordshire Regiment (7/Bedfords) in position between Mennessis and the intact Montagne Bridge. To their left was the 6th Battalion Northamptonshire Regiment (6/Northamptons) which was in turn in contact with three companies of 11/Royal Fusiliers. The line to the edge of the town was held by elements of 9/Scottish Rifles and the 3rd and 5th Dismounted Brigades from the 3rd Cavalry Division.

At 6.00pm that evening units of the 1st Bavarian Infantry Regiment, under the cover of a trench-mortar bombardment, made a determined effort to cross the canal using the Montagne Bridge and established a bridgehead on the western bank. It was during this attack that 29-year-old Second Lieutenant Alfred Herring, who had been attached to the Northamptons from the Army Service Corps, found himself cut off and surrounded. The former chartered accountant immediately counter-attacked with his men and a company of 7/Bedfords and in doing so regained the line of the canal and captured over twenty prisoners and six machine guns. The post was continually attacked through the night but Herring and his diminishing band of men hung onto the canal bank for over ten hours. There is little doubt that the initiative and personal bravery of this officer in preventing German infantry from using the Montagne Bridge held up the advance and assisted considerably in maintaining the line of the canal. But the fact remained that despite efforts to destroy the bridge and the courage of Alfred Herring and his men, it would not be long before the position would be overwhelmed, particularly as German infantry were already crossing the canal further south.

West of Jussy the Bavarians made two attempts to cross the canal on the evening of 22 March using the remains of the demolished bridges and light bridges which had been constructed by their engineers. Both attempts were beaten back by the Scottish Rifles and the King's Royal Rifle Corps – readers will recall that the 7 and 8/KRRC had retired from the 14th Division Forward Zone through the German lines on the evening of 21 March. Led by Lieutenant Colonel Julias Birch, the remnants of both battalions occupied a position 200 yards in front of the railway line between Jussy and Flavy-le-Martel. But it was a hopeless defence in the face of overwhelming numbers. Yet another German attempt to cross at Jussy in the early hours of 23 March was met with a counter-attack delivered by a mixed body of men from 5/Lancers and the KRRC led by 25-year-old Captain Maurice St Aubyn of 7/KRRC. St Aubyn had been left with the transport lines in the town after Lieutenant Colonel Birch established his headquarters in a cellar of a house on the level crossing on the Jussy-Flavy road. In the confusion of fog and darkness Birch tells us that after his adjutant pushed back the Bavarian infantry 'almost singlehandedly', he was mistaken for the enemy and shot by a sentry.

The morning of 23 March was greeted again by a thick fog which covered all the British positions along the canal and Bavarian infantry lost little time in using it to their advantage. *Gefreiter* Georg Maier, a machine gunner with the 1st Bavarian Division, crossed the canal west of Jussy:

> *'Thanks to the fog* [the enemy] *was not able to hit us hard, and our infantry stormed the position where the firing was coming from and we followed with our machine guns. The town was soon on fire. It looked grotesque through the dense fog, and we became confused by all the noise of shell fire, rifle fire, and the cries of the wounded. Because of the fog we couldn't see much of the enemy – or even our own forces – but we stormed on through the streets amongst the burning houses.'*[16]

According to Birch once a foothold had been gained by the German infantry and it was obvious they were not going to be stopped, there was a wholesale rush to escape:

> *'Reports were to hand that the enemy had effected crossings of the canal on both sides of Jussy. This was confirmed at daybreak by the garrison of the village retiring precipitately along the Jussy-Cugny road past my headquarters. This garrison was a general mixture of various units, some few were persuaded to stand fast on my line of defence, but the majority were panic stricken and there was no holding them. The mist mercifully sheltered their retreat, otherwise I doubt whether any would have escaped to fight again, as the country to our rear was flat and commanded by the German positions.'*[17]

Forced back to the railway embankment astride the Jussy-Flavy road near Birch's headquarters, the remains of the KRRC, along with the survivors of the Scottish Rifles and the 5th Dismounted Brigade, formed a last ditch defensive line. At the same time, under cover of the fog, elements of the enemy found themselves forward of the main force on the northern side of the embankment. The railway embankment offered a view across the countryside to Flavy-le-Martel and the need to keep the German infantry off this vantage point was of paramount importance. Birch's account again:

'German heads could already be discerned on the top of the bank and through the mist which was beginning to lift. I rallied what men I could by whistle and drove the enemy off. We were driven off in turn but counter-attacked once more successfully. As a result we were one side of the embankment and the Germans on the other, throwing hand grenades over the top until our stock was exhausted. During this curious state of affairs two grenades fell on my steel helmet but misfired, a third fell close by and on exploding damaged my leg and shook me up.'[18]

For a short time it was stalemate as Georg Maier remembered only too clearly before his unit was subjected to 'friendly fire':

'We were lying on one side of the embankment, the English on the other. What to do? We had no hand grenades, and neither did they. Soon we had lost three men out of four shot through the head by snipers – but the worst was still to come. Our own artillery began firing on the embankment. They were unaware that some fifty men and our four machine guns were already there. One shell dropped between the tracks on top of the embankment and killed a few of our infantrymen. Another man from one of the machine guns had his left arm torn away. Suddenly to our horror we got fire from machine gun teams in the rear. The thick fog of the morning had helped us take Jussy, but now we were unable to call off the artillery fire.'[19]

The continued Hotchkiss fire along the front of the embankment from 5/Lancers was all that was keeping the enemy at bay – by this time Batten-Pooll was also on the embankment having withdrawn from the canal line – and when their ammunition began to run out Birch and Lieutenant Colonel Herbert Cape, commanding the Lancers, were left with little choice but to withdraw to a partially dug trench about 300 yards west of the railway. By the time orders had been issued the fog began to lift, giving the German machine gunners the opportunity to fire at will on the retreating British. Shortly afterwards – around 11.30am according to Birch – both flanks were under attack and the garrison had been reduced to thirty officers and men. 'This situation could not last very long with fresh German troops constantly arriving. Machine gunners got round our flanks; we were shot down and the few survivors taken prisoner.' Birch was one of those taken prisoner, recording with some satisfaction that the 'battalion commander to whom I was led was incensed that our action had delayed his programme, as he said, by two hours'.

If casualties had been heavy on the German side, they had also been significant for the British. The 5/Lancers lost 24-year-old Lieutenant Richard Hearson and twenty-one other ranks killed but Birch's battalion had suffered enormously; at roll call that evening they could barely muster 5 officers and 130 other ranks, the Scottish Rifles were a little better off with 8 officers and 192 other ranks.

In the meantime, further south enemy units had crossed the canal at Mennessis and got into the communal cemetery, news which was compounded shortly after midday by word that enemy troops were in the Frières Wood, all of which told a story of potential envelopment. For the 54 Brigade troops along the canal to the south of Jussy a fresh line of defence was organised along the railway embankment and orders were sent out to retire onto this line. But fog and the general confusion that existed amongst units fighting on the canal line contributed to the fate of many isolated groups of infantry being left behind. One of these was Captain Brookling with men of 11/Fusiliers:

> *'The 11th Royal Fusiliers (or at least that part of it which actually held the front line – A, B and D Companies) did not receive the order to retire on the morning of 23rd. No such word reached me and we therefore held on and it was early afternoon before we were eventually withdrawn owing to the complete exhaustion of ammunition.'*[20]

Brookling and his company had defended their position on the canal for fourteen hours against repeated efforts by the enemy to cross the water, eventually he was badly wounded but still managed to stand his ground on the canal despite the casualties that were fast impacting on his men. When the orders to retire eventually reached them it was too late for many of them to avoid capture and Brookling was taken prisoner along with seven other officers, a conclusion to three days fighting that was only tempered by his award of the Military Cross. Surviving Fusilier officers returning from captivity after the war maintained that the left and right companies near the canal were surrounded and attacked from the railway line behind them. Eventually, wrote Second Lieutenant Arthur Snell, 'field guns and trench mortars were brought up against them and the survivors surrendered either late that night or early the next morning'. Interestingly, Snell – having managed to avoid capture himself – then fell back with a miscellaneous group of infantry and cavalry and joined the northern end of the line running through Frières Wood, a line that Snell maintains was held long after 6.00pm to enable the 'remnants of 54th Brigade and cavalry and other infantry to pass through them,' where they were collected up and formed into columns.[21]

The CWGC database lists over 50 NCOs and men of 11/Fusiliers killed in action between 22 and 23 March together with 19-year-old Second Lieutenant Charles Knott of C Company – who was reported to have killed four of the enemy with his revolver and was shot down whilst clubbing a fifth with the empty weapon – and Second Lieutenants Robert Simmonds and William Francis. The vast majority of these men are commemorated on the Pozières Memorial.

A little further to the east along the canal from Brookling, Alfred Herring and his men at Montagne Bridge did receive the orders to retire:

'We held onto our position in front of the bridge until 10.00am on March 23, when I received orders to withdraw to the railway embankment about 500 yards to the rear. We put the captured guns out of action and withdrew in good order. We just reached the railway embankment when I received the following order – previous order cancelled, you will return to your original position – I started back with my men, but during our withdrawal the Germans had got down to the canal and lined the bank with machine guns, and out of 50 of us only 2 men and myself succeeded in reaching our original position. We were subjected to a heavy machine gun fire and the Germans crossed the canal at many points in boats and captured us. We had no ammunition left.'[22]

Alfred Herring's Victoria Cross citation referred to the stand he and his men made in front of the Montagne Bridge, this final act of courage in the face of withering machine-gun fire was surely a more gallant act. Quite why Herring was ordered back to the canal line has never been explained; the general order to retire was given at 11.30am by Brigadier General Sadlier-Jackson but the local front on which Herring was fighting would have been commanded at battalion level by Lieutenant Colonel Reginald Turner, whose headquarters was on the railway embankment. No mention is made in the Northamptons' war diary of Herring's stand at the bridge or of any orders to return to the canal.

Shortly after midday it was obvious to all that a further withdrawal was necessary, both flanks had been pierced and the brigade was in danger of envelopment. Despite the arrival of 200 of the Canadian Mounted Brigade, Sadlier-Jackson's orders to pull back to the high ground south of Faillouel were soon compromised by the speed of the German advance, and the retirement continued towards Villeselve. But here we must leave the remnants of the Jussy defence and move northwest along the canal to St Simon.

St Simon is a little over three miles along the towpath from Jussy and is situated at the junction of the St Quentin and Somme Canals. The River Somme itself rises at Fonsommes near St Quentin and runs south to St Simon where, in its canalised form, it continues west towards Péronne and Amiens. It is here that we meet the 20th (Light) Division which had been placed in reserve but made available to Lieutenant General Sir Ivor Maxse and his XVIII Corps, one of the divisions Gough had originally wanted to move to the north of Ham on 18 March, a request that was refused by GHQ.

Despite Maxse's confidence on the eve of 21 March, his three divisions were now under severe pressure. Despite the fact that he still held six miles of his Battle Zone, eight battalions had been all but annihilated in the Forward Zone and both flanks of his sector were under threat by the loss of Essigny on the III Corps front and Maissemy on the left. Gough tells us that he found Maxse and his staff cheerful and active when he visited them late on 21 March:

> *'Maxse and I arranged, therefore, that he should continue to hold his Battle Zone as long as possible on Friday 22nd, but that he should draw back his right flank, to keep touch with the III Corps which was withdrawing to the line of the Crozat Canal, and that he should also throw back his left to cover the Omigon valley and keep touch with XIX Corps.'[23]*

After moving south from the Menin Road sector at Ypres in February 1918 the 20th Division was billeted in and around Ham and Ercheu to the west of the Crozat Canal. Divisional orders called for the three brigades of infantry to support the Rear Zone defences between the Somme and the Omignon Rivers – from St Simon to Trefcon – allocating one brigade of artillery to each of the 36th and 30th Divisions. By 3.00pm on 21 March the situation on the XVIII Corps front had become critical and 61 Brigade was ordered to the bridgeheads at St Simon and Tugny to cover the retirement of the 36th Division. With 60 Brigade forming a defensive line from the Somme to Vaux and 59 Brigade further north between Vaux and Trefcon, the division was scattered along a front of over ten miles; a situation that drew sharp criticism from Major Christopher Ling who was serving on the XVIII Corps staff:

> *'Was the 20th Division used for counter-attack? Not a bit of it! One brigade was put in to help the 36th Division and the other two were strung out all along the rear Zone to act as a net onto which, and through which, the corps was to retire. The 20th Division as an offensive unit ceased to exist. In my view this was the turning point between the active offensive-defensive visualized in the corps defence scheme and the passive defence which so quickly deteriorated into a disorganized retirement.'[24]*

Ling may well have been right in his judgement particularly as the corps defence scheme had identified the Essigny-le-Grand positions as a weakness and specified they should be regained by a counter-attack delivered by the 20th Division. To this end, the division had actually practised the attack some weeks before and, according to Ling, 'every platoon commander knew his line of advance and role'. But as we know, even the best of plans were discarded in the face of the strength of the German advance.

Brigadier General James Cochrane and 61 Brigade were in position on the eastern side of the canal by dusk on 21 March. The 7th Battalion Somerset Light Infantry (7/Somersets) were in reserve at St Simon with the 7th Battalion Duke of Cornwall's Light Infantry (7/DCLI) and the 12th King's Liverpool Regiment (12/King's) on the canal line from St Simon to Tugny. Later that evening the brigade was ordered to pull back over the canal; the DCLI being moved back to Ollezy in brigade reserve, the 12/King's deployed north of St Simon to protect the Tugny bridgeheads and the 7/Somersets taking over a line from the junction with the Somme Canal running southeast along the canal towards Jussy. Lieutenant Colonel Cecil Troyte-Bullock, commanding the Somersets, was informed by brigade headquarters that he would be able to get in touch with troops on his right flank – presumably units of the Royal Berkshire Regiment. 'As a matter of fact,' commented Troyte-Bullock, 'the only troops we ever did get in touch with in that direction was the Huns on the morning of the 23rd.'

Once the brigade was across the river on the west bank the sappers were able to begin the demolition of the bridges. Lieutenant John Stapylton Smith from 150/Field Company moved quickly to blow the St Simon bridges – four road and seven foot-bridges. The main bridge, close to the junction with the Somme Canal, was only demolished with seconds to spare; we are told German infantry were actually on the bridge at the time. At Pont de Tugny there was another heart-stopping moment at the main steel girder bridge which was in the charge of 29-year-old Lieutenant Cecil Knox and his section of sappers from 150/Field Company. Minutes before the bridge was blown and only just ahead of the pursuing German infantry was Major Kenneth Cousland with what was left of the 179 Artillery Brigade 18-pounders. With the Germans in sight up the road, Knox was preparing to demolish the bridge and was clearly reluctant to let him cross, but Cousland insisted. 'I had to use my authority to force him to let us cross over before he pressed the button. A few minutes later and we would have all been stranded.' Cecil Knox was a Nuneaton man and one of nine brothers, of whom six were serving officers. Andrew had been killed at La Boisselle in 1915 and his elder brother James was commanding 1/7 Royal Warwicks on the Asiago plateau in Italy. Two other brothers were also serving with the RE and Alexander was at sea with the Royal Naval Voluntary Reserve.

With Cousland safely across the bridge and the Germans about to set foot on the bridge, Knox 'pressed the button' which, to his horror, failed to detonate the charges. A split second later, Knox, a civil engineer in civilian life, rushed forward under heavy machine-gun fire and lit the stand-by instantaneous fuse located under the bridge. It was a suicidal act that should have concluded with the young sapper's death but incredibly he survived the encounter without serious injury – although his hearing was affected for the remainder of his life. His award of the Victoria Cross was announced in the *London Gazette* in March 1919.[25]

Trying desperately to rejoin the Somersets from the battalion transport lines at Dury on 22 March was the battalion chaplain, the Reverend Thomas Westerdale. His detailed diary adds much to the sketchy information that surrounds the last stand of the battalion and the disarray that was apparent in the back areas to the west of the canal. Forced to detour round Ollezy he pushed along the road towards St Simon:

'News spread down the St Simon road to Ollezy that the Boches were advancing rapidly and now began the general emigration of civilians from the villages right

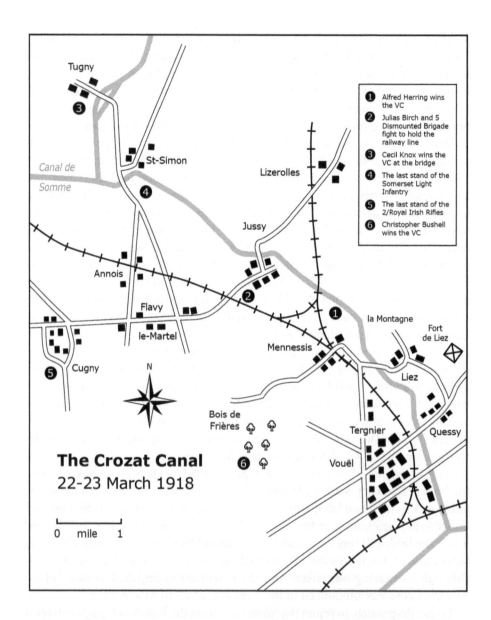

The Crozat Canal
22-23 March 1918

0   mile   1

Legend:
1. Alfred Herring wins the VC
2. Julias Birch and 5 Dismounted Brigade fight to hold the railway line
3. Cecil Knox wins the VC at the bridge
4. The last stand of the Somerset Light Infantry
5. The last stand of the 2/Royal Irish Rifles
6. Christopher Bushell wins the VC

Map labels: Tugny, St-Simon, Canal de Somme, Lizerolles, Jussy, Annois, Flavy, le-Martel, Cugny, Mennessis, la Montagne, Fort de Liez, Liez, Bois de Frières, Tergnier, Quessy, Vouël

back to Noyon and beyond, the most pathetic sight of a lifetime. Off they went, some in carts, but most on foot pushing wheelbarrows full of household goods and driving lowing cattle before them.[26]

The German machine-gun barrage from the east bank of the canal rendered the road from St Simon to Ollezy decidedly unsafe, forcing the chaplain to re-route through Flavy-le-Martel and Annois before he finally made contact with the battalion:

'The battalion had Lewis guns placed in the woods close to the canal. Further back the main body had dug itself in on a line of rough half-finished trenches running parallel with the canal. A few hundred yards behind this line was the village of Annois, which consisted of a pack of tumbled down ruins with a few wooden shacks among them. Across the canal were the Boches and towering over us was the stately spire of St Simon's Church not half a mile away and from this tower the enemy's watchmen could see every little thing we did.'[27]

The Somersets had three companies deployed along the canal with battalion headquarters a little under a mile further back on the D431- some 600 yards north of the railway line. Westerdale remembered the battalion headquarters dug-out being constructed after dark, 'near an old private tomb between the village [Annois] and the canal and screened from St Simon by a few trees'.

All through 22 March 1918 the battalion had been plagued by swarms of German aircraft flying low over the trenches and machine gunning anything that moved; 'How low their airmen came!' wrote Westerdale. But enemy aircraft were the least of their worries as German gunners began the 'softening up' process before the infantry delivered its attack across the canal. Westerdale was at the battalion aid post on the D431 when the barrage began:

'Over came the shells a dozen at a time. All night long until 7.00am he systematically shelled every part of the canal bank, roads and village. At every spot he had seen us during the previous day he made new craters. The Doc and [I] sat huddled together with the orderlies in the flimsy aid-post waiting for the direct hit which would end all – the direct hit which by the mercy of providence never came. Ten yards away they fell, then nearer and nearer, five yards, then one at the entrance three yards away, the strong blast of it sweeping across us and bringing the dirt down upon our heads.'[28]

The barrage continued, searching out the nearby battalion headquarters before moving onto the back areas of Annois, Flavy and Cugny. 'His shooting was amazingly accurate,' recalled Westerdale, who was delighted to see the face of Troyte-Bullock appear in the doorway of the aid post just before dawn on 23 March and 'cheerily enquire if we were all safe'.

Safe they may have been for the moment, which was more than the surviving men of the three companies of Somersets along the canal found themselves, now very much on their own and awaiting the imminent German attack from across the canal. At some point in the early morning, Captain James Scott, the transport officer, along with Quartermaster Sergeant Cox and Sergeant Betty limbered up and delivered much-needed small arms ammunition to the canal by riding straight through German units who had by this time advanced on both flanks from the direction of Jussy and Tugny. Unbelievably they successfully repeated the drama on the return trip. For their audacity under fire Scott received a bar to his Military Cross and Cox and Berry the Distinguished Conduct Medal. But despite their efforts in re-supplying the battalion, the end was close.

The regimental historian tells us that the Somersets, after finding themselves surrounded, attempted to fight their way back to the railway line but it appears that it was only A Company under Captain George McMurtrie – which was not deployed along the canal – which managed to escape by falling back onto the 7/DCLI west of Annois. McMurtrie was at battalion headquarters when they came under attack:

> '[The] *Huns attacked us and for about an hour we kept shooting at them and kept them at bay. The CO was shot through the neck by a rifle bullet, and Berry, [Captain Samuel Berry the battalion Adjutant] who was next to me firing away, got up to look over the bank, over which we were shooting. He got a bullet right through the head and was killed instantly, falling on top of me with a groan. I was very upset to see him killed. I now had to take command of battalion headquarters. Ammunition was given out and the Germans were gradually working round us and threatening to surround us at any minute. I considered it would be a waste of life to hold on any longer, having done all we could to delay the enemy for as long as possible ... I decided it was time to withdraw.'[29]*

Thomas Westerdale had by this time left battalion headquarters on his bicycle to try and reach the transport lines. It is likely that Troyte-Bullock was well aware of the possibility of capture at this point and sent him back before the serious fighting began. Westerdale's account confirms the extent of the German encirclement on that foggy March morning but also records a remarkable journey as he inadvertently repeated James Scott's epic drive by cycling clean through enemy lines under the cover of the fog that was still clinging to the landscape:

> '*Then* [I] *realized that the battalion must be practically surrounded, in fact less than an hour later it had suffered terribly, many men and officers being killed and soon was retiring forced back by impossible odds over the railway ... The Boches outnumbered us by twelve to one, and nearly every one of their men seemed to have a machine gun. The enemy had got across the canal somehow in the mist and had come in via Ham and Flavy, cutting through the outskirts of Annois they had jumped out of the mist right onto battalion headquarters. The CO and Adjutant and many others having fallen.'[30]*

The battalion war diary only provides casualty details for the whole of March 1918 and even these are at variance with other figures. However, the CWGC database does provide a total of forty-one officers and men killed between 22 and 23 March, of which only two – Captain Samuel Berry and Lance Corporal David

Jennings – have been positively identified. At least another seven died of wounds in the succeeding days, a register which included 19-year-old Second Lieutenant Marcus Hayward who is buried at Mezieres Communal Cemetery, Second Lieutenant Wilfred Guy, attached to 61/Trench Mortar Battery, and 21-year-old Captain Grahame Willstead who is buried at Grand Seraucourt British Cemetery with Berry and Jennings. Cecil Troyte-Bullock was wounded during the attack on battalion headquarters and managed to escape capture but nine of his officers were taken prisoner. We can only assume that any of the surviving other ranks from the three companies deployed along the canal were also taken prisoner.

But it wasn't quite over yet for George McMurtrie. Moments before the battalion was surrounded he and the remaining men from A Company and battalion headquarters escaped captivity to fall back on 7/DCLI behind the railway line west of Annois. Here the positions were held until 10.00am the next morning when Lieutenant Colonel Burges-Short, commanding the DCLI, gave the order to retire. Captain Frederick Allam, the DCLI adjutant had good cause to remember that day:

'Lt.Col. Burges-Short divided his command (which consisted of parties of other units as well as his battalion) into two portions. One half under myself withdrew under cover of the remainder of the battalion – the enemy at once attacked the right flank of the rearguard and heavy fighting ensued, D Company suffering many casualties. The battalion eventually took up a position on a ridge NE of Villeselve which afforded excellent fields of fire ... We were shelled in the afternoon by field guns and trench mortars and eventually outflanked. I was wounded at about 4.40pm but Lt.Col Burges-Short with a few men held on until finally, when practically surrounded, he was seriously wounded and taken prisoner.'[31]

McMurtrie and his Somersets were part of the rearguard referred to by Allam;

'Almost immediately they started withdrawing and after they had got clear I gave orders to withdraw too. I was determined not to let the men start running, for once they did in such a situation it was impossible to hold them. I had my revolver out and anyone who tried to run I immediately threatened to shoot. This stopped all running but it was the worst hour I had been through. The enemy was lining the right ridge and pouring a deadly fire into us, shells and shrapnel were bursting everywhere. German aeroplanes started flying over us and firing into our midst. Men were dropping everywhere, some were wounded and calling out for help, others were dying and groaning in their pain. It was a ghastly situation. Second Lieutenant [Stanley] Butler was killed. The Colonel had given me no place where we were to withdraw so I steered a course straight to our rear.'[32]

That course took McMurtrie slap-bang into what he describes as 'a huge number of German artillery and transport'. Quite how many of McMurtrie's men were captured with him remains vague although some sources suggest as little as nine of his company joined him into captivity. There is no doubt that 7/Somersets along with 7/DCLI and 12/King's had suffered enormous casualties, 61 Brigade had been reduced to a composite battalion of just four companies with a total strength of nine junior officers and 440 other ranks.

Chapter 10

Retreat to the Somme

People ask me if I was frightened, of course I was frightened, it was so like a nightmare that I thought it must be a nightmare, such a thing could not be happening and I'd wake up suddenly and find it was a dream.
Captain Maberly Esler, Medical Officer with the 2nd
Battalion Middlesex Regiment

Behind Gough's Fifth Army sector lay the River Somme and the network of canals that stretched north from the junction of the Crozat Canal through Ham to Péronne. All Gough's corps commanders were quite aware that circumstances may dictate a retreat to the line of the Somme to cover Péronne; indeed Lawrence's orders to Gough in February 1918 made it clear that if the Fifth Army fell back on the rear defences of Péronne and the Somme, the line of the river must be held at all costs. Thus at 10.45am on 22 March the order went out from Gough's headquarters to each of his four corps commanders that, should it be required, they were to make a fighting retreat to the line of the Somme but they must maintain contact with each other's flanks.

Around midday Ivor Maxse, concerned at the retirement of III Corps on his right flank and presumably by the German success on the Crozat Canal, rather prematurely ordered XVIII Corps to retire behind the Somme, failing, for whatever reason, to inform Herbert Watts of his intentions. Whether Maxse misunderstood or even misinterpreted Gough's original order is questionable but he opened up a dangerous gap between himself and Herbert Watts' XIX Corps on his left flank. Watts was suddenly placed in the unenviable position of not only fighting a battle on his front but now having to defend his right flank where XVIII Corps was supposed to be! Major Christopher Ling felt Maxse's retirement was almost entirely unjustified. Leaving aside his feelings regarding the deployment of the 20th Division, he felt XVIII Corps to be in a relatively strong position and despite the fact that the right flank was being threatened by the III Corps retirement they still held the front of the Battle Zone:

'Practically everywhere the corps front held. About midday [on 22 March] *I went along the Battle Zone from Roupy to the left flank at Holnon Wood and everywhere I found wonderful spirit and optimism and a determination and assurance that they could stay there forever. The 61st Division in particular ... had taken great toll of the enemy and was in fine fighting fettle.'*[1]

Maxse's decision may very well have baffled the officers and men who now found themselves marching the nine miles towards the Somme, none more so than the men of the unfortunate 24th Division who found themselves marching back towards the enemy to plug the gap between Maxse and Watts. In the circumstances there was little Gough could actually do once the machinery of movement had begun and the extent of the XVIII Corps retirement became apparent. Writing to Brigadier Edmonds in 1934 it is clear that Maxse placed much of the blame for his retirement on the 14th Division and the fact that he was 'allotted the 20th Division too late to do more than hustle it into a previously reconnoitred position on a wide front, instead of using it for a planned counter-attack from a flank'. A decision, if you remember, that had drawn criticism from Major Ling.

The need to maintain an unbroken line of resistance was paramount, however, and XIX Corps had little choice but to fall in with Maxse's movement towards the Somme, which incidentally may well have been instrumental in the reduction of 61 Brigade to a composite battalion and the desperate stand of 2/Royal Irish Rifles at Cugny. On the ground the situation certainly looked grim, particularly to the 61st Division which interpreted its retirement to the Somme in the worst possible light. By and large, however, Gough's front line was only bending with the pressure exerted upon it and not shattering as Ludendorff had expected.

Indeed, by nightfall on 22 March the Germans had fallen well short of their battle objectives and had not achieved the success they hoped for except in the south and it was this success that led Ludendorff to make a grave strategic error on 23 March, one that ultimately led to the failure of the March offensive. Readers will recall the original German objectives for the March offensive were clear cut: the Second Army would thrust towards Péronne and encircle the Flesquières Salient from the south, while the Seventeenth Army would drive into the salient from the north and pinch it out by linking up with the Second Army while even further south, Oskar von Hutier's Eighteenth Army would drive towards Ham on the Somme and form a buffer along the river against French reinforcements arriving from the south. Now, having studied the reports of the first two days of the offensive and studying the aerial photographs of a massive British retreat, Ludendorff was convinced the British were beaten and changed the overall battle strategy.

With his eyes firmly fixed on the south – where von Hutier had made significant inroads towards Noyon – he abandoned his aspirations in the north and sought to drive a wedge in between the French and British in the south by attacking along both sides of the Somme and pushing towards Amiens, a strategy that involved a confrontation with the French as well as the British. To make matters more complex Otto von Below's Seventeenth Army was now required to dilute its strength by attacking in three directions. By altering the entire axis of attack from the northwest to the southwest Ludendorff had eased the pressure on V Corps in the north and ignited the catalyst that would see Fifth Army command gradually whittled away as III Corps were placed under the direct command of the French Third Army commanded by General Georges Humbert.

Apart from resentment in some quarters at III Corps over the nationality of their new masters, however, the troops on the ground cared very little if Ludendorff had blundered or not, the retirement was still in progress and as far as the British Tommy was concerned there remained an enormous number of Germans who were intent on killing him. Private Alex Jamieson of 11/Royal Scots was convinced that the German artillery was targeting him and his mates. 'Even when we managed to get away our troubles weren't over, because we were shelled all the way back. In fact it seemed that we'd become a target for the German artillery'; a sentiment undoubtedly shared by the tired troops of the 36th Division as they crossed the St Quentin Canal late on 21 March and moved towards Sommette-Eaucourt via Cugny.

The 2/Royal Irish Rifles and 107 Brigade crossed the canal at Seraucourt-le-Grand at around 11.00pm on 21 March, falling back on the Le Hamel-Happencourt road where they dug–in for the night. The next morning the battalion moved to an old French trench system southeast of Happencourt where, despite being heavily shelled, they remained in position throughout the day. At 6.00pm Major Richard Rose, commanding the battalion, was badly wounded and evacuated. Rose had won the Military Cross in 1917 at Westhoek and was destined not to return to active service, command of the battalion falling to 26-year-old Captain Thomas Thompson. At dusk the battalion was ordered to retire and moved towards Sommette-Eaucourt but as they crossed the Somme Canal fresh orders sent them to Cugny, a small village a little over a mile southwest of Annois.

Early on 23 March the Germans forced the line of the Crozat and Somme Canals and as 61 Brigade began to fall back Lieutenant Cyril Lacey and his collection of troops from units of the 14th Division were ordered to take up a position along the Cugny-Flavy-le-Martel road facing north. By this time Ham, several miles to the northwest, had fallen and elements of the German 5th Guard Division were crossing the canal via the Pithon railway bridge, which was still intact despite the last-minute efforts of French railway engineers to destroy it. On the Cugny–Flavy road Lieutenant Lacey came under attack just before midday:

'At 11.45am I reported to the 42 Infantry Brigade that I was holding the Cugny-Flavy road in strength and that the enemy appeared to be pressing on through Flavy gradually. The enemy attack then developed more definitely and was pressed

vigorously from the east through Flavy and it was necessary to change front to meet this attack … A little later intense and sustained machine gun fire was commenced from the direction of Flavy and low flying aeroplanes dropped bombs and smoke signals indicating our positions; our line was then immediately in front of Cugny.'[2]

Lacey tells us he was still in place at 6.30pm when he again sent a runner to 42 Brigade informing them of his situation, unfortunately his account stops short at this point as shortly afterwards he was wounded. Lacey's men and the remnants of 14th Division presumably withdrew through Cugny before the attack on 2/Irish Rifles got underway.

Earlier that morning at 10.00am 2/Royal Irish Rifles had taken up a defensive position northeast of Cugny with D Company under the command of the Dublin-born Lieutenant John Boyle in reserve a little further to the northwest. At midday the battalion received reports that Flavy was in German hands and Thompson was instructed to hold Cugny at all costs to allow other retiring units to pass through their lines. Apart from the constant annoyance from low-flying enemy aircraft the afternoon passed relatively quietly – these aircraft were undoubtedly from the same *Geschwader* that Lacey remembered bombing his position further to the east and caused Kenneth Cousland and his battery to take cover in some ruined buildings near Flavy:

> *'The Huns came very low shooting through the roof with their machine guns. We tried to make ourselves as small as the bricks on the ground but several of our fellows were hit. Then the sportsmen on the planes leaned over the side and dropped bombs on us. One bomb made a hole in the one remaining wall beside me large enough for me to dash through and sprint across a small orchard with the Hun diving at me before I flung myself under a large hedge where they could no longer see me.'*[3]

However, at Cugny the lull was not to last long and at 6.00pm the Germans attacked the Irish Rifles in force, succeeding in driving a wedge between the battalion and Cugny village, a situation that was only recovered by the men of C Company led by Lieutenant Richard Marriot-Watson who drove them back with an energetic counter-attack. At 10.00pm Thompson and the battalion drew back to a line 300 yards west of Cugny.[4]

Thompson had been told the 12/King's Liverpool Regiment from 61 Brigade was on his left flank but there had been no evidence of their presence all day. Captain Cyril Wilkins, a staff officer with 107 Brigade, visited the battalion at Cugny on the evening of the 23 March and assisted with the reorganization of the line facing Cugny:

> *'The CO [Captain Thompson] and I reconnoitred to the right flank and did not gain touch with any of our units or the French. We then reconnoitred forward*

until we ran into the enemy who were holding a position just south of Cugny. On returning we reconnoitred from the left flank but failed to establish a connection with any of our troops nor did we find the enemy.'[5]

Wilkins returned to brigade to report the situation to Brigadier General William Withycombe, noting again that he did not encounter the 12/King's on his way back. He was clearly concerned as to the plight of Thompson and his men:

'*I suggested to the brigade commander that the 2nd Royal Irish Rifles, in view of their precarious and isolated position, should be withdrawn to a better defensive position in line with the remainder of the brigade and the troops on our right. General Withycombe decided that the* [battalion] *should remain in their positions as other troops of the 61st Brigade and 108 Brigade were reported to be still in position about Ollezy.'*[6]

Wilkins returned again at dawn on 24 March to report that the 1st Battalion Royal Irish Rifles (1/Royal Irish Rifles) were in position in and around the ground at Montalimont Farm to cover the battalion's withdrawal but after a conversation with Thompson it must have been obvious to both men that the chances of regaining the safety of the 1st Battalion's lines were poor. It was a prognosis that became all too apparent to Wilkins when he came under fire from German units who were already near Brouchy – over a mile to the northwest of Cugny. Wilkins was probably the last individual to visit the battalion before it was overwhelmed.

At 6.00am the war diary recorded that touch had been established with troops who had moved forward during the night – these may have been elements of the 36th Division counter-attacking towards Brouchy. Second Lieutenant Tom Witherow, who was part of the attack, reported that 'two wounded men came into our lines from the right; they belonged to my own battalion, the 2nd Royal Irish Rifles, and said that the remains of the battalion were surrounded and would shortly be captured'. Had Tom Witherow not been at the Fifth Army School at Caix attending a platoon commander's course on 21 March, he would almost certainly have been at Cugny with his battalion. As it was he was now within a mile of the beleaguered unit and powerless to help.

Back at Cugny heavy German machine-gun fire was directed on the Irish Rifles and enemy troops were clearly advancing on both flanks. Thompson drew in his flanks to form a more compact defence line but with 150 officers and men there was little he could do but stand fast and await the inevitable attack. The first assault took place just after 10.00am which was beaten off successfully but with ammunition running woefully short Thompson gave orders to his riflemen to make every round count. Second Lieutenant Edward Strohm was commanding Number 9 platoon in C Company:

'Daybreak on the morning of 24 March was foggy, our line being taken up behind Cugny, the fog lifted about 10.00am. Weather fine, visibility fair. We had no supports, none of our planes were apparent, enemy planes were over us from time to time. No. 9 Platoon was in support to C Company 50 yards in the rear of the front line. Enemy machine guns were established on both our immediate flanks, he advancing his men in short rushes all the morning, our fire was very damaging.'[7]

Thompson was magnificent, deliberately exposing himself to fire to encourage his men on the menaced right flank which was being attacked again and again. According to the 107 Brigade war diary messages were sent out from 1/Royal Irish Rifles for the battalion to withdraw; but it was too late and none of the runners reached Cugny across the mile-and-a-half of open ground that lay between the two battalions. Had they have done so it is unlikely the 2nd Battalion would have been in a position to withdraw in the opinion of Captain Joseph Bryans, a retirement across open country with the Germans on at least three sides was impossible. By early afternoon the enemy had brought up trench mortars, Edward Strohm was also aware of 5.9-mm shells also being registered on their line:

'About 2.00pm the enemy was observed about 2,000 yards to our right and well to our rear. About 3.00pm he was well in our rear on the left. About this time his trench mortar and machine gun fire was very persistent, my men were running short of ammunition. About 4.00pm he put down an intense barrage comprising the former with the addition of artillery which lasted about half an hour.'[8]

Captain Bryans described their final position as a ditch some 300 yards south of Cugny. We were 'in remarkably good spirits,' he wrote, 'although it was evident our position was hopeless'. They didn't have to wait long: having softened up the Irish positions with a barrage courtesy of the German gunners, the final infantry assault was pressed home with determination. Strohm again:

'Then he [the enemy] came over, I observed an officer and about 20 men falling back on our left, this apparently gave him [the enemy] an opening which he followed up and was through on our left. Seemingly within a few minutes he was through our line and we were all mixed up. He seemed to pass right through and we were all mopped up by the second wave and I was taken [prisoner] at about 5.00pm. I had no ammunition and what remained of my men had none.'[9]

Strohm does not say whether he saw Captain Thompson and Lieutenant Marriot-Watson killed or indeed the 24-year-old Lieutenant Morgan Moore, but when the end came many, according to Bryans, 'had only their bayonets left to fight with and rather than wait for the end they jumped from their entrenchments and met it gallantly'. From a 'trench strength' of 18 officers and 551 men on 1 March, only 150 officers and men had marched into Cugny on 22 March, and of these, over 100 were killed or wounded.

Bryans tells us that after the battalion had been overwhelmed the German officer commanding the attack gave his word that the bodies of Thompson and Marriot-Watson would be buried locally. 'The German officer commanding, who spoke in congratulatory terms of our stand, assured me personally that they would be accorded a Christian burial in the village cemetery some 200 yards away.' If this did take place their bodies were subsequently lost and both men are commemorated on the Pozières Memorial along with the majority of those who lost their lives at Cugny. Only the body of Lieutenant Morgan Moore remains locally, after being evacuated to Flavy he died of his wounds the following day and is buried at Grand-Seraucourt British Cemetery, six miles to the northeast. Taken prisoner with Bryans was Captain John Boyle whose wounds may have contributed to his death in captivity seven months later but fortunately Second Lieutenant Strohm survived his spell behind the wire and was repatriated in December 1918, a month later than Joseph Bryans.

All through the day the indomitable Father Henry Gill had been trying to reach the battalion at Cugny. Arriving at brigade headquarters – which by this time was at Guiscard – he was a little alarmed to be asked to take some maps with him as several dispatches 'had failed to reach them'! Finally he met a ration party about to set out in an attempt to find the battalion:

'I told them that I feared they had gone. I was unfortunately right. The order had been given that Cugny was to be held at all costs. And they had done so. Of the whole 750 (sic) or so only a very few came back. They had been killed or taken prisoners. One felt a lump in one's throat. The battalion had of course been gradually renewed many times, but no such sudden extinction as this had taken place.'[10]

Officers and men who had just returned from leave or, like Tom Witherow, had been on courses, were collected together and reformed into a battalion of eight officers and forty men under the command of Lieutenant Colonel Patrick Cox. On 30 March at Maisnieres near Abbeville, Father Gill held a Mass for those who had survived. 'Instead of the hundreds who had filled the church before,' he lamented, 'there were less than thirty.'

Apart from the Germans forcing the passage of the Somme at Ham and Pithon, 23 March also saw the formation of 'Harman's Detatchment'. The German attack across the Somme had effectively driven a wedge between two divisions of Maxse's XVIII Corps and at the same time threatened the left flank of Butler's III Corps. In order to have some control over his flank, Butler ordered those cavalry units from the 2nd and 3rd Cavalry Divisions that were still mounted to form a combined mounted unit under the command of Major

General 'Jacques' Wentworth Harman. Born in 1872 the 42-year-old Harman had been commissioned into the 3rd Dragoon Guards in 1894 and twenty years later, as a squadron commander with the Queen's Bays, he was in France with the BEF. Badly wounded at Néry during the retreat from Mons he took command of the 18th Hussars in 1916 and a year later – now a brigadier general – was appointed to command the 6th Cavalry Brigade. When summoned by Butler to cobble together a mounted flank guard he had only been in command of the 3rd Cavalry Division for a month.

Each regiment from the two cavalry divisions was ordered to contribute fifty mounted men to which were added 600 infantry who had been collected together under Lieutenant Colonel Courtney Theobald, eight Lewis guns and their teams from 13/Balloon Company and 'O' Battery Royal Horse Artillery (RHA). Butler's orders to Harman was for his unit to provide mounted reconnaissance patrols reporting to III Corps Headquarters, a vital role that the scattering of the cavalry divisions into dismounted reinforcements had rendered largely impossible. However, there was one local action involving Harman's Detachment that brought them into close contact with the Germans north of Collézy.

During the early afternoon of 24 March the two German divisions which had been hounding the 36th and 20th Divisions were converging on the Villeselve area where remnants of both divisions and elements of French infantry were still dug in and about to be outflanked. According to Lieutenant John Bickersteth it was about 2.00pm when the detachment from 6 Cavalry Brigade was ordered 'to make a mounted attack on some hostile infantry and machine guns' near Hill 81 and re-establish the defensive line around Villeselve. The infantry were said to be 'very shaky' and the attack it was hoped would regain some of the lost ground and restore a little confidence amongst the infantry.[11]

The detachment of three troops – no more than 150 in total – under the command of Major Evelyn Williams of 10/Royal Hussars, moved north along the main road to Villeselve taking the sunken track which runs north into Collézy. Here they ran into heavy machine-gun fire from the direction of Golancourt, which, after taking cover in the nearby farm buildings and a rather hasty reconnaissance, was seen to be directed from two small copses 600 yards to the north. The farm buildings were situated between the British infantry who were to the east and the French who were in the sunken road to the rear. There was no time to lose if they were to profit from the element of surprise.

The plan of attack was quite straightforward; Lieutenant Arthur Vincent and his troop of 3/Dragoon Guards would charge towards Copse B and secure the right flank while the two troops of 10/Hussars and Royal Dragoons would make the main attack towards Copse A on the left. Passing through the British infantry lines, the three troops broke into a charge with 3/Dragoons bearing off to the right in the hope of distracting attention from the main attack. Farrier Sergeant

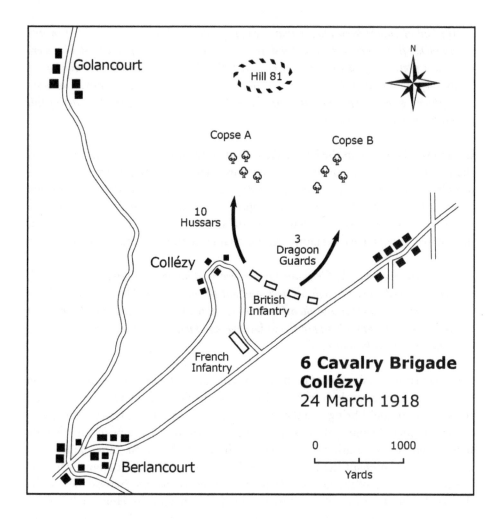

Golancourt

Hill 81

N

Copse A

Copse B

10
Hussars

3
Dragoon
Guards

Collézy

British
Infantry

French
Infantry

**6 Cavalry Brigade
Collézy**
24 March 1918

0   1000

Yards

Berlancourt

Albert Turp was riding with the Royal Dragoons towards Copse A on the left, he recalled an officer of 10/Hussars giving the order to draw swords:

> [We held them] *down along our horses' shoulders, so that the enemy would not catch the glint of steel, and we were told to lean down over our horses' manes. A moment later we were wheeling into line. I can't remember if I was scared, but I know that we were all of us very excited and so were the horses.*[12]

The 3/Dragoons almost immediately came under fire which was maintained until the horsemen were some 200 yards from the edge of the copse, but as their swords came down for the final rush the German infantry bolted, many being shot down at point blank range as they were pursued through the trees:

'We had of course been taught that a cavalry charge should be carried out in line
six inches from knee to knee, but it didn't work out like that in practice and we were
soon a pretty ragged line of horsemen at full gallop. We took the Germans quite
by surprise and they faced us as best they could, for there can't be anything more
frightening to an infantryman than the sight of a line of cavalry charging at full
gallop with drawn swords.'[13]

It was a similar story on the left flank, as the two troops galloped straight towards
the copse with swords 'in line' the German infantry either put up their hands
or bolted. But for the unfortunate infantrymen it was too late, they were ridden
down and sabred ruthlessly. It was an opportunity seized upon by the cavalrymen
to strike a blow against an enemy who up until this point had looked almost
unbeatable. Albert Turp certainly had no qualms at running the enemy down:

'As our line overrode the Germans I made a regulation point at a man on my offside
and my sword went through his neck and out the other side. The pace of my horse
carried my sword clear and then I took a German on my nearside, and I remember
the jar as my point took him in the collarbone and knocked him over. As we galloped
on the enemy broke and ran.'[14]

Although largely insignificant to the wider strategic picture it was a demonstration
of just what a good cavalry action could achieve using the element of surprise and
the stability it could bring to a dangerously porous line. The cavalry casualties –
73 were reported wounded, mostly non-serious wounds – had been surprisingly
light given the strength of the German infantry. Amongst those killed was
22-year-old Lieutenant the Hon William Cubitt of the Royal Dragoons who was
one of six children of the Second Baron Ashcombe. It was another sad day for the
Ashcombe family as one of his older brothers, Lieutenant the Hon Alick Cubitt,
had been killed serving with 15/Hussars in November 1917 during the Battle of
Cambrai.[15]

Had the British infantry attempted to cross the ground over which the cavalry
charged they would have been all but wiped-out by the four or five machine guns
positioned in the two copses. As it was, between 70 and 100 German infantry
were sabred and 107 prisoners handed over to the infantry who were following
close behind. Williams' charge provided a much needed tonic for the troops
on the ground who held onto their positions with a little more vigour until the
unavoidable retirement abandoned Villeselve to the enemy. Shortly before the
Germans arrived, the advanced dressing station run by 62/Field Ambulance
had been packed up and sent on its way to Guiscard, but a small party under
Lieutenant Colonel Stack remained behind attending the British and French
wounded. Even when shells began bombarding the house where Stack and his
party were based he refused to move until all the casualties had been evacuated.

There had, in fact, been another mounted cavalry action on 22 March – two days earlier – at Roisel, some twenty miles further north of Villeselve, that had involved A Squadron of 15/Hussars. Late on 21 March the regiment had been bivouacked at Roisel although on this occasion the squadron's horses had remained saddled up all night in case an immediate call for reinforcements was required. The call came at 7.45am the next morning when the regiment was ordered to retake the Brown Line to the east of the village. At the time Roisel was under a heavy artillery attack and the enemy could be seen advancing in large numbers on both flanks. The orders given then appeared to have had a certain inevitability about them – a point the regimental historian does not fail to make:

'Owing to the very unfavourable situation in other parts of the line, it did not seem likely that the attack, even if successful, could effect any material change, as it appeared the party making it would become quite isolated. Nevertheless, the situation was desperate, the counter-attack was ordered to take place, in spite of the hopeless conditions under which it had to be carried out.'[16]

A Squadron under 32-year-old Captain John Godman, led the attack with the intention of securing the high ground north of Hesbécourt before turning east to attack the Brown Line. In spite of the heavy fire the sheer audacity of the squadron's attack succeeded and Godman and the men of A Squadron had occupied the shallow trenches of the Brown Line somewhere east of Haut Woods. Once in place the squadron had seen German infantry to the north and south advancing in huge numbers while to the northeast Templeux-le-Guérard where 2/6 Lancashire Fusiliers had counter-attacked the previous day, was clearly visible. Godman must have realized that his position was totally isolated and any attempt to hold the line would be doomed to failure, particularly as the Germans were well-established to the north beyond the railway line and Roisel had already come under a heavy artillery bombardment.

At 1.30pm Roisel had been abandoned and the regiment had moved to the marshy ground west of the village near Marquaix. Unable to establish any form of communication with A Squadron, Godman and his men were left to their fate. The regimental historian tells the rest of the story:

'Although soon surrounded on all sides, the squadron continued to fight on alone and unaided, and manfully upheld the traditions of the regiment. The enemy attempted time after time to rush and annihilate this small handful of men, whose determined resistance was causing them so much loss. Our own artillery, quite unaware that there was a part of men still holding out, so far behind the advance of the enemy, shelled the area thoroughly, and the plight of the squadron soon became desperate in the extreme. But the men refused to surrender, and accounted for very large numbers of the enemy.'[17]

Towards evening, with ammunition virtually expended and exhaustion setting in, the Germans brought up a trench mortar battery to surround the position before finally rushing the trench and overwhelming the surviving cavalrymen. The CWGC database lists twelve 15/Hussars killed on 22 March, eleven of which are commemorated on the Pozières Memorial and one, Private G McFarelend – who had been with the regiment since it landed in France in August 1914 – buried at Roisel Communal Cemetery Extension. This number concurs with those listed in the regimental history and we can assume that these men died with A Squadron that day. Godman had been taken prisoner along with Lieutenants Lowe and Pickering and no survivors were reported to have returned to the regiment.

* * *

Reinforcements in the form of the 50th Division were placed on stand-by as early as 4.30am on 21 March but no move was made until the evening when the three brigades marched to Guillancourt having been ordered to provide immediate support for Major General Neill Malcolm's 66th Division by assembling along the Rear Zone Defences. This was accomplished by 8.00am on 22 March after a march through Brie that left the majority of the men tired and hungry; hot food we are told did not arrive until 8.40am by which time orders had been received to man the defences immediately. The hurried deployment of the division drew criticism from the divisional staff which was somewhat dismayed over the length of the line the division was expected to hold. One staff officer in particular felt they had been placed in an impossible position:

> '*It would have required seasoned troops with the very highest morale to have offered any effective resistance on a line which existed more on the map than on the ground; more especially seeing since daybreak the men were subjected to the trying ordeal of a constant stream of men passing through their ranks, spreading tales of alarm and despondency.*'[18]

The Green Line – or Rear Zone – was five miles east of the River Somme and ran from the crossroads one mile southwest of Villévèque on the southern bank of the Omigon River to Boucly on the banks of the Cologne River in the north – as far as the 50th Division was concerned the line they now occupied would very shortly become the front line.

It had been Watts' intention for the 24th and 66th Divisions to retire from the Battle Zone through the Green Line and reorganize under the protection of the 50th Division and their artillery. The reader will recall that the Rear Zone had only been partially dug and there was very little wire in place, thus any improvements that might have been made by the three brigades of the 50th Division before troops began passing through their lines on the afternoon of 22

March were negligible. The 150 Brigade commander, Brigadier General Hubert Rees – having carried out an inspection of his sector – was so concerned as to the state of the Green Line that he felt it necessary to inform his divisional commander of the poor state of the defences immediately. His assessment was blunt and to the point. 'The single uncompleted trench was impossible to hold and [I] urged the necessity of withdrawal of 1,000 yards so that the division could avoid annihilation to no purpose the next morning.'[19] Rees had scant evidence to suggest the defences were any better elsewhere along the line. Gough's view on the deployment of the 50th Division – albeit written in 1930 – was strikingly similar to that of the divisional staff:

> *'If they had been moved up when I asked, their men would not have had to enter on a terrific fight without rest after long and harassing marches, their officers could have reconnoitred their positions, and a little more time would have been available to strengthen them ... To move them up was not to commit them.'*[20]

But there was little or no time to make much of a difference, less than two hours later at 4.30pm 149 Brigade on the right flank was under heavy attack, the enemy advancing in eight waves down the Omigon valley.

Commanding the 5th Battalion Durham Light Infantry (5/DLI) was Major Alwyn Raimes. On arrival at Brie the battalion had been 'lent' to the 66th Division and was sent up to prevent the enemy from advancing out of Roisel – by this time already abandoned – in a rather pointless exercise which left the DLI tired even before they arrived back on the Green Line and took up their position on the right flank of 151 Brigade:

> *'After considerable trouble caused by the constant stream of men, horses, tanks, guns and limbers retiring through us, the companies found the positions allotted to them and eagerly awaited the coming of the enemy. They had not long to wait as the German infantry in great numbers soon became visible, and, between 4.00pm and 5.00pm, could be seen forming up for attack. We telephoned for artillery support. It quickly came, but unfortunately the barrage was right on our own line instead of on the Germans, and we had a number of casualties. To make things worse telephone communication broke down, and we were unable to get word through to the batteries.'*[21]

It had not been a good start but there was little time to curse the gunners before the German infantry attack was unleashed on the line; a protracted defence against such a heavy attack was practically impossible in such poorly-constructed defences. On the right Caulaincourt was lost and in the centre 150 Brigade was pushed back near Bernes and from the high ground east of Nobescourt Farm. Second Lieutenant John Fleming-Bernard was with U Battery, RHA near

St Quentin Copse and fortunately his 13-pounder gun crews had little difficulty in finding the correct target:

'At 5.00pm our attention was rudely drawn to our own front and we were soon firing in good earnest to cover Nobescourt Farm. The Huns seemed to come on, despite our efforts, and about 5.45pm we spotted masses of men on the Vraignes-Nobescourt road ... and gave the Huns 15 rounds per gun over open sights, the range being about 1,500 yards. The shooting must have told frightfully on the mass of men on the road, our shrapnel seeming to burst right amongst them.'[22]

It didn't stop their advance but as Fleming says, 'each shell left a gap as if a tooth had been drawn'. However the wire in front of the DLI was good and as the enemy strained to force their way through they were cut down by the Lewis gunners. The attack was held by A and C Companies but on the right, D Company and part of B Company, were forced to give ground, retiring to the outskirts of Nobescourt Farm where battalion headquarters had been established amongst the ruins of the farm buildings:

'Owing to the enemy's success at this point, battalion headquarters found themselves practically in the firing line, and for a time there was great excitement as it looked as if the Germans were coming right through. Every available officer and man – commanding officer and adjutant, signallers, runners, pioneers, batmen, cooks – quickly turned out, and manned the ruined walls and buildings ready for a last stand.'[23]

The expected assault never came, for whatever reason the Germans appeared content with the capture of the ridge which, with the onset of darkness, provided a very welcome opportunity to reorganize. On the Durham's right the 4th Battalion Yorkshire Regiment (4/Yorkshire) had suffered badly. Having lost its forward trenches the battalion gave ground some 800 yards to the west of the line and it was there that the commanding officer, 32-year-old Lieutenant Colonel Bernard Charleton and his adjutant, Captain James Bainbridge, were killed leading a counter-attack.[24]

With Caulaincourt and the high ground near Nobescourt Farm now in German hands the Green Line was in great danger of being overwhelmed when the German attacks resumed the next morning. Maxse's XVIII Corps was already retiring towards the Somme and there was little the units of the 50th Division could achieve by remaining in situ, consequently at 10.40pm Brigadier General Arthur Stockley – who was temporarily in command of the 50th Division – issued orders for the division to retire to the line of the Somme.[25] For Raimes and his men this meant a 2.00am retirement on 23 March to new positions near Catelet Wood. For once the fog worked in favour of the British:

'*This was not an easy matter as the fog was so thick that they could not see more than five yards in front of them, and it was difficult getting the scattered companies together and on the road in column of route. It was only by frequent references to their compasses that they succeeded in their object ... we cursed the fog at the time, but there is no doubt that if it had been a clear morning we should have had many casualties as our position and the road would have been in full view.*'[26]

The 5/DLI had got away lightly but for the 4/East Yorkshires and the 6/Northumberland Fusiliers there were heavy casualties, the Northumberland Fusiliers losing two companies who were unable to withdraw after being surrounded. At Le Catelet the DLI fell back again along the line of the D88 road to the wooded area northwest of Mesnil-Bruntel where orders finally arrived at midday to retire across the Somme using the bridge at Eterpigny; the 6th and 8th DLI were to lead off with Raimes and his battalion providing the rearguard:

'*We at once took up a covering position astride the main road at the west end of Le Mesnil. [Mesnil-Bruntel] The 8th soon came along and passed through us, but we waited in vain for the 6th. Time passed. The enemy were by this time in the east end of the village and their machine guns were making themselves extremely unpleasant. At last we were forced to the conclusion that the 6th must have retired by another route.*'[27]

They had indeed taken another route and one that resulted in the battalion unintentionally walking into an ambush. Captain Ralph Ainsworth, the battalion adjutant, takes up the story:

'*After about two hours, however, orders came to cross the river by the Eterpigny footbridge. A route was taken across country towards this bridge, but there being no gap through the marshes and undergrowth, the Battalion was forced to turn aside through Le Mesnil [Mesnil-Bruntel] village and, incidentally, to pass under a light shrapnel barrage. It was not known that the village was in the enemy's hands, but as soon as Z Company, who were leading, had reached the far side, the remaining Companies were attacked. Again Y Company distinguished itself, as did W and X Companies. They at once deployed, and though driven towards the marshes, successfully checked the enemy and eventually followed Z Company over the partially destroyed footbridge, about 300 yards long.*'[28]

It had been a close run thing but thanks to the quick thinking of Captain John Aubin, he and his company deployed into a firing line and with rifle and Lewis gun fire fought a rearguard action across the marshes to the bridge, enabling the battalion to escape across the river relatively intact. John Aubin received the DSO for his part in the action, adding to the Military Cross and bar he had already received since his arrival on the Western Front in July 1915. The two remaining brigades of the 50th Division were also engaged as they fell back to the canal. 150 Brigade crossed the canal at Brie, Brigadier General Hubert Rees described the confusion that met the men of his brigade on their arrival:

> *'23 Brigade had arrived and took up a position on the west bank of the Somme, sending one battalion across the river into Brie village. When the 5th Yorks and 4th E Yorks retired this battalion also retired. This mob of men crossing the bridge was covered by Lieutenant Ginger and the 4th Yorks. Before the 4th Yorks could retire somebody blew up the bridge and Lieutenant Ginger had to construct a footbridge to get his party and wounded across the river under fairly heavy fire.'*[29]

According to Buckland the officer responsible for blowing the numerous Brie bridges and marooning the young officer on the east bank was Lieutenant George Begg from 239/Field Company. Faced with a stream of infantry crossing the bridge and a German aeroplane flying low along the river, Begg waited until the bridge was clear – or so he thought – and charged the electrical exploder. Nothing happened – the silence that followed must have been deafening! A second attempt failed – German infantry were now visible on the opposite bank – he tried again for a third time. This time the resulting explosion announced a successful detonation, the fleeting look of relief on the young RE officer's face shattered only by the realization that Lieutenant Thomas Ginger and his rearguard were still on the other side of the canal! But as Rees says, the party managed to escape and get across the river. Thomas Ginger was the signals officer with 4/Yorkshire and his reward for his part in the action on the canal came in July when his award of the Military Cross was announced in the *London Gazette*.

* * *

In Chapter 7 we left the 16th Division after it had abandoned the Battle Zone on 22 March and was retiring on Villers-Faucon. The retirement was covered by 11/Hampshires who, despite being designated divisional pioneers, now demonstrated they could fight as well as they could dig. The rearguard action at St Emilie and Doingt by the Hampshires was another of those almost forgotten actions where a small unit was able to delay the German advance quite significantly, unfortunately we have very little detail apart from the battalion war diary and regimental histories to provide much more than an outline of what took place.

At Villers-Faucon the initial attack fell largely upon D Company of the Hampshires which was commanded by Major Thomas Thyne. The company occupied the line of trenches to the east of the village where they remained until their right flank had been turned, withdrawing through A and B Company's lines near the station. The attack then focused on Captain George Howson and

B Company who, in their turn, were forced back after a desperate fight during which Second Lieutenant Walter Elkington was killed. With the St Emilie flank now completely turned, the battalion began to fall back to Villers-Faucon making another stand along the railway line which ran south from Épehy and again on the high ground just to the north of Villers-Faucon.

At 3.00pm the 16th Division was on the Green Line with the right flank just to the east of Tincourt-Boucly and the left near Tincourt Wood – Bois de Boucly on present day maps – where it was in touch with the 39th Division.[30] The Hampshire's headquarters were now established in a small quarry on the northern outskirts of Tincourt – close to the junction of the D184 and D6. That night the quarry headquarters sheltered Lieutenant Colonel Basil Crockett, commanding 11/ Hampshires, Captain Harry Molyneux, the adjutant, Captain William Tyndall, the battalion medical officer and Major Cecil Hazard. The war diary reported a quiet night with the exception of occasional shelling and machine-gun fire. Nonetheless, it was a lull that came to an end sharply at 6.00am on 23 March 1918 as German infantry attacked again under cover of the morning fog.

Inevitably a further withdrawal was on the cards; confusion, lack of communication and the fog all contributing to the battalion's movement back to the high ground covering the approach to Doingt and Péronne. At 1.00pm the battalion again came under heavy attack and 'after severe fighting orders were received from 48 Brigade to withdraw'. The war diary continues: 'A and B Companies then retired to a position half way down the slope in some rear trenches, A Company employing covering fire from outlying houses and huts in Doingt.'

Also at Doingt was Lieutenant Colonel Rowland Fielding with his remaining Connaught Rangers, now part of a composite battalion with two companies of Leinsters and one made up of the numerous 48 Brigade units retiring towards the Somme. From Fielding's account it appears that his men must have first retired through the Hampshires near Carnival Copse and, along with the sappers of 157/Field Company, successfully held off the advancing German infantry just east of Doingt before retiring through the village towards Péronne:

> *'I formed up the few men of the Connaught Rangers at the foot of the hill on the edge of the village of Doingt – the same village where I had taken tea so short a time before, and, in conjunction with Colonel Crockett and his men, and Major Whittall's sappers, fire was brought to bear upon the enemy, who were already descending the near side, and whose machine guns were already shooting from the slopes of the ridge we had just occupied.'[31]*

Remaining in the village were two companies of the Hampshires under Major Hazard and the sappers of 157/Field Company with their commanding officer Major Perceval Whittall. By employing classic street fighting tactics amongst houses and garden enclosures they fought a delaying rearguard action against the enemy allowing the 49 Brigade units to cross the Somme. During the fighting Captain George Howson was captured after holding on too long to a building which was eventually surrounded by the Germans. He later managed to escape, rejoining the battalion in Péronne.

It was this stand at Doingt that drew such admiration from Lieutenant Colonel Jackson, the senior staff officer (GSO1) with the 16th Division; in his opinion the Hampshires were responsible for holding the enemy in check at a most critical time and allowing 48 Brigade to withdraw relatively unscathed. Jackson's praise also credits the Hampshires gritty stand – in which Cecil Hazard played such a vital part – with facilitating the retirement of 47 and 49 Brigades on the left. Perceval Whittall was awarded a bar to his DSO and Cecil Hazard – despite Jackson's personal recommendation – received no official recognition whatsoever! If ever there was an unjust allocation of awards, the exclusion of Cecil Hazard must rank highly amongst them.

But it was not quite over yet. From Doingt the Hampshires retired to what the war diary describes as a light railway cutting on the outskirts of Péronne where they again held off several violent attacks before all three companies withdrew across the Somme, Cecil Hazard reported as being the last man to cross the bridge before it was destroyed. The bridge that Hazard crossed was in fact the Bristol Bridge which was held by men of the 5th and 6th Manchesters until 24 March when Péronne fell to the Germans after a furious bombardment which fortunately fell on an almost deserted town. The Bristol Bridge was the last structure over the Somme at Péronne to be demolished, a task which was carried out by 180/Tunnelling Company at 6.00pm – this time there was no possibility of the bridge being used again by German infantry – the explosion blew a gap of 150 feet in the span.

The Bristol Bridge is not the last we shall hear of the Hampshires as they were involved in another testing rearguard action near Morcourt on 27 March. The Hampshires' casualties over the two days of 22/23 March were remarkably light given the intensity of the fighting the battalion was involved in. By far the greater number were killed on 22 March at St Emilie – one officer and twenty-one other ranks – while on 23 March the battalion only suffered eight other ranks killed. The number of wounded went unrecorded.

Chapter 11

The Somme Crossings

Most of the men were lying like dead men, tired out ... Some of them were shaving off five days' growth of beard. There could not have been more than 1,500 able-bodied men left out of each division.

Paul Maze on passing the remnants of the 20th and 36th Divisions

At the beginning of March 1918 the 8th Division was in the Steenvoorde area to the west of Poperinge. Up until this point the possibility of a German offensive south of Arras was purely academic, a situation which occupied passing conversation and speculation, all of which changed on 13 March when the division was moved to Tilques and was officially placed in GHQ Reserve. Suddenly the time and nature of the much talked about German offensive became of great interest and, as many now realised, the division was highly likely to be drawn into the battle at some point. That moment came at 9.00am on 21 March when orders were received to begin preparations immediately for the division to entrain for the south.

Commanding the division was 51-years-old Major General William 'Billy' Heneker, a Canadian national who had accepted a commission with the 1st Battalion Connaught Rangers as a second lieutenant on 5 September 1888. Although he had been in command of the division since December 1916, the briefing he received at Fifth Army Headquarters must have given him and his staff some cause for alarm. The division was to be deployed on the XIX Corps front along a line east of the River Somme; all the available reserves had been thrown in to the battle; the third and last defensive zone had been breached and an immediate retreat to the bridgehead positions west of the Somme was in progress. The retiring troops of the 50th Division and the remnants of the XIX Corps divisions were to retire through them and after blowing the bridges, the German advance was to be held on the line of the river.

For Heneker's division this meant only one thing, it was going to be placed in the same situation that the 50th Division faced on the Green Line, in that it would be given little time to put the Somme line into a state of defence. No time would be given for any reconnaissance of the positions it was to occupy and, like the men of the 50th Division, its troops would be turned straight into battle. It was an unenviable prospect which was exacerbated considerably by a change in orders at the last minute, switching the divisional line from the east to the west bank of the river! One can only imagine the difficulties this caused Heneker's staff as they feverishly sought to issue new orders. Captain Richard Brooke recalled the exasperation that was apparent at divisional headquarters:

> *'The difficulty of intercepting the units of the 23rd and 24th Infantry Brigades now on the march to their allotted areas east of the Somme on a pitch black night with the roads crowded with troops and transport can better be imagined than described, but somehow or another by about 5.00am on 23rd* [the] *advanced troops of the 24th Brigade began to arrive at the Somme line and the division gradually filtered into its 15,000 yards of front.'*[1]

In fact 23 Brigade was not in position until the afternoon of 23 March with 24 Brigade arriving even later. According to Captain Maurice Toye, serving with the 2nd Battalion Middlesex Regiment (2/Middlesex), the advance parties of 24 Brigade which had crossed the Somme were surrounded by the enemy and had to fight their way back to the positions on the west bank, 'with the result that the division went into action piecemeal'. The Somme frontage that was finally occupied by the 8th Division now ran from the confluence of the l'Ingon stream with the Canal du Nord at Rouy-le-Petit in the south, to Eterpigny in the north, a line of defence correctly estimated by Brooke as roughly eight miles and considerably longer than that previously allocated to the 50th Division on the Green Line.

There was however, one problem. The integrity of the river line did not only depend on the 8th Division, the Crozat Canal had already been crossed at Tergnier on 22 March and early on 23 March the railway bridge east of Ham had been taken by German infantry enabling their units to link up with the German bridgehead at Jussy and St Simon. Thus the whole front from the River Oise in the south to the Somme Canal at Ham was now being advanced, endangering the west bank of the river and threatening to roll up the whole of the Fifth Army line from the south.

Brigadier General Ferdinand Stanley commanding 89 Brigade – whom we last met near St Quentin – had effectively lost his brigade on 22 March when his three battalions were split up to reinforce the XVIII Corps divisions. After moving his headquarters to Villers-St-Christophe as ordered, he heard nothing more until he was ordered to Ham:

> *'I arrived there about 10 o'clock, I should imagine, and found the Corps Headquarters staff just clearing out. Soon after our arrival I was told that, being free, I was to*

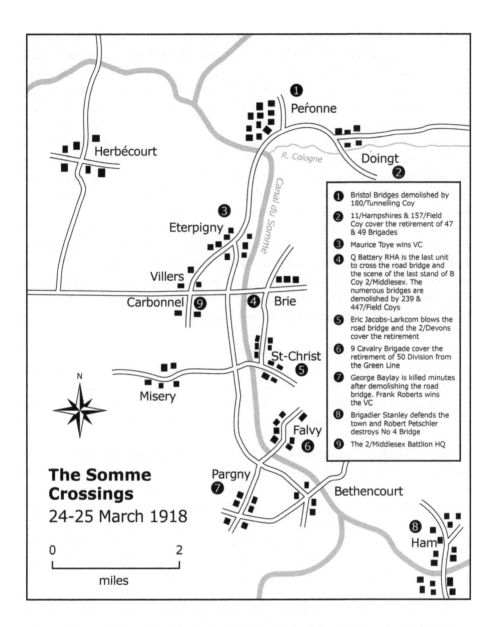

The Somme Crossings
24-25 March 1918

Herbécourt

Péronne

R. Cologne

Doingt

Canal du Somme

Eterpigny

Villers

Carbonnel

Brie

St-Christ

Misery

N

Falvy

Pargny

Bethencourt

Ham

1. Bristol Bridges demolished by 180/Tunnelling Coy
2. 11/Hampshires & 157/Field Coy cover the retirement of 47 & 49 Brigades
3. Maurice Toye wins VC
4. Q Battery RHA is the last unit to cross the road bridge and the scene of the last stand of B Coy 2/Middlesex. The numerous bridges are demolished by 239 & 447/Field Coys
5. Eric Jacobs-Larkcom blows the road bridge and the 2/Devons cover the retirement
6. 9 Cavalry Brigade cover the retirement of 50 Division from the Green Line
7. George Baylay is killed minutes after demolishing the road bridge. Frank Roberts wins the VC
8. Brigadier Stanley defends the town and Robert Petschler destroys No 4 Bridge
9. The 2/Middlesex Battlion HQ

0   2
miles

undertake the defence of Ham. Certain troops had already been dug in. On asking what troops would be available, I was informed that the only troops for this purpose were the two entrenching battalions, two companies of special RE, five platoons from the Corps of Reinforcements and a corps of cyclists.'[2]

Stanley's dismay at the hurriedly cobbled together force was further added to when these troops were suddenly withdrawn leaving him with the small body of men from his brigade headquarters and the sappers detailed to blow the bridges. To Stanley's credit he deployed his meagre force on the bridges and established a small group of volunteers to harass the enemy as they gained entry to the town. Late in the afternoon of 22 March, a much-relieved Stanley was told to reform his brigade and bring them all back to Ham to assist in the defence. The 18th King's Liverpool Regiment (18/King's) arrived first at about 7.30pm taking up positions south of the town, two hours later the 17/King's were established in the centre of the line while the remnants of 19/King's, having fallen back through the 20th Division, arrived in the early hours of 23 March, forming up north of the town on the left of the line. Stanley recalled his dismay on being reunited with his 'much knocked about' battalions: 'The 19th Battalion were so knocked about that one could hardly count them. They had lost all their officers except one, and he was wounded. Poor fellow! He was killed the next day.'³ In reality there was very little the brigadier could do at Ham apart from ensure the bridges were destroyed, a task he proceeded to carry out with his usual methodical style. At 3.00pm on 22 March Lieutenant Robert Petschler was summoned to Stanley's headquarters and given very clear written instructions:

> *'I saw the general and he gave me personal orders about the blowing up of one of the bridges: "Your only duty is to blow up Number 4 Bridge in the event of the enemy being in possession of the bridgehead – ie that there are none of our troops who can prevent him from getting over" … the bridge had to be left to the last, as it was the main line of retreat. It spanned the canal at Ham on the main road.'*⁴

Number 4 Bridge – on the present day D932 heading south towards Guiscard and Noyon – was, in 1918, a substantial double girder construction designed to take heavy military traffic. A second bridge further to the east had been blown earlier in the morning by sappers from 200/Field Company. When Petschler arrived with his three sappers he discovered the bridge had already been prepared for demolition but the wooden foot-bridge close by had not. He and his men immediately set about dislodging the timbers and dropping them into the canal, a canal which Petschler noted was 'almost dry in places and was passable for determined men'.

The road was now crowded with retiring troops and transports, 'they came in endless streams for hours on end,' wrote Petschler, who soon found himself acting as an impromptu traffic controller. As always, the retirement was continually harassed by German gunners who appeared to have access to an endless supply of ammunition. When Lieutenant Herbert Asquith and C/149 Battery entered Ham twenty-four hours after leaving Holnon Wood, he noted the bombardment was falling on a largely deserted town:

'The Germans were firing on the town with long-range guns, some of which were aiming at the bridges of the Somme Canal. The civilian population had vanished and there were many signs of the haste with which they had fled ... while we were marching down the main street a man ran out with a box containing a large number of eggs and gave it to the captain to prevent it falling into the hands of the enemy. We crossed the bridge over the Somme Canal and halted a short distance away on the south side of the town.'[5]

Asquith and his battery crossed the canal in daylight, but as the sappers on the bridge were only too aware, the stream of men and transports continued all night, prompting Robert Petschler to wonder if everyone would cross before the Germans arrived. His thoughts were much along the same lines as Brigadier General Francis Duncan as he and his brigade major stood at the bridge collecting the remnants of 60 Brigade until the early hours of 23 March – but we will return to his part in the story shortly.

At 12.45am on 23 March the German advance broke through southeast of Ham at Aubigny and with the dawn came news that the railway bridge at Pithon had been crossed by units of the German 5th Guard Division and the right flank at Ham was now under pressure. The demolition of the Ham bridges had already begun and Petschler was becoming quite anxious:

'The position was now desperate. The stragglers got fewer and in smaller parties, and I continually asked NCOs or officers if there were more to follow ... in the distance I saw an officer leading about a platoon of men. When he approached he said he was the last of the infantry. I began to be very much on the alert. I called my sentries and waited. The officer came running back and said that his commanding officer ordered the bridge to be blown up. I did not do it immediately and waited for at least a quarter of an hour. Then I heard a tremendous burst of cheering – it was the Huns entering the town. Bullets were flattening themselves on the walls and road near me. Through the mist I thought I saw movement and then it was unmistakable – a small part of Huns were rushing the bridge. I waited until they had just set foot on the bridge and then pressed down the handle of the exploder for all I was worth. Up went the bridge with a terrific crash and it was quite some minutes before the pieces stopped falling.'[6]

The bridge was blown at 8.00am, the explosion had cut the girders in the centre but the ends remained on the abutments and the hanging ends rested on the lock walls. Clearly infantry would still be able to cross but Robert Petschler and his men had done their job and were heading towards Verlaines to rejoin their field company:

'Taking cover behind the railway wagons I ran down the road for all I was worth and did not stop until I had covered a fair distance and found a corner in the road where I was sheltered from fire; the men who had been with me had bicycles and soon got away. I continued to walk rapidly until I reached Verlaines where I caught up with columns on the move and saw our infantry extending in open order to make a fresh stand.'[7]

Barely an hour later Brigadier General Duncan apparently received a telegram from Gough ordering him to counter-attack the bridge immediately! Quite how Gough knew that enemy infantry were still able to use the bridge is not mentioned by Duncan, but as he later recalled:

'Quite by chance I found one or two (I cannot remember how many) of the 61st Division behind a wall quite close by to me. I got hold of the senior officer amongst them and wrote out some orders for the counter-attack, lent them my brigade major and sent them off to Ham Bridge. They were able to hold the Germans for some time, but had to fall back and I collected them in the afternoon. I gathered from the German officer afterwards, whom we had taken prisoner, that Ham Bridge had not been completely blown up by our engineers.'[8]

From Duncan's account we can assume he remained on the south side of the canal for most of the morning as his rearguard kept the bridge free of German infantry traversing the damaged girders. Herbert Asquith and his guns were providing support from their position near Esmery-Hallon and using the church tower at the eastern end of the village as an observation post; a vantage point from which they were also able to observe Duncan's rearguard at the bridge, who, Asquith tells us, had to fall back in the face of heavy machine-gun fire. C/149 Battery were firing on crossroads and road junctions in an attempt to delay the German onslaught, moving the next morning only after the enemy advance from Golancourt threatened their positions.

Meanwhile, as soon as the Germans entered Ham the 89 Brigade battalions began withdrawing towards Eppeville on the southern bank of the Somme Canal. At Eppeville the 11th Battalion South Lancashire Regiment (11/South Lancs) had been in position since late on 22 March with orders to cover the retirement. Lieutenant Colonel Herbert Fenn had been in command of the battalion since May 1916 and as pioneers, they had dug their way along much of the British sector of the Western Front, moving with the 30th Division to the Fifth Army Front in January 1918. Trench warfare at least had some order to it – unlike the situation they now found themselves in where circumstances changed almost as rapidly as the wind. Fenn's frustration is expressed in the war diary: 'I had received no orders of any kind and did not know what was happening on either flank or even if it was intended to hold the line of the canal.'

Remaining in position, Fenn heard the explosion signifying Petschler's bridge had been blown, an event which was followed by a large number of units retiring down the Ham-Eppeville road towards the line of the Canal du Nord. With them was a staff car carrying, amongst others, Lieutenant Colonel John Haskard, the senior staff officer from the 20th Division. An indication as to the level of confusion that existed that morning is contained in the movements of 11/South Lancs after Haskard was questioned by Fenn as to what was happening on his front. Haskard was of the opinion that the line of the Somme Canal was to be held by the 30th Division prompting Fenn to begin moving the battalion towards Canizy, a move that was halted by further information from the 19/King's indicating the Germans had crossed the canal – presumably this referred to the canal at Ham – and were advancing in the direction of Eppeville. Accordingly Fenn moved two companies back to the line of the railway embankment. On his left were some of the 19/King's and part of 23/Entrenching Battalion which was holding a section of the railway line towards Canizy. He had no idea who was on his right, if indeed anyone was:

'About 10.00am I received information that the enemy appeared to be massing on the north side of the canal and then until about 12.20pm there was a considerable number of the enemy moving about in the wood [on the north bank of the canal] *and fairly heavy rifle fire. The enemy appeared to have intended to attack but did not succeed in reaching our line.'*[9]

Shortly before 2.00pm Fenn received word that his right company on the railway embankment was in danger of encirclement, enemy infantry were now on the outskirts of Eppeville and there was little choice but to fall back south of the railway. That evening Fenn failed to get in touch with his right flank. A sucrerie, which was supposed to be in British hands, was occupied by the enemy and there was no sign of 23/Entrenching Battalion, that is until 7.00am the next morning, when Fenn observed them retiring towards Canizy. For the South Lancs, however, time was running out and German infantry were closing in rapidly:

'The two companies holding [the ground south of the railway line] *were almost entirely surrounded; their only line of withdrawal was across a stream which was lined with barbed wire. Owing to the magnificent way in which Lewis gunners remained firing at the enemy until they were either killed or wounded, parts of the two companies withdrew and fought a rearguard action, across the canal near Moyencourt.'*[10]

The stream – the River Allemagne – was a rather small but steep-sided waterway and the scene of a rather magnificent action that led to the award of the Victoria Cross to Corporal John 'Jack' Davies, a Lancashire lad who had joined the

11/South Lancashire Regiment on the outbreak of war in 1914. Originally dubbed the St Helens Pals, his battalion had crossed to France in November 1915 as part of Kitchener's New Army which seven months later would find itself embroiled in the 1916 Battle of the Somme. Davies was wounded twice during the Somme battles returning to duty after each period of recovery and recuperation. Needless to say by March 1918, after more than two years in uniform, the 22-year-old Jack Davies had been hardened to the horrors of war and the loss of his comrades. As a Lewis gunner his role was to provide covering and supportive fire, a role that in March 1918 when the confines of trench warfare burst forth into the mobility of open warfare, had become all the more vital.

As his comrades moved to cross the stream, Davies began to put down a heavy fire from his Lewis gun with deadly effect to delay the German advance. Writing to Davies' mother in April 1918 and unsure as to the fate of the young corporal, Herbert Fenn described what he knew of the final action:

> *'He was last seen kneeling on the trench parapet in order to get a better view of the enemy, and kept firing his gun until the enemy were so close on him that he could not get away. By his very gallant conduct he no doubt saved the lives of many of his comrades ... I need hardly say how proud all officers and men were to have such a gallant NCO in their battalion ... very few, if any, would have been able to get away alive had not your son held up the enemy with his Lewis gun.'*[11]

Davies was fortunate in that he was captured alive after wreaking such havoc on the enemy but he would have been well aware his decision to remain behind had placed his life in jeopardy if he was lucky enough to survive. What marks this action above many others is the clear sense of duty that this young man possessed: when asked after the war to describe his role in the fight at Eppeville, Davies simply replied, 'that's what I was there for'.

* * *

As the British units fell back from the Green Line towards the Somme the 1st Cavalry Division was directed north of the confluence of the Canal du Nord with the Canal de la Somme in order to fill the gap between XIX Corps and Maxse's XVIII Corps and hold the bridges at Béthencourt and Pargny until relieved by the 8th Division. After crossing the Somme at St Christ Briost 2 Cavalry Brigade was dispatched to Béthencourt – where it was in touch with units of the 20th Division – and 9 Cavalry Brigade was ordered to cover the double bridgehead at Pargny and Falvy where another Victoria Cross would be won on the night of 23 March.

There were five bridges numbered 61–65 along the causeway that crossed the Somme marshes between Pargny and Falvy, Number 61 spanned the canal at

Pargny while the other four crossed branches of the river towards Falvy. The five bridges had been prepared for demolition by 1/Siege Company whose sappers were on hand at each location. Early on 23 March units of the 24th and 50th Divisions began their retirement on Falvy, to support their crossing were the 8th Hussars who crossed the river at Pargny and moved north towards the crest of the high ground above the village of Falvy where they were joined by the 1st Battalion Worcestershire Regiment (1/Worcesters), under the command of 26-year-old Lieutenant Colonel Frank 'Cully' Roberts. Roberts crossed the river and deployed his men to the east of the village from which point they could see the retiring troops falling back towards them with the advancing German units of IR 52 some way behind. They soon came under a heavy fire from the forward machine-gun teams of IR 52 as they closed in on the rearguards of the retiring troops, but Roberts held his ground until the last moment and then pulled slowly back towards the bridge.

Meanwhile 8/Hussars had been ordered to join 19/Hussars in a chalk quarry close to Falvy Copse to the north of the village and wait for the opportunity to counter-attack. No sooner were the Hussars across the river when they were met by a pandemonium of thirty stampeding horses of 19/Hussars, which,when combined with enemy shellfire, quickly turned the intended counter-attack into a retreat – particularly as both regiments were also under fire from enemy machine guns – all of which prompted a sharp return to Falvy bridge.

Initially the forward companies of IR 52 thought the Worcesters were about to make a stand on the high ground above Falvy, noting with some alarm that they even advanced against the right flank of the regiment. 'Nevertheless the heights east of Falvy were taken by about 3.00pm and the Somme crossings lay under our fire. But the English tenaciously defended the villages and the bridges themselves.'[12] There may very well have been a determined defence of the bridge at Falvy but according to Lieutenant Thomas Evans-Lombe, the retirement back over the bridge was far from straightforward:

> 'The village and bridge were being heavily shelled. In order to cover the retirement of the remainder of the regiment, one squadron was sent across the river to Pargny. When the remainder tried to follow the bridge had been blown up by German shellfire. The horses were consequently sent across at St Christ. On their way they were met by a party of the 19th who reported that the bridge at St Christ had also been blown up. Attempts were made to repair the bridge at Falvy with material found in the village and also to swim the horses over. The bank was so boggy that the horses stuck the moment they got into the stream and swimming had to be abandoned.'[13]

By this time a heavy fire from the IR 52 machine gunners was targeting the village making it impossible to make any repairs on the bridge. Evans-Lombe was standing on the bridge as planks were being put in place over the gap. 'No horses were got across,' he lamented, 'and it was decided to get the men across and abandon the horses.' For the cavalrymen this must have been a heartrending process as they retired dismounted to the eastern edge of Pargny. With the Germans now practically in the village and the infantry falling back along the causeway, bridges Number 63 and 64 were blown at 2.30pm, leaving only the canal bridge intact. On the bridge Sergeant George Crossley was in a quandary, with no orders to blow the bridge and no communication from the 24th Division, he bravely took it upon himself to detonate the charges. As Reginald Buckland wrote in his account of the incident, 'for some reason, possibly because the charges had been loosened by the previous explosions, [from bridges 63 and 64] the demolition was not successful'. At which point Lieutenant George Baylay from the 1/Field Squadron RE stepped forward to finish the job:

> *'Lieutenant Baylay, seeing that the canal bridge had only been partially destroyed, sent for more explosives, and with Corporal* [Selwyn] *Regester and six of his sappers laid fresh charges under heavy machine gun fire and set them off. Accompanied by his corporal, he went forward to see the result, which was satisfactory, but on his way back he was unfortunately killed by a machine gun bullet.'*[14]

As dusk closed in that evening the situation was precarious to say the least. Constant sniping and intermittent machine-gun fire ensured little sleep was had by the men of 1/Worcesters who were now deployed along the western canal bank between Pargny and Epénancourt. At 8.00pm Frank Roberts visited all his posts along the canal, unaware that units of IR 52 had crossed the canal on the debris of the bridge and entered Pargny village, a situation Roberts only became aware of when he reached the village outskirts:

> *'I found the post there very excited as they were being shot at from the houses in the north portion of Pargny, and had also seen Bosche in the village before dark. I was also told that all posts between them and the bridge had ceased to function (afterwards I found a number of men in them had been shot in the back and that the local defence south of the bridge had been broken through about dusk).'*[15]

Realizing that 2/Rifle Brigade must have withdrawn from his right flank and that the canal line would soon be taken by the enemy, he immediately resolved to counter-attack, reasoning that, 'unless the village could be taken back, we should be mopped up during the night, if the enemy continued to advance NW of the canal'.

Gathering together all his available force – some 45 NCOs and men – he led them to the crossroads on the south western edge of the village. The main attack would drive straight down the main street with two flanking parties on either side to mop up any stragglers. It was a straightforward plan and its boldness relied very much on the element of surprise. At 9.00pm he gave the order to attack:

> '*For the first 100 yards or so we went in two parties in single file on each side of the main road at a walk and as quietly as possible. The first intimation that I had of the Bosche was some shouting from houses we were passing, and then both machine gun and rifle fire (very wild) from windows and doors, with small parties of the enemy dashing into the streets and clearing off in the direction of the bridge. Once this started we all went hell for leather up the street firing at anything we saw and using the bayonet in many cases. From beginning to end every man screamed and cheered as hard as he bloody well could and by the time we reached the church the village was in uproar and Bosche legging it hard to the bridge or else chucking his hands up (we only took very few prisoners as I'd told our men to kill so as to prevent the brutes ... coming up in our rear). In the churchyard itself the hardest fighting took place, tombstones being used as if in a game of hide and seek. Here, after clearing it, we had a few minutes rest and then went smack through to the bridge where a mass of Bosche were trying to scramble across, some did and some didn't.*'[16]

The attack was an outstanding success with Roberts and his men retaking the village, capturing six machine guns and taking about 15–20 prisoners. The announcement of the award of the Victoria Cross to Frank Roberts appeared in the *London Gazette* in May 1918. As for the battalion on the right referred to by Roberts, it had indeed withdrawn but, according to the Rifle Brigade historian, withdrew only after the enemy had succeeded in crossing the canal and working round both flanks. Its retirement to a sunken road east of Morchain apparently took place a little after midnight on 25 March, four hours after Roberts stated his right flank had been abandoned.

Further south along the canal line, German infantry were making repeated attempts to cross the canal early on 24 March. At Offoy, despite the thick fog, 12/Rifle Brigade was able to frustrate any attacks with their rifle and machine-gun fire until that evening when they were forced to withdraw to Quiquery. At Béthencourt German infantry had more success against the defences held by 11/Rifle Brigade and enough of them were on the western bank of the canal by 8.00am to consolidate a bridgehead. An hour later Béthencourt was reported in enemy hands despite the efforts of 2/East Lancashire and C Company, 11/Rifle Brigade, which, although 'hopelessly outnumbered' counter-attacked; an attack – the regimental historian tells us – from which 'the majority failed to return'.

Three miles north of Pargny at St Christ Briost were a collection of wooden pile bridges that had been erected in 1917 after the retreating Germans demolished the road bridge. These were destroyed at 11.00am on 23 March with gunpowder and petrol but the main road bridge that crossed the canal and two branches of the river was of a far more substantial construction. Recently completed by

American engineers, the bridge was one that had been constructed using steel girders and was designed to carry tanks. Lieutenant Eric Jacobs-Larkcom from 15/Field Company was detailed to carry out the demolition with his section of sappers:

> '*I proceeded to the site of the bridge and obtained a covering party from the infantry unit holding that sector. The Germans had not attempted to cross the bridge, but the roadway was under accurate fire from machine gun positions on the far bank. A reconnaissance of the bridge showed it consisted of two heavy steel girders supporting the roadway. I judged that the available explosive would not make a thorough job of both girders – so decided that most damage would be done by concentrating all the explosive on one girder. The charge was laid and the leads brought back to an exploder … The explosion brought down a hail of machine gun fire on the approaches to the bridge, but we managed, by waiting our opportunity and using whatever cover there was, to withdraw the firing party without casualties. Unfortunately the charge was insufficient to bring down the whole girder although the bridge had been considerably weakened, it was, however, the best we could do.*'[17]

Covering the bridge was C Company of the 2nd Battalion Devonshire Regiment (2/Devons) who successfully beat off all attempts by the Germans to cross the bridge, each attempt being repelled by Second Lieutenant William Maunder and the counter-attack platoon. Continually under attack from across the canal, William Maunder, a former warrant officer who had fought with the battalion since landing in France in August 1914, repeatedly led his men forward in response to German attempts to gain a foothold on the west bank:

> '*Three times the enemy came on, and only after most severe fighting were they held at bay. One strong party of Germans waded across just above the bridge and tried to outflank its defenders. Once again Second Lieutenant Maunder's platoon met them, charging across the road and up an embankment beyond and got well into them with the bayonet. Second Lieutenant* [James] *Huntingford and another platoon supported him, and between them they drove off the attackers … nearly 20 prisoners were taken.*'[18]

Already the holder of the Military Medal, Maunder's award of the Military Cross was announced in the *London Gazette* in July 1918.

The 2/Devons were holding the canal line from St Christ Briost to a point just north of Happlincourt Château, their left flank platoon being in sight of the road bridge at Brie. On the night of 24 March 2/Middlesex relieved the West Yorkshires in the defences of the Brie and Eterpigny bridges. Lieutenant Colonel Charles Page established his battalion headquarters in an old trench some 700 yards east of Villers-Carbonnel a little to the north of the road to Brie. A regular officer, Charles Page was gazetted into the Middlesex Regiment in 1901 and almost immediately found himself fighting in South Africa with his battalion. At the outbreak of war in 1914 he was a 34-year-old captain with little prospect of advancement much before 1919 – all of which changed in May 1916 after his promotion to major and his award of the Military Cross. In October 1917 he was appointed second-in-command of 2/Middlesex and two months later was in command of the battalion. Page was another individual who excelled when facing huge odds, never losing his grip on command, his poise and composure under fire proving inspirational to the officers and men in the battalion. His orders to the battalion as they deployed along the Somme were quite simple: hold on at all costs and do not retire until ordered.

The first attack by the German 208th Division came at 7.00am on 25 March. Captain Maurice Toye commanding C Company had positioned one of his four platoons on the bridge at Eterpigny, a post that quickly became the focus of the German attack. Twice they were driven off the bridge and twice they counter-attacked to regain possession, the last message indicating they were practically surrounded. Half-an-hour later a patrol sent along the canal also vanished without trace leaving Toye – a former boy bugler who enlisted in the RE in 1912 – with only one conclusion: the Germans had crossed the river and canal in some force. He didn't have to wait long before the whole company came under a heavy assault from both north and south of the bridge, an attack which forced 7/DLI in Eterpigny village to retire – the Middlesex war diary noting with some distain that they did so 'without fighting at all'.

The DLI's retirement had exposed C Company's left flank to the extent that Toye and his men soon found themselves surrounded, but mindful of Page's orders to hold on at all costs they did exactly that – but at a terrible cost. Second Lieutenant Francis Mahany who was stranded in the village attempted to reach Toye with his platoon, fighting his way through 'at the cost of all but three of his men'. Eventually Toye and Mahany together with the six remaining men of the company forced their way through from the village onto the Villers-Carbonnel road. Here, finding some seventy men of 7/DLI, Maurice Toye formed them up with his own men and counter-attacked back across the road towards the village. Once again the element of surprise caught the enemy unawares and Toye was able to hold onto his newly won position until relieved by the 2/West Yorkshires. This desperate action undoubtedly temporarily held up any advance west but could not prevent Brie from coming under attack by the German 19th Division.

With the Eterpigny bridgehead now in enemy hands German infantry quickly moved down the west bank of the canal towards Brie where two companies of the Middlesex were defending the crossing. Possibly the last unit to cross the river ahead of the enemy was Q Battery, RHA. Signaller Herbert Quick was with the guns as they arrived on the eastern bank of the canal at the Brie road bridge:

'I hold that [Q Battery] were the last battery to cross the Somme at Brie in our retreat; further I think Gunner Fisher and myself can claim to be the last British troops to cross the bridge at the same time …The enemy were advancing very fast, as they hadn't many men holding them; our troops kept coming back in twos and threes and when I thought the last few had crossed the bridge and the enemy were getting very near, I reported to HQ, but could get no answer. When I could discern the uniform of the Bosch, and machine gun bullets began to fly around, I decided to retire.'[19]

It wasn't long before heavy fighting enveloped the Middlesex positions. The left post of B Company was the first to be overwhelmed and a platoon from A Company sent to support them suffered the same fate. Private Frederick Curtis thought 'the earth was turned into hell', as the company came under fire from German gunners on the far side of the river:

'After four or five long hours had passed away our position became very hot, because not only were we under shells and rifle fire, but a big warehouse that was about 20 yards away from the end of our trench was set alight by the German gunners. Besides this we had to cope with a German aeroplane that kept flying over our trench and firing a machine gun onto us.'[20]

Curtis was serving in the Lewis gun section at Brie and was one of the more fortunate who were lucky enough to survive to fight another day. From all accounts it was a desperate defence:

'Only the right platoon of B Company and the last support platoon of D company got away. The other six platoons of these two companies perished at their post … The right platoon of B Company was in the bridge defences with two Lewis gun sections. They fought under Second Lieutenant W J Martin there for one and a half hours. Captain [Hugh] Wegg then posted them on the Amiens road near his company headquarters overlooking the bridge. When the rest of the company was destroyed Second Lieutenant Martin fell back upon A Company at Happlincourt and withdrew through the outskirts of Villers-Carbonnel with the left of the 2/ Devon Regiment.'[21]

At battalion headquarters news of the attacks reached Charles Page at 9.00am. On being told of the demise of C Company and the close-quarters fighting at Brie, he realised it would be only a matter of time before his headquarters would be under siege. His position was hardly a good one, the Roman Road from Brie to Villers-Carbonnel rises from the river valley at the Pont les Brie spur before it continues west towards Villers-Bretonneux and Amiens. The first solid evidence that German infantry had taken Eterpigny arrived in the form of Second Lieutenant

Cawdron who confirmed the village was lost: the second came shortly afterwards as German machine-gun teams appeared on the ridge, prompting Major Charles Drew to counter-attack with a party of twenty-six cooks, signallers and runners. Drew's men drove the gunners back from the ridge and into the valley, beating off a further enemy attack in the early afternoon and holding on to their position for four hours before retiring.

In the meantime Charles Page had sent Lieutenant Ernest Frayne on to the ridge to protect Drew's right flank but Frayne and his men never arrived; after walking into a German machine-gun team they were nearly all killed or wounded, Frayne himself being wounded and taken prisoner only to die from his wounds in captivity. The only man to return after escaping his captors was Sergeant W Fox. The last news Page received from B Company at Brie was at 4.15pm in the form of a hastily-scribbled message from Second Lieutenant Alexander Liversedge. Even as the young subaltern wrote the message he was watching the long lines of enemy troops descending into the river valley opposite and he and his remaining men must have realised there was little chance of any reinforcements and they had but a short time left:

> 'My left is about 200 yards to the left of the Brie road. Several lines of the enemy can be seen coming down the slope of ridge opposite and to the left of our front. Reinforcements and ammunition urgently required.'[22]

'Fred' Liversedge was 23 years old when he was killed on the banks of the Somme Canal, a former telegraphic clerk from Paddington he enlisted into the London Regiment in 1914 arriving on the Western Front in March 1915. His service record indicates he was promoted to acting corporal and transferred to the Royal Sussex Regiment before being recommended for a commission. A similar message was received from Second Lieutenant George Ball who appeared to be the only remaining officer in B Company still on his feet: 'Enemy preparing to attack again, both from left flank and direct front. Reinforcements required.' Ball signed himself the 'Officer Commanding B Company'. Like Fred Liversedge, the 20-year-old George Ball died on the canal with his men, he too was a former NCO who had been commissioned in 1917 and is one of only two Middlesex officers killed on 25 March who have a CWGC headstone. He and Captain Roy Launceston can be found at Assevillers New British Cemetery near Péronne along with sixteen of the battalion's NCOs and men.

Page's men at battalion headquarters now prepared to sell their lives dearly. Reinforced by two Vickers machine guns the headquarters party kept the enemy at bay for nearly two hours before German gunners subjected them to an intense barrage. At 6.45pm a runner arrived from 23 Brigade ordering the battalion to withdraw. For the three companies on the canal the order was too late, six platoons from B and D Company had already fallen at their posts or had been taken prisoner and one platoon from A Company had vanished without trace. The remaining men from C Company with Captain Maurice Toye were still fighting with the West Yorkshires near Eterpigny. The battalion had been all but destroyed.

At 7.00pm German infantry had approached unseen to within 450 yards of battalion headquarters. Page quickly began his retirement, sending parties of men off in batches while he and a small party of men maintained a rapid rifle and machine-gun fire covering the movement of men towards Estrees. In the closing moments of the retirement Charles Page dispatched the last two men and, after a final volley from the rifle he had been using for the past hour, left the trench. Three minutes later the first Germans arrived.

The Middlesex had lost heavily, the war diary recording 12 officers and over 300 other ranks killed, wounded or missing. From 7.00am when the bridge at Eterpigny was rushed, to 7.25pm when Charles Page successfully withdrew the remnants of battalion headquarters, the Middlesex had fought against odds of at least five to one. In all, eleven platoons had been lost to enemy action leaving fewer than 160 men to be reorganized into four composite companies, each barely larger than a full strength platoon. Such gallantry and sacrifice cannot go without recognition and the award of the Victoria Cross to Maurice Toye – who had managed to escape from Eterpigny intact – was announced in the *London Gazette* in May 1918. Although his citation refers to 'two further occasions' when he demonstrated his gallantry under fire, the action at Eterpigny was the most outstanding:

'When the enemy had captured the trench, at a bridgehead, he three times re-established the post during the 25th March 1918. The position was later taken by the enemy after new attacks. When three of his posts had been captured, Captain Toye, another officer and six men fought their way through the enemy. He then collected 70 men of the Battalion, who had been retiring, and took up a position which was maintained until reinforcements arrived. Without this action, the defence of the bridge would certainly have failed.'[23]

Charles Page's leadership was recognised with the award of the DSO which cited his 'conspicuous gallantry and devotion to duty during many days of intense fighting, in which by his high standard of military leadership, he kept his battalion together under the most difficult circumstances'. What the citation neglected to mention was the 200 rounds of rifle ammunition the commanding officer had fired at the enemy whilst covering the retirement of his men. As the war diary concluded, 'thank God all ranks did their duty'.

A little further to the north at Barleux 5/DLI were told to 'hang on to the death'. Major Alwyn Raimes, in questioning the wisdom of this instruction, was told again to remain in position and to stay and fight it out. They could see

German troops at Villers-Carbonnel moving past their right flank without any apparent opposition and as Raimes said afterwards, 'the only conclusion we could come to was that we were to be sacrificed to cover the retirement'. Later in the evening as the other units to their left and right withdrew, all attempts to contact brigade headquarters failed, it was obvious to all they had already packed up and left! Slowly it dawned upon the DLI that orders for them to retire had perhaps not reached them, it was only the discovery of a platoon of Northumberland Fusiliers who had been instructed to cover the Durhams' retirement that Raimes realised his suspicions had foundation:

'As can be imagined, no time was wasted, and it was not long before the Battalion was moving in single file, as quickly and quietly as possible down the sunken road skirting Barleux. It was an awesome business. There was a bright moon, so the Germans had a good chance of discovering that our line was being withdrawn, and of closing up and cutting off our retreat. It is extraordinary what a noise three or four hundred men make on a still night, however hard they are trying to move quietly.... . We got away without a shot having being fired at us, and eventually reached the new line established in front of Estrées and Assevillers.'[24]

But there was no rest to be had; almost as soon as the DLI arrived they were again withdrawing. This time their destination was Rosières.

During the afternoon of 23 March Douglas Haig finally visited Gough's Headquarters at Villers-Brettoneux and perhaps for the first time began to develop some idea of the seriousness of the situation facing the Fifth Army, although, it must be said that his diary entry for that day still betrayed a failure to grasp the extent and intensity of the German advance. Less than twenty-four hours later his apparent complacency was shaken to the core after a meeting with General Pétain at Dury where it emerged that – despite the earlier agreement to mutually support each other in the event of a German attack – the two men now had very different priorities:

'I explained my plans and asked him to concentrate as large a force as possible about Amiens astride the Somme to cooperate on my right. He said he expected every moment to be attacked in Champagne, and did not believe the main German blow had yet been delivered. He said he would give Fayolle [General Marie Émile Fayolle, commanding the French Army reserves] *all his available troops. He also told me he had seen the latter today at Montdidier, where the French reserves were now collecting, and had directed him in the event of the German advance being pressed still further, to fall back south-westwards to Beauvais in order to cover Paris.'[25]*

Although Haig's diary implies that this came as a complete surprise which he immediately interpreted as a separation of the French from the British right flank, there is evidence to suggest that Pétain was left with the impression that the BEF would break with the French left flank and retire to the Channel ports and not the other way round. Tim Travers writes that Pétain underlined the vital necessity of the two Allied armies remaining together; pointing out that the French Army had all of France to fall back on whereas the BEF would not be so well-situated if they retreated northwest to the Channel ports. In his diary Haig confirms that the conversation with Pétain at Dury touched on the consequences of a separation of the two armies:

> *'I at once asked Pétain if he meant to abandon my right flank. He nodded assent, and added, "It is the only thing possible, if the enemy compel the Allies to fall back still further" ... In my opinion, our army's existence in France depends on keeping the British and French Armies united.'*[26]

Here again there may well have been a cloud of misinterpretation. Pétain apparently meant that *if* the BEF did begin to fall back towards the Channel ports then it *may* be necessary for the French reserves at Montdidier to fall back towards Paris. Certainly the balance of evidence strongly suggests that Haig had considered the worst possible scenario which included the possibility of retiring to the Channel ports – in effect abandoning the Fifth Army – and it was this scenario that was uppermost in his mind at Dury.[27] Haig's diary tells us that he hurried back to Beaurepaire to instruct Lawrence to telegraph the Chief of the Imperial General Staff (CIGS) and Secretary of State for War to report the serious change in French strategy and ask them to come to France immediately. Again there is an aura of uncertainty as to whether the telegram was actually sent or indeed what version of events was relayed to England, but whatever interpretation we choose to place on the meeting between the two commanders-in-chief, it marked the beginning of the rise to prominence of Ferdinand Foch.[28]

Both the Secretary of State, Lord Alfred Milner, and the CIGS, Henry Wilson, were strong advocates of Foch as overall supreme allied commander, a notion that Haig was persuaded to support in the light of Pétain's announcement and the prospect of what he saw as a disintegration of the BEF and the Western Front. At the Doullens Conference on 26 March a Franco–British agreement gave Foch overall command of Allied forces along the entire Western Front. It had taken a crisis but political will had finally triumphed and the Alliance now had a supreme commander who 'was without the dual responsibility for a particular national army'.[29]

It was not going to be an easy task. Already von Winckler's XXV Reserve Corps had crossed the Somme at Béthencourt and Pargny and driven a wedge between Watts and Maxse, opening up a gap of over a mile and like it or not, Watts' XIX Corps was being prised away from the line of the Somme. The 8th Division had been forced to give up Eterpigny and Brie and was now falling back on Estrées along with the remaining XIX Corps divisions. Further south a very weak and threadbare 61 Brigade was covering another one-and-a-half miles of front and although Péronne had fallen, Watts was still clinging to the south bank of the Somme as it meandered its way west towards Cerisy. The news further north from Tudor's 9th Division was no less encouraging, the South African Brigade had fought to the last round at Marières Wood and Byng's VI and V Corps – which had only regained touch with the Fifth Army on 25 March – had been pushed back onto the desolate 1916 Somme battlefields. What worried Gough was that the right flank of the Third Army was now over four miles *behind* the left of the Fifth Army.

Gough had little choice but to counter-attack in an attempt to regain the line of the Somme about Pargny. The plan involved the British 8th and 24th Divisions attacking simultaneously at 8.00am on the morning of 25 March along with the French 122nd Division under General Félix Robillot. It was an unmitigated disaster. British troops who were in the process of forming up in their jumping off positions came under heavy fire from ground they presumed was held by the French – Robillot had neglected to inform Maxse and Heneker of his request for a postponement of the attack! Caught again by the strength of the German assault the French infantry were driven back, forcing Maxse to conform and Watts to order a similar retirement late that afternoon – it was this order that Charles Page received at Villers-Carbonel instructing him to withdraw his battalion.

25 March was also significant in that Sir William Congreve's VII Corps Headquarters and all troops north of the Somme were transferred to the Third Army and VII Corps troops south of the Somme were transferred to XIX Corps. Interestingly at 3.00am on 25 March the Fifth Army passed from the overall command of the British to General Marie-Émile Fayolle and the boundary between the French and British Armies was realigned along the Somme. This did not mean Gough was no longer in command but he was now under the orders of the French.

Gough's first encounter with Marshal Foch after the Doullens Conference was not a happy one. Accompanied by General Weygand, Foch arrived at Gough's headquarters at Dury in a bombastic frame of mind:

> *'He began at once by asking "why I was at my Headquarters and not with my troops in the fighting line?" He then said, "why could I not fight as we had fought in the first battle of Ypres in 1914?" "Why did the Army retire?" "What were my orders to the Army?" He waited for no replies to any of these questions, and he did not expect one, except possibly the last'.*[30]

Gough's indignation at this verbal assault on his command is well documented; he had not been invited or indeed informed of the Doullens Conference and found Foch 'excitable and evidently apt to jump to conclusions'. However, having been given overall command, Foch made it clear that there should be no further retreat and British and French troops must remain in touch to cover Amiens. It now remained to see whether he could stem the German advance and provide the unity of strength and purpose that was so desperately needed.

Chapter 12

The Rosières Pocket

The troops on our right are retiring at a great pace. Unless orders to the contrary are received Major Drew will at 5pm send back the right half company to battalion HQ in preparation of a defensive flank and the possibility of a withdrawal.

Message to brigade HQ signed by Captain Maurice Toye
from the 2nd Battalion Middlesex Regiment at Caix – 28 March 1918.

Von Hutier's Eighteenth Army was now intent upon advancing from Nesle, separating the French and British Armies and preventing French reinforcements from using the railhead at Mondidier. The British 20th Division had been ordered to conform to the retirement of the French towards Roye. An officer with 12/KRRC remembered his arrival at Roye and the news that welcomed him:

'*At 3.00am the battalion with the remainder of the 60th Brigade, arrived at Roye, where sentries had been posted to direct them to grassy fields south of the Carrepuis-Roye road … The whole brigade sat down to rest in the field, while in a gutted building adjoining it, by the light of electric torches, the Brigadier held a conference of battalion commanders. The French, of whom weak detachments had taken over the front held by the 20th Division, were retiring and the division had to march at once to the neighbourhood of Le Quesnel nine miles to the northwest of Roye. Of the officers and men who had left Offoy with the battalion on the 21st, 8 officers and about 160 men were left.*'[1]

Roye was not without incident. As one of the last men to leave with the RAMC detachment the Reverend Thomas Westerdale was witness to 'one of the most exciting incidents of this exciting week' although his method of escape from the town was one he would remember for some time:

'*As the last four patients were leaving the CCS – two walking and two being carried by RAMC men, the enemy arrived and set machine guns to work. At the psychological moment a French armoured car rumbled along from Montdidier and dashed straight into the enemy scattering him to the winds and enabling the four sick men to get away. On the Roye-Montdidier road we stopped all traffic and pushed the sick and wounded on everything that came along. The padre rode for some miles on a heavy gun behind a motor lorry. Except in a case of great urgency we do not advise anyone to attempt the experiment, it will shake even the tags off your bootlaces.*[2]

Ordered to act as flank guard for this retirement was Brigadier General James Cochrane's 61 Brigade – now reduced to little more than 400 rifles. The march from Roye to Le Quesnel began shortly before dawn and over the course of 26 March; 61 Brigade – organized into four under-strength companies under the command of Captain Kenneth Stoker – occupied in turn the villages of Parvillers, Damery and finally Le Quesnoy, establishing posts and pushing out patrols to the north to maintain touch with the 24th Division. All went well until just after 10.00am when Kenneth Stoker and the brigade major, Captain Edmund 'Eddie' Combe were preparing to retire from Le Quesnoy towards Bouchoir. As the company was being formed up a dispatch rider from brigade headquarters brought fresh orders: they were to hold the village until relieved by the 30th Division.

Exactly how many men were at Le Quesnoy that day is uncertain; Westerdale's diary tells us there were fifty men of the Somersets, King's and DCLI while the divisional historian writes that there were 100 men of 7/DCLI – a figure confirmed by the brigade war diary. What we do know is that the 30th Division carried out their relief of the 61 Brigade troops in Bouchoir at 1.00pm, the latter heading in the direction of Beaufort-en-Santerre thus leaving the Le Quesnoy garrison isolated and in the path of the German advance. Whether this was intentional or not is again unclear, but at 12.30pm German infantry were seen moving towards the village from the direction of Parvilliers. Armed with their rifles and two Lewis guns, Combe's men waited until the first company of enemy troops came into range at 500 yards and opened fire. Four drums of Lewis gun ammunition were enough to stop the advance in its tracks as the grey-clad infantrymen were cut down in the flat, open countryside between the two villages. But it was only a temporary respite, forty minutes later the Germans came on again – this time by sectional rushes and estimated to be at least two companies strong – accompanied by a trench mortar barrage which eventually put the two Lewis guns out of action. By 2.00pm, after close-quarters fighting, the eastern edge of the village was in enemy hands, a point in the battle that coincided with orders from Brigadier General Cochrane to retire via Bouchoir to Beaufort.

Cochrane's orders couldn't have come at a worst moment. German infantry were moving forward on both flanks and had machine guns trained on the three other exits from the village, rendering escape practically impossible during the hours of daylight. An hour later the enemy attacked in strength and this time pushed Combe's men back to the centre of the village where fighting raged around the church at the crossroads. With assistance from British aircraft the attack was halted but enemy infantry had succeeded in establishing themselves near the church and attempts to dislodge them were unsuccessful.

By 4.00pm the survivors were clinging to the western edge of the village where they put up a stubborn resistance for the next two-and-a-half-hours by which time the enemy were attacking from three sides. At 6.40pm Combe and Stoker decided it was now or never and gave the order to the nine remaining men to retire. As they abandoned their positions the war diary notes that a number of the enemy were dressed in British uniforms. There is no record of how many men reached the safety of Beaufort but that evening at roll call only 4 officers and 126 NCOs and men of the 61 Brigade Composite Battalion answered their names, two of those officers were Combe and Stoker.[3]

Thomas Westerdale recorded the event in his diary, his information would have been second or even third-hand and despite the fact that his account suffers from some exaggeration of the facts, it stands as a testament to a little-known rearguard action that has been buried away in time and almost forgotten:

'Still the heroic band fought on, until at last only two or three rifles were left to crack. At 5pm the two officers and nine men alone remained, and most of these were wounded. In the gathering dusk this little company of eleven got away to the main body of troops behind, having held up the German Army in this sector for four precious hours! Who knows but that those four precious hours saved Amiens and perhaps the British Army itself!'[4]

Recommended for the Victoria Cross for this gallant stand, Eddie Combe eventually received a bar to his Military Cross.

A little further north 9/East Surreys were a few miles southeast of Rosières defending a line from Hattencourt to Hallu, on their left were 8/Royal West Kents still under the command of Herbert Wenyon but now reduced to two companies. At 8.00am on 26 March the line came under fierce attack from IR 110. Second Lieutenant William Austin was in command of A Company of the East Surreys near Hallu Wood:

'The Germans made a bayonet attack and I was shot through the right shoulder and lungs by a point blank rifle bullet. When I saw it was useless to resist further at this point I ordered the company to retire to the communication trench 50 yards in the rear. This was done in a very orderly manner.'[5]

There is an underlying note of concern in Austin's account, and well there might have been as his right flank had been turned and the whole line was now in trouble. Commanding the battalion was Major Charles Clark, who – recognising the critical point in the encounter – sent a warning to Herbert Wenyon and the Royal West Kents that he may be forced to withdraw and deployed his signals officer, Lieutenant Maurice Blower and thirty men to secure the flank:

> *'This position I held for over 2 hours during which time I lost over half my party, this left me with 15 men, chiefly youthful signallers and runners ... After keeping up a steady fire under these desperate conditions where retreat was impossible our ammunition was finally exhausted. When we were ultimately taken we had an opportunity of seeing the damage we had done which was considerable.'*[6]

Blower's flank guard action was doomed from the start but the young subaltern would have known that when he received his orders. As for the battalion, having held off repeated assaults Clarke commenced his retirement only to find the Royal West Kents had already gone, leaving his remaining flank unguarded – a situation the enemy had already capitalized upon and cut off their retreat:

> *'The enemy began to surround us, so I decided to fight it out. We took up position in an old communication trench and used our rifles with great effect. [Lieutenant Stanley] Grant was doing excellent work until shot through the head and [Captain G W] Warre-Dymond behaved admirably. It was a fine fight and we held them up until the ammunition gave out: they then charged in and mopped up the remainder. They were infuriated with us. I'm afraid I presented a curious looking object at this time, my clothing had been riddled with shrapnel, my nose fractured and my face and clothing smothered in blood.'*[7]

Clark, a former regimental sergeant major with the 4th Battalion, was taken prisoner along with Warre-Dymond and the remaining officers and men of whom only about 60 were unwounded. The East Surreys had hung onto their positions doggedly and only gave ground reluctantly, a factor acknowledged by the IR 110 historian:

> *'The countless trenches aided the tough resistance of the English. Everywhere there were opportunities to deploy machine guns where they would be well hidden from the attackers. Thus the advancing companies soon came under strong machine gun fire from the old German trenches along and east of the Hallu-Hattencourt road which the Kaiser Grenadiers were able to overcome.'*[8]

The escape of the remaining units of 72 Brigade was almost entirely down to the sacrifice made by Clarke and his battalion. That evening at Warvillers 72 Brigade was reorganised as a composite battalion under the command of Herbert Wenyon. They were not alone; much of XIX Corps was now fighting under the unfamiliar banners of 'composite battalions'. Exhausted and dishevelled, the surviving men of Watts' corps had been hard-pressed by the enemy for nearly thirty miles since their retirement began on 21 March, now they were about to fight again in the Rosières pocket.

To the north the nine mile frontage held by XIX Corps between Rouvroy and the Somme was being held by six divisions, there were no reserves – apart from the mixed bag of units united under the name 'Carey's Force' which had been organized the previous day. Attacking Watts' line were eleven German divisions of which six were comparatively fresh to the fighting. The immediate danger to XIX Corps lay not to the south where we know a weak XVIII Corps – including the 61st Composite Battalion – was battling with the German thrust towards Mondidier, but to the north, where the right flank of the Third Army lay six miles further west than the Fifth Army flank. This rather premature retirement of Third Army units from Bray in effect abandoned the Somme crossings between Bray and Sailly-le-Sec forcing a retirement of XIX Corps south of the Somme to come into line. The crisis point came early on 27 March when two regiments of the 1st Königsberg Division were instructed to wheel 90 degrees left, cross the Somme at Chipilly and advance south to the Rosières line, more of which later.

Just to the south of the wide, looping meanders of the Somme units of the 16th Division were still struggling to remain intact as they were bundled from one action to the next trying desperately to stay one step ahead of the enemy. Since 21 March 1918 the division had lost 203 officers and 5,340 other ranks, its units being all but destroyed in the first two days of the offensive. Typical of these much depleted battalions were the 290 survivors from 2/Munster Fusiliers whom we last heard of in action at Malaisse Farm near Épehy. The battalion was now under the command of Major Hubert Tonson-Rye, a former regular officer with the regiment who had been serving on the 34th Divisional Staff. On 23 March the four companies of Munsters began to fall back from Tincourt Wood onto Doingt, fighting its way through the Hampshires' rearguard and crossing the Somme at Péronne just before the Bristol Bridge was destroyed.

On 26 March the battalion – now reorganized into one company of four platoons under Captain Cecil Chandler, north and east of Chuignolles – was under fire from units of the German 4th Guard Division which moved quickly to cut the battalion off by occupying the road to the west. Tonson-Rye moved with equal speed and under the cover of darkness managed to extricate his small force to join up with the remainder of 48 Brigade which was in position between St Germaine Woods and Méricourt. But their troubles were just beginning. Under repeated attack the next day the Munsters were again surrounded, the Germans having pushed on up the Proyart-Morcourt road and joined up with units north of the Somme:

'*The Munsters and the two Irish detachments* [100 men from the Dublin Fusiliers and South Irish Horse] *were left like a rock surrounded by the incoming tide. And rocklike was their determination. A quiet consultation was held between the three commanding officers, and after another ineffectual effort had been made to get into touch on the right flank, it was decided to withdraw and fight a way through.*'[9]

The way through involved an attempt to cross to the north bank which, at the time, was thought to be still in British hands. Leaving Corporal Reginald Padfield with a Lewis gun in the trenches with orders to fire occasionally until 10.00pm the party made their way north. Finding the Eclusier bridge occupied the column retraced its steps following the canal towpath along the south bank until it reached the bridge at Chipilly where, once again, they found the bridge was guarded and to make matters worse, it had been destroyed. Undeterred they rushed the bridge:

'*The quiet night march became an inferno. Everyone rushed forward shouting, firing, cursing … On rushed the column to the bridge, which was found to be broken, the girders cut and lying at the foot of the pier on the far side of the river. The Irish charged down, and rapidly became jammed at the bottom. The more that arrived the tighter the crush. Gradually a few men were hoisted up, then more; the enemy was smashed or swept aside … the bridge was secured and the column passed over.*'[10]

From Chipilly they avoided the canal path and the minor road north of the river by striking west through the boggy marshlands that ran between the two waterways. Just before they reached the canal bridge at Sailly-Laurette they encountered a German patrol. An attempt to bluff their way past resulted in an exchange of shots and a Dublin Fusilier was shot dead. Surrounded by irate Irishmen the patrol was disposed of before the party crossed over the canal and launched themselves southwest across country, navigating by the stars and expecting at every turn to be discovered by German patrols. At 3.30am on 28 March, near the Bois de Hamel, they were challenged by a sentry, the familiar cockney tones announcing they had indeed reached the British lines. The Munsters had travelled over seventy-five miles in forty-eight hours, eight of which had been through German-held territory at night, an episode which, despite the casualties – 5 officers and 100 other ranks – must be regarded as one of the most remarkable achievements of the 1918 retreat and one that underlined the crucial role of the regimental officer. As in the retreat of 1914 where battalions were often thrown back on their own resources, the Munsters had once again demonstrated their resolve and determination in the face of overwhelming odds.

At the same time as the Munsters were contemplating their future after finding themselves surrounded, the 11/Hampshires and the remaining units of the brigade – now under attack from their left and right flanks – were falling back on Morcourt and taking up a new position on the high ground to the south of the village. During this rather hasty and confused withdrawal Major Thomas Thyne and the men of D Company were surrounded and either killed or captured, a fate that also overtook Major Cecil Hazard who was commanding a mixed group belonging to various units of 49 Brigade:

> 'This is the last that was heard of him and it cannot be ascertained what his ultimate fate was. Whilst the battalion was withdrawing to new positions it was found that large bodies of the enemy had crossed the River Somme apparently at Cérisy completely outflanking the withdrawal of the division, and our left flank came under heavy shell and machine gun fire.'[11]

Hazard had in fact been taken prisoner along with Thomas Thyne but it was some time before the battalion heard of their capture. Fearing the worst, Lieutenant Colonel Crockett withdrew the battalion to Lamotte where it joined forces with Major Perceval Whittall and his sappers to hold up the German 3rd Grenadier Regiment thus allowing the brigade to withdraw to Le Hamel which was where the Munsters finally rejoined in the early hours of 28 March.

While the Munsters had been making good their escape along the line of the River Somme the strategic picture further south was changing quickly. The 8th Division – now with its headquarters at Harbonnières – was able to report that it was in touch with the 24th Division on its right and the 50th Division on its left and was withdrawing towards Rosières. Although the British Tommy might well have disagreed, after a week of impressive advances the first signs that the German offensive was slowing down began to surface. Contrary to expectation Ludendorff had not yet achieved his breakthrough and had certainly not crushed the resolve of the British to fight on. As tired and exhausted as he may have been, the British soldier was rapidly adjusting to the demands of open warfare and little by little was beginning to hold his adversary. Not that the soldiers of 6/Northumberland Fusiliers would have noticed as much as they fell back on Foucaucourt to be greeted by huts and stores on fire – albeit with the reassuring presence of a military policeman:

> 'If the place could not be held at any rate nothing of value was to be permitted to fall into the hands of the enemy. At Foucaucourt crossroads, two runners had been left with a message for all officers who had not yet passed through. Later in the day the writer learned that these runners had waited at the crossroads with the military policeman on duty until the Germans were entering the village a couple of hundred yards away. The policemen then ordered the runners to leave. When they came away the policeman remained. He was standing at his post as cool as a cucumber and calm as the constable who stands at the foot of Northumberland Street. Shells

were bursting round him and the approaching enemy were but a stone's throw from him. Apparently he had no orders to quit his post and he stood fast.'[12]

Early on 27 March the attacks resumed and while the 8th Division held its sector of the line, further north at Proyart there was a breakthrough where the line was thinly defended. At 11.00am 23 Brigade received an urgent request for their counter-attack battalion to retake Proyart and an hour later 2/Devons were on the move, reaching Harbonnières at 1.00pm. Harbonnières was in almost total confusion when Major Arthur Cope arrived with his battalion; guns, limbers and men were moving back in disorder and there was little anyone could tell Cope as to the whereabouts of the 39th Division which was holding the line to the north. Although Proyart is not visible from Harbonnières, the urgency of the situation demanded that Cope begin his attack without any prior reconnaissance. Supporting him were three companies of the 22nd Durham Light Infantry – the divisional pioneers – and a composite battalion of RE with other troops from the 50th Division:

'The advance was carried out splendidly, the men moving as if on parade. As they topped the rise North east of Harbonnières they came under machine gun fire and lost heavily, but they forged ahead though quite without artillery support ... They encountered thick belts of wire but somehow found gaps, pushed through and closed with the Germans who were occupying old trenches and buildings just south of the Amiens-Péronne road.'[13]

Arthur Cope was a regular officer who had been commissioned into the Devons in September 1911, at the age of 26 he was more than thirty years younger than Lieutenant Colonel Cecil Morgan who commanded 22/DLI. By any standards Morgan was an elderly commanding officer and may well have been one of the oldest battalion commanders on the Western Front. Despite his advancing years, however, he wore the ribbon of the DSO – won in Sierra Leone in 1899 – and was described as an able and popular commanding officer. Morgan was severely wounded in action two days later on 29 March and it is likely that he died without having received the tragic news that his son, 19-year-old Second Lieutenant Basil Morgan, serving with 1/Hampshires, had been killed the previous day near Arras.[14]

In Rosières itself the 8th Division infantry units were now under the command of Brigadier General Clifford Coffin. Coffin provided a much-needed rallying point for the scattered units of the division that until now had been dogged by poor and ineffectual communication and a lack of overall command and control. If the German advance was to be slowed down it was imperative that all three infantry brigades operated together; circumstances sharpened by instructions received from the French Generalissimo, Ferdinand Foch, ordering the Rosières line to be held at all costs. In passing on Foch's orders Watts undoubtedly knew they would be greeted with a degree of soldierly disdain, after all, how many times had the British soldier been told to hold on at all costs during the past week? Yet this time there was a greater urgency in the instruction, an urgency intensified by the gap in the line along the Somme River which had laid open the Fifth Army's left flank to attack.

Ordering exhausted units to hold the line at all costs was all very well but the intense battlefield fatigue and poor communications that handicapped many of the retreating British units had the potential to turn stratagem into disaster. Such was the case in the centre of the line between Rosières and Vauvillers. What has been termed as a misunderstanding on the part of 5/Northumberland Fusiliers resulted in a premature withdrawal towards Harbonnières. Caught up in this movement were 6/Northumberland Fusiliers and 5/DLI who, on seeing their neighbours falling back to the rear, issued orders for their own companies to conform to the 5/Northumberland Fusiliers line. The Germans lost little time in pushing through the gap and taking Vauvillers. By 3.00pm long lines of German infantry were sweeping across the open fields towards Harbonnières with the intention of rolling up the British line. It looked very much as if the Fifth Army was about to fall back in disarray yet again.

Salvation came in the form of a British general on a rather ungainly artillery horse – but that was not how the last of the British reserves viewed it as they were pushed into the gap – what they saw, and responded to magnificently, was a red-tabbed general gallantly leading them into battle. A former Northumberland Fusilier himself, Brigadier General Edward Riddell was no stranger to the front line and already had a reputation for his almost complete disregard of danger. In June 1916 he had been appointed as commanding officer of 1/1 Cambridgeshire Regiment, four months later after the fighting around the Schwaben Redoubt north of Thiepval on the Somme he had been awarded the DSO to which he had added a bar in July 1917. Three months later he had been appointed to command 149 Brigade.

As the retiring troops were stopped and posted along the light railway line east of Harbonnières, Riddell sent out instructions to 7/DLI to counter-attack towards Framerville and led the remainder out towards the German line. From their jumping off point on the railway line 5/DLI took up their place in the line:

'*There was no panic, and on receipt of orders we quietly took up our positions … After a while, orders from the Brigadier were passed along from officer to officer instructing us and the Northumberland Fusiliers to advance in line with the counter-attack on our left, and recapture the position we had held during the night. We accordingly pushed on, platoon by platoon and section by section, in quite the old field-day style, the men firing freely at the Germans, who could now be seen advancing towards us five or six hundred yards away. We came under machine gun fire, and the bullets were kicking up the dust all along our line. We had many casualties, and as one looked back over the level ground behind, one could see the motionless forms of many men who had fought their last fight, while here and there were wounded men trying to make their way to the rear. After a while it became very exciting as we could see the enemy halt and turn back through the trees near Vauvillers. Our men gave a sort of grunt and advanced ten times as quickly as before.'[15]*

Also on the railway line was Lieutenant Eric Jacobs-Larkcom who remembered being deployed at midday:

'We were told to hold the railway northeast of Rosières. We held the railway but the Boche was there in multitudes and attacked with great persistence. We held him back and got a machine gun up on the factory roof but had many casualties. Some of the other companies went over in a counter attack, my section sergeant, Sergeant Cowan, got killed. A lot of men were laid out that day by 5.9s.'[16]

Although Vauvillers was recaptured it was lost again when the Germans counter-attacked later in the day and the British were forced back onto the light railway line again. But crucially the line had been held and the enemy advance checked. It had not been without cost. The two battalions of Durham Light Infantry lost some forty other ranks killed on 27 March but more seriously for 5/DLI the loss of Major Raimes and two other officers wounded was a significant blow. Raimes had seen them through some of the bitterest fighting and held the battalion together, now he was gone. The survivors were collected together by Second Lieutenant Frederick Williams and brought out of action to join A and D Companies which had remained on the railway line.

The line may have held – thanks largely to the efforts of the 8th Division – but the Rosières position had now taken on the shape of a pronounced salient – a pocket of resistance that had seen each of its two flanks pushed back. To the south the front had been driven back alarmingly and Montdidier with its rail and road network had fallen to the enemy, while to the north there was an even greater danger about to be unleashed by the German Second Army.

Von der Marwitz's advance north of the Somme on the morning of 27 March had been blocked by the 1st Cavalry Division together with a combination of artillery and air attack. In what could have been the decisive move of the whole battle, two 1st (Königsberg) Division infantry regiments from von Gontard's XIV Corps were ordered to cross the Somme at Chipilly and Cerisy and advance south to attack the Fifth Army around Rosières in the rear. While IR 43 forced its way across the river and overcame the token British opposition, the German 3rd Grenadier Regiment (GR 3) captured the villages of Lamotte and Warfusée. Karl Goes described the movement of German troops over the Somme:

'*Two regiments – IR 43 and* [Grenadier Regiment] *3 – are given command to carry out a daring thrust beyond the Somme and attack the enemy's left flank. Advance to the left! Thrust via Chipilly-Cerisy toward Hamel! … The dagger thrust is aimed right into the back of its withstanding foe. Oberstleutnant Dorndorf's IR 43 troops are in the vanguard. Cleverly arranged he has led them behind the frontline to Chipilly. Rifle fire opens up from the other bank of the Somme. East-Prussian fists bring on wood and planks, building footbridges, while the 6th battery of the Königsberger – Field Artillery Regiment 16 – being circled by English planes, smashes the MG positions beyond. Over wavering planks the Musketiere jump over, infiltrating Cerisy, mopping it up. The flat Hill 66 is taken. Leutnant der Reserve Böhm and his 3rd Kompanie are in full pursuit of the English for Hamel, but receive heavy fire. Running out of ammunition he is forced to go back a little. This is like stirring up a hornet's nest, because the English fight for his supply routes from Proyart further back. From all sides it cracks and bangs, and a hail of bombs and shells falls from above.*'[17]

XIX Corps was now in an extremely dangerous position, the German advance had gained the road to Villers-Bretonneux – the modern day N29 – the line to north of which had been driven back, away from the Somme. German forces were now directly behind the Rosières line and less than ten miles from Amiens and the only British troops standing between the Germans and their seizure of Amiens were a miscellaneous collection of men under Major General Carey, in position along a line running north from Demuin to the Somme itself. Hamstrung by Foch's orders to stand fast, the situation demanded urgent action if the three divisions in the Rosières pocket were not to be isolated and cut off completely. Shortly after midnight on 27 March their extreme plight was communicated first to Watts and then to Gough whom, it is said, woke Foch and obtained permission to withdraw some time after 3.30am.

It was almost too late and only prompt action by the three divisional commanders enabled the beleaguered troops to swing back and meet the threat from the north. For the 50th Division this meant taking up a line from Caix to Guillaucourt where, almost before it had time to deploy, found itself under attack all along its line. Guillaucourt soon fell as the German 3rd Grenadiers advanced towards the high ground overlooking Caix and the Luce valley. For a second time in twenty-four hours the irrepressible Brigadier General Edward Riddell – still in possession of his artillery horse – seized the initiative:

'*I galloped out of Caix along the Guillaucourt road. As we breasted the hill, we saw our men coming back along the western side of the valley to our right, and over the crest near the little wood south of Guillaucourt. They were running all doubled up as men do who are under machine gun fire. The bullets flicked up little spurts of dust as we galloped across the plough. Near the crest of the hill we managed to stop some of the men, but only for a moment as the Boche machine guns had got into the wood southeast of Guillaucourt and raked us in enfilade. Our machine gunners stood fast in the little wood on the crest left of us, their guns rattling in those bursts so comforting to the infantryman. A glance towards Guillaucourt showed me the Boche infantry eight hundred yards away. He was coming our way, and would soon reach the crest overlooking Caix through which troops of all sorts were now passing.*

Below me, to the south, under the shelter of one of those remarkable steep-sided banks which abound in this country, were the 22nd Entrenching Battalion [DLI] calmly eating their dinner, and, as is the custom of the British soldier during meal times, quite oblivious of what was happening around them. I galloped to them shouting 'Fall in!' Fortunately the men were extended in a long line at the bottom of the bank with the officers in a group. I shouted the order to fall in in two ranks, and told them it was a race for the crest of the hill. As they climbed up the steep sides of the bank, away behind me, near the Harbonnières road, I heard the sound of a hunting horn. It was General Jackson, the divisional commander, blowing his 'pack' towards him. 'Forrard away', and up the hill and over the crest went the Entrenching Battalion and back to Guillaucourt went the Boches.'[18]

Major General Henry Jackson was by this time in command of the 50th Division having relieved Brigadier General Arthur Stockley of his temporary command. His timely arrival along with Edward Riddell on his horse had, for the time being, kept Caix in British hands.

But it was a different story at Lamotte where an attempted counter-attack by 184 Brigade failed miserably in the face of enemy machine-gun fire. Still fighting with the brigade were the 2/4 Ox and Bucks whom we last met at the Enghien Redoubt on 21 March. Lieutenant Colonel Harry Wetherall had been in temporary command of the brigade until a few days previously when he was badly wounded in the neck by a piece of shrapnel and the battalion was now commanded by Major Jack Bennett. On 28 March, 184 Brigade, having been held in reserve at Mezières, was on the move to Villers-Bretonneux when they were diverted to Marcelcave:

'At Villers-Bretonneux Bennett received orders from a staff officer to go to Marcelçave, where the 61st Division was being concentrated for a counter-attack at dawn against the village of Lamotte. In the darkness the route was missed and the convoy drove straight into our front line. Marcelçave was reached eventually, but so late that a dawn attack was impossible. At 10am on March 28 the forlorn enterprise, in which the 183rd Brigade, the Gloucesters, and the Berks shared, was launched from the station yard. The troops were footsore, sleepless, and unfed. They were mostly men from regimental employ – pioneers, clerks, storemen – to send whom forward across strange country to drive the enemy from the village he had seized on the important Amiens-St Quentin road was a mockery. Such efforts at counter-

attack resulted in more and more ground being lost. Still, the men staggered forward bravely, to come almost at once under fierce enfilade machine-gun fire. The losses were heavy. Craddock, a young officer now serving under Bennett, moved about among the men, encouraging them by his example of coolness and gallantry. When 350 yards short of Lamotte the advance was driven to take cover. It was useless to press on; in fact, already there was real danger of being surrounded. Bennett, whose leadership throughout was excellent, with difficulty extricated his men by doubling them in twos across the open. Towards evening those that got back were placed in trenches outside Marcelçave.'[19]

While the Ox and Bucks failed to get into the village, others clearly did and those who were not killed were taken prisoner by the infantry of GR 3 who now occupied the village:

'Leutnant der Reserve Röhnisch lowers his binoculars. His 11th Kompanie is ready to provide a hearty welcome. Lamotte is deserted in a moment, but behind every hedge and bush sharpshooters and machine guns are lying in ambush. The English march into the village, totally clueless – and all of a sudden Königsberger Füsiliere stand in front and around them and [take them] prisoners ... An English column gets caught at the eastern entrance of Lamotte, its drivers beat the horses to escape from ... but suddenly it cracks from everywhere: death or captivity is the slogan of the moment!'[20]

However, while the Lamotte attack may have been a disaster, the 20th Division counter-attack on Mezières later that afternoon was a little more successful. An officer with 12/KRRC described his battalion's part in the assault:

'At 2pm orders were received from 60th Brigade that the Rifle Brigade and ourselves should counter-attack Mezières. As soon as the orders could be given, the three leading companies advanced in co-operation with the battalion on our left, while the right was secured by the French on the high ground south of the village. At the crossroads a number of prisoners with two heavy trench mortars, several machine guns, and two teams of horses with limbers were taken; at the crossroads 400 yards farther east we were held up, and after several attempts could not pass this point. D Company, which had been in reserve, now advanced round the southern edge of the village to a quarry, and began to work forward so as to take the eastern crossroads from the south. In the meantime, however, the enemy was continuing to advance north of us, and was beginning to occupy the western side of the woods northwest of Mezières, and the brigade was forced to retire from the left. We withdrew again across the valley, and through Villers-aux-Erables under considerable machine gun fire, leaving behind the machine guns and mortars which we had put out of action.'[21]

The XIX Corps withdrawal from the Rosières pocket had been a confused, costly and rather messy daylight retreat in which the commanding general of 118 Brigade was captured. Brigadier General Edward Bellingham and his brigade major were taken prisoner whilst supervising the right flank and rearguard as 118 Brigade retired southeast of Villers-Bretonneux. Being taken prisoner was a fate that Second Lieutenant Frank Warren was contemplating as he and his platoon of 17/KRRC became increasingly convinced that they were surrounded. It was an impression that quicky changed after the RFC dropped a message with orders to retire towards Ignaucourt. Now it became a case of every man for himself as groups of men left the cover of their trench to expose themselves to enemy machine-gun fire:

> *'Immediately a thin stream of men begin to bolt from the trench, according to orders, running the gauntlet of machine gun fire from two quarters – the road to the southeast and the ridge to the east. When my men, who have waited their turn, are clear I am cornered by an officer of the Gloucester Pioneers, who tells me to wait to give covering fire for the withdrawal of his men! Having had definite orders from my own company commander, I remind him that all my men have gone, and prepare for my quick dash to cover. I have been watching the flick of machine gun bullets in the dusty ground and have noted where the stream of fugitives is thickest. Then I make my bolt, keeping to the edge of the stream of men and running zig-zag.'[22]*

By midday the five 'divisions' of XIX Corps were established on a line parallel to the River Luce, they had escaped the net which was closing around the Rosières pocket by the skin of their teeth, aided no doubt by the German failure to exploit the Königsberg Division's success. Fortunately for the British, the German XIV Corps were unaware of the Cerisy success and did not capitalize on a move that – for a while – had threatened the whole of the British line south of the Somme with encirclement. Now the retirement was about to focus on the River Avre and Moreuil Wood.

Chapter 13

Moreuil and Rifle Wood

When we reached the village, there were rifle shots close at hand; as we rode down the street, bullets whizzed over us or struck with a clap on the walls of the houses; but there was no one to be seen, no inhabitants, no soldiers, on either side.

Herbert Asquith crossing the River Avre at La Neuville

Hubert Gough was adamant that Foch's orders to XIX Corps to hold the Rosières line nearly brought about its destruction. The question of retirement, felt Gough, should have been the responsibility of the British GHQ. 'Haig was still responsible for the security of British troops', he wrote, 'and I cannot say that I approved of the Fifth Army being handed over body and soul, to the French even if Foch was Generalissimo.'[1] Despite having a personal axe to grind, there were many senior officers who shared Gough's feelings on the Rosières retirement:

'*If the order to retire could have been issued in time to enable the divisions to withdraw the previous night, they could have retired from their dangerous positions and taken up a new line before daybreak on the 28th with little loss, and with much better prospects of holding it. Foch knew, or ought to have known, that my troops were extremely exhausted after a week of desperate fighting, that their left flank was very exposed to attack for five miles, and that no reliefs were coming up for several days yet ... That Foch's hasty and ill-considered order did not lead to a disaster was only due to the gallantry of the exhausted fragments of the British divisions and the steady tactical leadership of their officers.*'[2]

28 March 1918 was not only Hubert Gough's last day in command of the Fifth Army but also marked the first day of the German 'Mars' attack along thirty-three miles of the Third Army Front from the Somme River to Arleux, north of Arras. Byng's Army faced an offensive spearheaded by nine fresh divisions and, as with the larger 21 March offensive, the attack was opened with a bombardment of gas and high explosive. But on this occasion there was one essential difference – by

5.00pm the offensive had ground to a devastating halt in the face of a stubborn and effective British defence. 'Mars' had been a complete and very costly failure and in cancelling the attack that evening, Ludendorff – despite the initial success of the 'Georgette' Offensive in Flanders ten days later – effectively signed away any further German pretensions of overall victory on the Western Front. It was the day Germany lost the war.

The disaster that overshadowed the 'Mars' offensive was indicative of the overall failure of the March offensive. Ludendorff's plan to turn the flank of the British and move swiftly on the Channel ports had almost been negated by his change of strategy to reinforce the Eighteenth Army in the south where the gains were of little consequence. But despite the initial – and yes, impressive – territorial gains, German assault troops had sustained enormous losses and senior commanders witnessed not only a corresponding plunge in battlefield morale but a growing Allied recovery in the field as German lines of supply to their forward troops came under an intolerable strain:

> *'The Große Schlacht* [Great Battle] *is turning into a disaster for the attacker. The entire front is trembling from an overwhelming cannonade, the English and French gunners load their guns ceaselessly from huge stacks of ammunition, while the Germans have to count every shell. The German infantry is exhausted, their battalions counting no more than regular companies.'*[3]

The responsibility for maintaining the momentum of the German advance fell on two of the oldest forms of transport available – manpower and the long-suffering horse. The distinct lack of motorized transport – capable of transporting troops en masse and the all important supplies of ammunition – were largely absent from a battlefield where the pace of advance was dependent on the stamina of the infantry and the horse. To make matters worse a large percentage of motorized lorries were shod only with iron-bound wheels which added to the destruction of road surfaces between railheads and forward positions. Moreover, as the advancing German troops overran British supply depots, the gradual realization that their own resources were, by comparison, of poor quality, compounded a problem that would eventually see the euphoria of success being replaced by despondency as the promised breakthrough ground slowly to a halt.

But for the time being we must leave aside the waning morale of the German soldier on the battlefield and Ludendorff's strategic worries and return to the Fifth Army where Gough was about to be replaced by General Sir Henry Rawlinson. Gough's own account of his sacking in his 1931 account reveals little of the intense personal hurt and betrayal he felt at the time, and indeed continued to feel long after the event. However, on the day of his dismissal he wrote a private letter to Colonel Clive Wigram which hinted at the stinging rebuke he felt his dismissal to be:

'You can imagine my feelings at being removed from my command and handing it over to Rawly. I cannot as yet find out much as to the causes or persons responsible for removing me, but I have been told it was political and that it was due to a letter from Derby ordering it.'[4]

He was right. In spite of initial attempts by Douglas Haig to save his protégé from the inevitable, a telegram from Lord Derby, the Secretary of State for War, sealed the issue and Gough became the government's scapegoat for what was seen as the Fifth Army disaster.

We are told that the first Gough knew of his impending fate was at 5.00pm on 27 March when Major General Harold Ruggles-Brise, Haig's Military Secretary, arrived at Gough's Dury Headquarters with the news that he was to be replaced by Henry Rawlinson. It is hard to believe that the Fifth Army commander had no idea of the political storm that was brewing around his command, particularly as he had already been dealt with severely by Foch and had been excluded from the Doullens Conference. According to Brigadier General Henry Sandilands – commanding 104 Brigade – who had just returned from leave, Gough's removal was already on the cards by the morning of 26 March – before the Doullens Conference was convened that afternoon. Sandilands was outside Fifth Army Headquarters when:

'a large limousine drove up, out of which, to my astonishment, stepped Sir Henry Wilson, followed by Lord Milner in an overcoat and a bowler. Sir Henry Wilson, who knew me personally, asked me if it was safe to drive through Amiens and I told him as far as I knew it was perfectly safe, as I had not heard the slightest sound of shelling or bombing the whole morning. I naturally assumed that he was looking for Fifth Army Headquarters and told him that General Gough was inside the villa, at the gate of which we were standing. He replied, "Oh he is here is he? Well good morning". Both he and Lord Milner got back into their car and drove off. I thought at the time "that's the end of Gough".'[5]

At 4.30pm on 28 March 1918 Rawlinson arrived to take over command. Gough wrote of the occasion, 'I told him all I could of our situation, and as I felt I should only be an embarrassment to him in exercising his new command, I left Dury, not at all sure where I was to get a bed or dinner that night.' Paul Maze who had worked so closely with Gough since 1914 wrote of his sadness as he witnessed the 'lorries of the Fourth Army marked with a boar which were unloading, while the lorries of the Fifth Army marked with a fox were loading up. I needed no further evidence.' Maze recounted his final conversation with Gough in the small garden of his former headquarters:

*'He at once informed me that he had ceased to be in command of the Fifth Army …
and quite simply he told me of Marshal Foch's visit, how abrupt and short he had*

been to him and the depreciatory terms [with which] *he had referred to the conduct of the Fifth Army. During the moments we were together in the garden he neither made a complaint nor passed an opinion. His thoughts dwelt upon the problem the Fifth Army was still facing.'*[6]

Rawlinson had inherited five exhausted infantry divisions and one of cavalry, prompting a communiqué to Foch expressing his concern that unless reinforcements arrived within the next 48 hours, Amiens would fall. His divisional commanders could only muster a tenth of their original strength, some battalions had been almost completely annihilated while others were now part of composite battalions composed of a mixed body of men from all arms – in short anyone who could shoulder a rifle. It was hardly an auspicious start to a new command.

Rawlinson's diary entry for 30 March recorded one of the most significant cavalry actions to be fought on the Western Front involving the British 2nd Cavalry Division, which at the time included the Canadian Cavalry Brigade. The 2nd Cavalry Division had only arrived in the Avre valley on 29 March after a long march from Mondidier. Major General Thomas 'Tommy' Pitman, now in command of the division, established his headquarters at Boves, southeast of Amiens:

'This quiet little village, through which we had passed on the march only a few months previously, was now a mass of seething transport and all the paraphernalia which congests traffic in the area behind a battle. There were at least three other divisional headquarters in the same street, and the French, who had commenced to arrive, had taken over the château, which had formally been the headquarters of a corps school. It was nearly midnight before the last units of the Division reached their destinations.'[7]

But there was very little rest to be had. Shortly after 7.00am on 30 March, orders from XIX Corps were received by Pitman to cross the Avre and move southeast across the River Luce and clear the enemy out of Moreuil Wood on the right flank of the 20th Division. British infantry were holding a line running from Moreuil along the southern edge of Moreuil Wood to Demuin.

Commanding the Canadian Cavalry Brigade was Brigadier General John 'Jack' Seely, a larger-than-life character who counted Winston Churchill amongst his personal friends and was the only British cabinet member to serve for practically the whole period of the war on active service. Seely had already been awarded the DSO in 1900 for his services with the Imperial Yeomanry in the Boer War and would be mentioned again in despatches for the attack on Moreuil Wood. In his memoirs he describes his conversation with Tommy Pitman:

'[Pitman] told me that the German advance continued, and that the situation was grave in the extreme; we must do what we could to delay the continued onslaught;

the German advanced guard had already captured the Moreuil Ridge, and were pouring troops into the Bois de Moreuil on the Amiens side of the ridge. Villers-Bretonneux, on the ridge further north, was still held by us, but was being heavily attacked. I remember his final words, 'Go to the support of the infantry just beyond Castel, this side of the Moreuil ridge. Don't get too heavily involved – you will be needed later.' Pitman was a cool hand if ever there was one. From the way he spoke I knew things were pretty desperate.[8]

Whether the conversation was exactly as described by Seely – a man according to George Paget prone to an embellishment of the facts – is debatable, but there was no doubt that the situation at Moreuil Wood – a mere twelve miles southeast of Amiens – was of vital tactical importance to the Germans.

The pear-shaped wood stood on the southern end of the ridge and was typical of many French wooded areas – thickly planted with a good deal of undergrowth, although today the battlefield visitor will find the wood covers less than half its original acreage. In 1918 it had a northern face, a south western face running parallel to the Avre River, and a south eastern face running along the Moreuil – Demuin road. Each was approximately a mile-and-a-half in length. There was a small protrusion of woodland at the north western corner – the modern day Bois de la Corne. Significantly, the ridge upon which it stood was the point at which the French and British sectors came together and commanded the river crossings of the Avre and Luce. If this high ground was captured by the Germans the British line along the Luce would be compromised and the future of Amiens put very much in doubt. It was a strategic point that had not escaped the attention of the enemy. German infantry had been gradually moving forward since 4.30am on 29 March and under cover of the early morning mist had been pushing their units into Moreuil Wood from the southeast.

As 3 Cavalry Brigade and the Canadians were closest to the wood, Pitman ordered Brigadier General John Bell Smyth commanding 3 Cavalry Brigade to cross the Avre with Seely's Canadians and seize the ground north of Moreuil Wood and then 'restore the situation up to the line of the Moreuil-Demuin road'. The situation was deemed to be so serious that no further orders were given, once in the field the two cavalry commanders were to act upon their own initiative and support each other. Seely arrived first:

'I asked the French general what the position was. He said that strong detachments were already on the outskirts of Moreuil, some two miles to our right; that his flank was unprotected and that he had already sent orders to his troops to fall back ... I knew that moment to be the supreme moment of my life.[9]

Supreme moment or not, Seely had persuaded General Diebold – who spoke gloomily of the allies' prospects – to hold his positions and established his cavalry

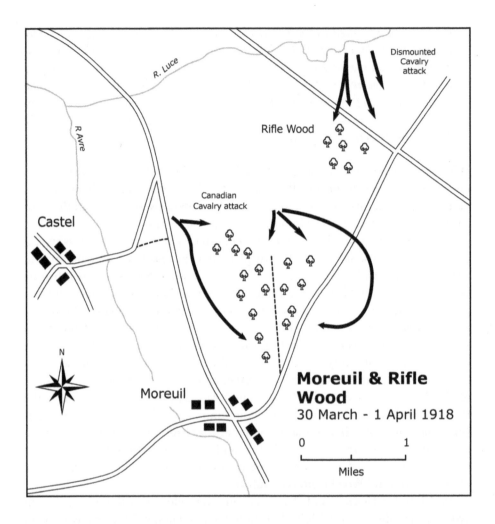

Moreuil & Rifle Wood
30 March - 1 April 1918

headquarters on the northern edge of the smaller wood which had not then been entered by German infantry. Seely's orders were for Captain Albert Nordheimer's A Squadron of the Royal Canadian Dragoons to clear the northwest corner of the wood and attempt to link up with the French at Moreuil village. According to Major Charles Connolly – Seely's brigade major – Nordheimer's squadron came under heavy enemy fire:

> '[They] *succeeded in getting into the wood and engaging the enemy in hand-to-hand combat. Many of the enemy were killed, all refusing to surrender, but a large party, estimated at about 300, retired from the wood south of the point where the squadron had entered it.*'[10]

Entrenched in the wood at this point was a company of II/IR 101, many of whom were taking part in their first serious action of the offensive. Taken almost completely by surprise by this unexpected cavalry intervention they were unable to prevent the Canadians penetrating their defences. The second squadron, led by Captain 'Newky' Newcomen entered the wood about halfway down its southwest side with the objective of gaining touch with Major Reginald Timmis' squadron which had been ordered to gallop around the north eastern corner towards Moreuil village. At the northeast corner of the wood, Major Timmis and B Squadron suffered a number of casualties from heavy fire and were forced to wheel to the left. They too then entered the wood. According to Reginald Timmis, B Squadron was very much under-strength, although his estimate of the number of machine guns operating against him is probably incorrect:

> '*My own squadron.... instead of being 160 strong was about 98.... The Boche had here over 40 machine guns, the lighter ones of which were up the trees. After we had gone past all these machine guns I turned around in the saddle and saw only two men out of 90 down. After we got into the wood we had to practically walk because it was very thick and many of our horses were shot and killed.*'[11]

Meanwhile Lord Strathcona's Horse were now ordered to send one squadron round the north-east corner of the wood to support Nordheimer's squadron of dragoons while the remaining two squadrons of the regiment were to follow up the main attack south-eastwards through the wood. Seely tells us that as he saw the dragoons and Lord Strathcona's Horse approach him he galloped up to Lieutenant Gordon Flowerdew who was in command of C Squadron:

> '*As we rode together I told him that his was the most adventurous task of all, but that I was confident that he would succeed. With his gentle smile he turned to me and said: 'I know sir. I know it is a splendid moment. I will try not to fail you.*'[12]

Flowerdew's task was to make a mounted attack in support of Nordheimer's squadron, disperse the German reinforcements entering the wood from the south and kill or capture those attempting to leave the wood by its eastern edge. As his men began their charge up to the edge of the wood the horsemen rose out of a dip in the ground and took the full force of the enemy's fire:

> '*Just as they reached the high ground, they found a large group of the Germans, perhaps 300 strong, retiring from the wood. They were from the 101st Grenadier Battalion that were withdrawing and other troops that were approaching. There was one howitzer and several heavy machine guns with them. In a split second, Flowerdew gave the order: 'It's a charge boys, it's a charge!' The trumpeter, Reg Longley, riding behind Flowerdew raised his trumpet to blow the call, it never*

sounded. Longley was the first casualty of the charge. In the excitement, many of the horses simply bolted. Private Dale of 4th Troop, riding behind Longley, had to jump over the trumpeter. He recalled that everything seemed unreal, 'the shouting of men, the moans of the wounded, the pitiful crying of the wounded and dying horses'. It was difficult to recall what happened and when. C Squadron approached the Germans with sabres raised; sabres against rifles and machine guns. They rode into two lines of Germans. Steel cut into flesh; bayonets and bullets answered. Casualties were high on both sides. Once the two lines were passed, the surviving horsemen turned back toward the wood. There, through the smoke and enemy was Harvey and his men. The survivors fought furiously to get back to them. Sergeant Tom MacKay, MM, the Troop Sergeant of 1st Troop was acting troop leader since Lieutenant Harrower was on patrol. The flesh was practically stripped between the knees and thighs of both his legs. The doctors later counted some 59 wounds in one leg alone. Sergeant Wooster also of 1st Troop, survived charging through both lines of Germans but at the second line forgot his sabre drill, and tried to club a German soldier to death. After bypassing another group of Germans, he moved back to the woods. While doing so, he found a wounded member of 4th Troop, Private Harry Hooker and tried unsuccessfully to assist him. He then made his way to where Seely had spoken to Flowerdew and reported to the General that the squadron had been destroyed in a charge.'[13]

The German account testifies to the savage cost of the charge:

'An artillerist cries out: 'Enemy in our backs, Help!' 'Kavallerie attacks' shouts another. The Saxon Kaisergrenadiere [GR 101] are attacked by the 1st Canadian Cavalry Brigade with full force, but rapid rifle fire holds them off, supported by mines. In several places sabres fight against pistols, a 15cm gun of FAR 93 rips terrible gaps into the squadrons of Lord Strathcona's Horses. It is a massacre, horses are wallowing in blood and mud, their riders shot off their backs. Not many Canadians manage to escape.'[14]

Sadly, the German version of events is the correct one and contrary to opinion, and no doubt the popular press of the day, Flowerdew's charge – however gallant it may have been – did not secure the wood. By 11.00am the two brigades of cavalry had only established themselves on three sides of the wood – the centre and southern sectors were still in enemy hands. Gordon Flowerdew's posthumous award of the Victoria Cross appeared in the *London Gazette* in April 1918. The 32-year-old former Framlingham College schoolboy who immigrated to Canada in 1902, is buried at Namps-au-Val British Cemetery. C Squadron probably had fewer than 100 men available on 30 March, with Lieutenant Harvey's troop detached it would seem likely that the charge took place with seventy-five officers and men. With twenty-four killed in the charge and subsequent action and another fifteen dying from wounds over the next few weeks, Flowerdew's squadron had been reduced to little more than a troop. Promoted to captain in the field by Seely, Gordon Flowerdew was hit almost immediately in the chest and legs and, after the battle, was moved to Number 41 Casualty Clearing Station. He died on Monday 31 March 1918. Reflecting on the Moreuil action forty-two years later, Major General James Lunt felt Seely's attack on the wood was hopeless from the start:

> '*He was pitting men on horseback, armed with swords, against men in trenches, armed with machine guns. But the theory of war is often a very different thing from its practice because the human factor, which plays such a dominant part in battle, is an uncertain and ever-varying quantity. The Seelys and Flowerdews of this world have proved time after time that we should honour them for having done so.*'[15]

In the meantime, 3 Cavalry Brigade, which had crossed the Avre behind the Canadians, had arrived and Seely ordered Lieutenant Colonel Geoffrey Brooke and 16/Lancers to drive the remaining 200 Germans out of the wood. Brooke was no stranger to Seely, having recently been the brigade major of the Canadian Cavalry Brigade. He had begun his war as a subaltern in August 1914 and, like so many of the successful regular officers who had survived the war to date, he had profited from rapid promotion and now commanded his regiment. Using the wide ride that runs north-south, Brooke's Lancers – in an action reminiscent of a pheasant shoot – cleared the rest of the wood leaving only the fringes of the southern and eastern edges in enemy hands. While Brooke and his men were engaged in the wood, the remaining units of 3rd Cavalry Brigade, the 4th (Queen's Own) Hussars (4/Hussars) and 5/Lancers, moved into the western extremities.

The only remaining threat was artillery fire. Both German and British guns were firing into the wood and although the British guns were eventually silenced, German artillery fire continued throughout the day. One casualty of this desultory shelling was Lieutenant Colonel MacDonald, commanding Strathcona's Horse, who was slightly wounded. Despite his loud objections, he was evacuated and Lieutenant Colonel van Straubenzie of the Royal Canadian Dragoons took command of the squadrons in the wood. Other casualties of the day included the loss of Lieutenant Colonel John Darley, commanding 4/Hussars, together with two other officers and fourteen other ranks killed and forty-four wounded.[16] The Queen's Bays lost one officer killed, two wounded and twenty-five men wounded or missing, while 8/Hussars lost eleven killed and twenty-two wounded.

With the wood practically cleared of hostile troops, Seely sent messages to Pitman, Diebold and the 8th Division confirming the wood was now largely in British hands. By 2.30am on 31 March three composite battalions of the battered 8th Division had relieved the cavalry. The 2/West Yorkshires, who by this stage of the offensive could only field 100 men, had already been sent up to Moreuil Wood where they were joined by units from 23 and 24 Brigade under the command of Brigadier General George Grogan. Grogan found the Germans were in possession of Moreuil village and the British line to the north running along the western edge of the wood. It was still an extremely delicate position and daybreak brought the first of a series of heavy German counter-attacks.

In the face of the supporting fire from British gunners the German infantry broke through on the left of the divisional front shortly after 1.00pm, driving 2/Devons out of the wood. On the right 1/Worcesters held on until 2/East Lancashires and 2/Royal Berks were in a position to counter-attack. Fierce fighting saw the line temporarily restored but by the evening most of Moreuil Wood and all of Rifle Wood – which lay a mile to the northeast – were in German hands again. Pitman's account sums up the situation south of the River Luce on the evening of 31 March:

'*Both the 8th and 20th Divisions had been driven back off the line which we had re-established for them on the previous day. They [German infantry] had been dribbling back in twos and threes throughout the day, and by the evening the Germans had taken out the whole of Moreuil Wood and Rifle Wood, except the north-western corner of the former, in front of which the 3rd Cavalry Brigade line was established through the neck which joins the corner with the main wood. On the left the 20th Division had been driven back to Hourges village and to Hangard, which was held by a company of French.*'[17]

By this time the 3rd Cavalry Division had arrived in the Avre valley and Pitman was ordered to retake Rifle Wood – Bois de Hourges on modern day maps – with a dismounted attack on 1 April. The wood was held by II and III/IR 74 from the German 19th Division with I/IR 74 in reserve. It was not going to be a particularly easy task.

Pitman's plan was to attack the wood from the north in three waves. The first – comprising of a 4 Cavalry Brigade Composite Regiment – was to attack towards the north eastern corner; the second wave – a dismounted company of 20/Hussars – was to follow and form strong points on the north eastern edge of the wood, while the third wave – a dismounted battalion of Canadian Cavalry – was to go through the wood, clear it of the enemy and consolidate its positions along the eastern and southern edges where it was planned they would be relieved by 6/Dragoon Guards. With the attack to be preceded by an artillery and machine-gun bombardment, tactical command on the ground was again given to Jack Seely.

At 9.00am the men of 4 Cavalry Brigade dumped their British warms at the assembly points along the River Luce and worked their way south of the river towards the wood. As the first line came into view a German artillery SOS burst above them and a heavy machine-gun fire opened up. Major the Hon Arthur Child-Villiers was commanding the Oxfordshire Hussars:

> *'Our regiment advanced on a front of less than 150 yards. For the first 40 yards or so we were not shot at, but then we were fired at, as we expected, from the wood. Batches of Germans could be seen running to their positions on the edge of the wood, and we did a good deal of firing at them with rifles. Three of the Hotchkiss rifles also fired at them during this advance, though it was difficult to reform the teams, which had all suffered casualties, during the actual advance. When we got near the corner of the wood, the Germans could be seen running away from some of their machine guns, and we entered the wood from the crossroads.'*[18]

The first wave reached its objective at 9.10am and the cavalrymen were able to bring more of their Hotchkiss rifles into action. The 20/Hussars, which made up the second wave, began their attack from the sunken lane which ran along the edge of the wood and here they took several casualties from enfilade fire before Captain Walter Hall collected together his three dismounted squadrons and rushed the objective. Hall had only recently returned from leave and on his return had taken command of the dismounted detachment. In his haste to find his regiment he mislaid his revolver and had bought another in Amiens. 'The only one he could get was of Spanish make', wrote a fellow officer, 'however, he armed himself with this and rushed into the fray.' As the Hussars consolidated their positions in Rifle Wood the Spanish revolver is said to have accounted for more than one of the enemy.

Following on behind the Hussars came the Canadians, who pushed on to take the remaining portion of the wood. It was all over remarkably quickly and by 11.00am the wood was secured. Of the 138 officers and men of Hall's command 3 men were killed and 3 officers and 39 men wounded. The Oxfordshire Hussars who had attacked with the first wave, took thirteen machine guns and twenty-three prisoners but suffered twelve men killed and forty-seven wounded. Three officers, including Major Child-Villiers were wounded. As for the Canadians, the fighting in Moreuil and Rifle Wood had cost the brigade 488 casualties and many of their horses were dead; their casualties accounting for nearly half of the 1,079 casualties suffered by the whole of the 2nd Cavalry Division.

The Rifle Wood operation had been very successful, all objectives had been achieved and any further German counter-attacks were largely broken up by the artillery. Pitman was delighted; both actions had vindicated his belief that the cavalry, when used correctly, could be exceptionally successful. Like Pitman, many of the officers and NCOs serving with the cavalry were pre-war soldiers and had been largely spared from the Allied offensives that cut through the ranks of the infantry. These professional soldiers had shown their worth during the March offensive and would do so again in the coming months. Although von

Hutier's units regained Moreuil and Rifle Woods they had almost reached the limit of their advance. Moreuil Wood was retaken some four months later, on 8 August 1918 – the opening day of the Battle of Amiens – by the French and Canadians and the 43rd Battalion of the 3rd Canadian Division recaptured Rifle Wood on the same day. However, it must be said that the battle for the woods north of Moreuil did not – as some writers have stated – win the war! What it did in fact was to blunt the German advance long enough to enable Foch to move up vital reinforcements and provided the vital breathing space which allowed the first of the Australians to arrive in time to fight at Villers-Bretonneux – a town shortly destined to become a shrine to the Australian soldier and nation. The war still had seven-and-a-half bloody and destructive months left to run but the failure of the March offensive was the beginning of the end.

Chapter 14

Aftermath and Beyond

We climbed the crest of a hill where the road rose high, and far on our right was Amiens cathedral, touched with fire in the glory of the morning, outlined against a pale green sky. Here was surely something to fight for, a symbol of France.
Sergeant 'Jimmy' Downing – 57th Battalion Australian Imperial Force.

After the actions at Moreuil and Rifle Wood there was a lull in the fighting, the junction between the French and British on the river Avre was strengthened and over the next two days the French gradually relieved the British 8th and 14th Divisions. On 3 April at the Beauvais Conference the Allied command met again to confirm Foch's appointment and decide on the immediate strategy both north and south of the Somme. Two days later the Fifth Army became the Fourth Army, Gough's command had been completely erased.

As far as the German offensive was concerned it was becoming increasingly clear to all that the breakthrough and swift success promised by Ludendorff was not going to materialize, added to which the enormous human cost of the advance had, in many respects, already outweighed any territorial gain. Despair replaced exuberance as Germany braced itself for who knew how many more bloody years of war.

With Amiens still firmly fixed in his sights, however, Ludendorff made one further attempt to take the town, an attack that was halted at Villers-Bretonneux on 5 April by the Australian 9 Brigade and the British 14th and 18th Divisions. The heavy fighting was almost too much for the battered 14th Division and, to the dismay of many, numbers of British troops and their officers were seen to be retreating in disorder. Aware of what their British counterparts had already suffered during the German offensive there was a degree of sympathy amongst the Australian ranks, Jimmy Downing thanking his lucky stars that 'we had escaped the hell they had already endured'. Buoyed up by the French and Australian reinforcements the Germans were held less than ten miles from the outskirts of Amiens. The offensive had come to a complete halt; the failure of both 'Michael' and 'Mars' had effectively ended Ludendorff's ambitions on the Rivers Somme and Scarpe.

By 5 April 1918 the BEF had been strengthened by over 100,000 infantry replacements hastily despatched in response to the German offensive, many of them were as young as eighteen. Private Frederick Hodges – en-route to join 10/Lancashire Fusiliers – remembered being addressed in Northampton by an elderly general who told them that despite not completing their training and still being boys of eighteen they were going to play the part of men. Fred Hodges and his reinforcements were badly needed as the total British losses given for the March offensive numbered 177,738 men, of whom at least 72,000 were prisoners. With a daily attrition rate of over 10,000 casualties the BEF had haemorrhaged men; the Fifth Army alone had lost over 90,000 from its sixteen infantry divisions. From the four Fifth Army infantry corps engaged during the battle the hardest hit was Watts' XIX Corps which reported losses of over 32,000 of whom some 19,000 were missing. The French reported losses of around 77,000 from the twenty divisions engaged. Although German losses were marginally less than the combined Allied total, the 239,000 casualties still averaged over 11,000 men per day, the larger army group of von Hutier's Eighteenth Army – thirty-five divisions - had taken 84,800 casualties, offset a little by the 51,000 Allied prisoners taken in the first seven days of the offensive. Von der Marwitz's Second Army – twenty-four divisions – reported over 73,000 casualties while von Below's Seventeenth Army – twenty-nine divisions - which was principally engaged in the costly 'Mars' offensive around Arras incurred over 81,000 casualties.

Even though the Allied losses were higher, with a greater number permanently lost to the war effort in captivity, taken as a whole, the loss to the Germans was much greater in terms of resources and morale. The *Kaiserschlacht* offensive had taken some 1,200 square miles of Allied territory in a remarkable advance of over forty miles, a result that none of the later German offensives would match. But this newly-won ground contained little of strategic value, much of the area comprised of the sterile 1916 Somme battleground and the wastelands created by the German withdrawal to the Hindenburg Line in 1917. Amiens remained in Allied hands and the ball was now firmly back in Ludendorff's court.

On 9 April Ludendorff's attentions were directed on the valley of the River Lys where once again the offensive strike – this time codenamed 'Georgette' - made significant ground before it too was finally brought to a halt. His judgement perhaps still clouded by visions of victory, Ludendorff once again turned his attentions to Villers-Brettoneux where he opened his assault on 24 April. By the end of the day it looked as if his gamble might just pay off; German units occupied much of the village and dug in to prepare for the inevitable Allied counter-attack. It came almost immediately with the Australian 15th Division attacking to the north and the British 18th Division to the south. The final stroke was launched on the night of 24/25 April in an attack which sealed the fate of the

German defence and set the name Villers-Bretonneux firmly up on the pedestal of Australian legend alongside those of Gallipoli and Poziéres.

Perhaps one of the greatest casualties of the March offensive was Hubert Gough whose performance during the retreat was arguably his finest hour. Up until March 1918 his record of command was one that had been pitted with controversy and it is ironic that it was the Australians, whom Gough had handled so badly at Pozières in 1916, who were finally brought up to bolster the line at Villers-Bretonneux in April 1918. Given the circumstances he found himself in in 1918, Gough fought relatively well but was made a scapegoat for problems that were not entirely of his own making and over which he exercised little control. His dismissal consigned him to a wilderness from which he only temporarily emerged in May 1919 when he was appointed Chief of the Allied Military Mission to Russia, an appointment from which he was sacked again the following October only five months later.

Returning home he was awarded the CBE, and spent the last months of the war as a student on an agricultural course at Cambridge University. In October 1922 he retired from the Army to take up pig and poultry farming at Burrows Lea at Gomshall in Surrey. This career change may have prompted his purchase of land in Kenya in 1925 but the move to Africa was never made and in 1927 he sold Burrows Lea. During this time he also briefly dabbled in politics, a career which ended in March 1922 after he was defeated as an Asquith Liberal in a parliamentary by-election in Chertsey.

Gough's Fifth Army colleagues continued to lobby the government for him to receive an award similar to that given to the other army commanders at the end of the war, but the Prime Minister Stanley Baldwin refused, preferring in 1937 to sanction the award of the Order of the Bath (GCB) in what was seen as a vindication of Gough's reputation. In May 1940 Gough was back in uniform when he joined the Home Guard as commanding officer of the Chelsea Home Guard detatchment. News of his professional performance apparently reached Churchill's ears, and in June 1940 he was promoted to Zone Commander in the Fulham & Chelsea area. Sir Hubert Gough died in London on 18 March 1963, aged 92.

If an ephitaph is needed for this old soldier it may lie within his obituary: 'Had Gough been removed from command during the battles of the Somme or of Ypres not much surprise would have been aroused. That he should now be recalled – on March 28 – by Mr Lloyd George's government, after hard fighting against great odds, appears the height of injustice.'

Gough's four corps commanders all survived the war and those that had not already received knighthoods did so soon after the Armistice. In 1919 Richard Harte Butler was appointed to command the 2nd Division, a post he held until 1923 when he became GOC Western Command. He retired from the army in 1929 to live in Shawbury, in Shropshire, where he died on 22 April 1935 aged 65. He is buried at St Luke's Churchyard at Hodnet, Shropshire.

Walter Norris Congreve, who had won the Victoria Cross at Colenso in December 1899, was appointed GOC of the Egyptian Expeditionary Force between 1919 and 1922 and then GOC Southern Command between 1923 and 1924. From 1924 he served as Governor of Malta, where he died aged 65. Walter Congreve's son, Major William de la Touche Congreve, was also awarded the Victoria Cross shortly after his death in July 1916, making father and son one of only three such pairs to be awarded the coveted cross.

Ivor Maxse was moved from command of XVIII Corps in June 1918 to become Inspector General of Training to the British Armies in France and the United Kingdom. After the War he became GOC of IX Corps, stationed with the British Army of the Rhine in Germany. He went on to be GOC Northern Command before retiring from the Army in 1926 to establish a successful fruit growing business appropriately called the Maxey Fruit Company. He died in 1958 aged 96. Herbert 'Teeny' Edward Watts who held the remnants of the Fifth Army together in the final days of the offensive, lived until 1934 when he died at home in Bournemouth aged 76. A very private individual who specifically asked that his funeral be kept within the family circle and who was described in his obituary as: 'A wise, a brave, and a modest man, and a very gentle and perfect knight.'

The unfortunate 59-year-old Major General Victor Arthur Couper, who commanded the 14th Division, was sent home in April 1918 and retired from the army a year later. In 1927 the former Greenjacket officer became Colonel Commandant of the 1st Battalion Rifle Brigade. He died in 1938. Although Lieutenant Colonel Arthur Kenlis Maxwell was not disgraced, his surrender at Boadicea Redoubt and subsequent captivity did raise a number of eyebrows, aparently not enough to prevent his award of the DSO being announced! After the war he retired to his estates in County Cavan and occupied his time with golf, hunting and sailing and was frequently to be found on the ski slopes of Switzerland. His son, Lieutenant Colonel the Hon Somerset Maxwell, was killed at the Battle of El Alamein in 1942 whilst serving with the Royal Corps of Signals. Arthur Maxwell died in 1957 aged 79.

The unlucky 8th, 21st and 50th Divisions found themselves again on the receiving end of the third major German offensive in May 1918, this time in the Aisne sector. Moved to what was considered to be a quiet part of the front, they bore the brunt of the Blücher-Yorck offensive which opened on 27 May 1918. The fiery Brigadier General Edward Puis Riddell who commanded 149 Brigade was badly wounded at Beaurepaire Wood with Brigadier General Cuthbert Martin, who was regrettably killed. Fortunately Riddell survived the war adding a second bar to his DSO before he retired from the army in 1925. He became chairman of the Hexham Conservative Association and was heavily involved in the British Legion. Knighted in 1945 he died at Hexham in August 1957 aged 82.

Brigadier General Hubert Rees, who commanded 150 Brigade, became another casualty of the Blücher-Yorck offensive when he was captured on the first day of the German advance. Rees had the rather dubious pleasure of meeting the Kaiser before being marched away into captivity. Repatriated in December 1918 he retired from the army in 1922 and died in January 1948. Lieutenant Colonel Charles Alexander Shaw Page was also taken prisoner on the Aisne after another epic stand with his battalion of Middlesex which, once again, was practically wiped out on 27 May. Page was repatriated in October 1918 and retired from the army in 1920 to take up Holy Orders in 1921. He died at home in East Dereham, Norfolk in August 1953 aged 76. In the Second World War his son, Flight Lieutenant Harry Page was shot down and killed in January 1942 flying with 61 Squadron.

Brigadier Hanway Robert Cumming, who commanded the Leicester Brigade at Épehy, emerged unscathed from the Blücher-Yorck offensive but was killed aged 54 during the Anglo-Irish War in the infamous Clonbanin ambush on 5 March 1921. His body was brought back to England and cremated at Golders Green. Amongst the long list of dignitaries in attendance was Field Marshal Sir Henry Wilson – who himself was assassinated by two IRA gunmen in 1922. Another casualty of the Anglo-Irish conflict was Lieutenant Colonel Gerald Smyth who commanded 6/KOSB. He finished his war with the DSO and bar commanding 93 Infantry Brigade; tragically he was gunned down in Cork by the IRA in July 1920. Brigadier John Edward Bernard Seely returned to England in 1918 and was appointed Under-Secretary of State for Air and President of the Air Council in 1919, posts he resigned from at the end of 1919 after the Government refused to create a Secretary of State for Air. On 21 June 1933 he was raised to the peerage as Baron Mottistone. His son, Second Lieutenant Frank Reginald Seely was killed in action with the 1st Battalion Hampshires in April 1917 and is buried at Haute-Avesnes British Cemetery. Jack Seeley died in November 1947.

The casualty rate amongst battalion commanders during the March offensive was high, on the first day alone eight were killed in action and a further fifteen were taken prisoner. Of those that survived the conflict several remained in the army as serving soldiers through to the Second World War. Probably the most renowned of these was Lieutenant Colonel Vyvyan Vavasour Pope whose arm was so badly shattered in his encounter with German infantry near Vadencourt that it had to be amputated. He transferred to the Royal Tank Corps in 1923 and on the outbreak of war in 1939 was appointed Chief of Staff to II Corps which had been mobilised at Salisbury under Alan Brooke's command. At the end of September he joined the BEF as Lord Gort's tank advisor and took a leading role in the armoured counter-attack at Arras on 21 May 1940. He was evacuated from Dunkirk after which he was posted to North Africa in 1941 as GOC XXX Corps. However, on 5 October his aircraft ran into trouble on taking off from Heliopolis. All those on board were killed.

Captain George Douglas James McMurtrie also remained in the army and served in Africa, retiring after the Second World War with the rank of lieutenant colonel. He died in 1994 having achieved the grand old age of 96. Many, such as Lieutenant Colonel Algernon Lee Ransome, who retired in 1938, were recalled on the outbreak of war in September 1939; in Ransome's case it was to command the 46th Division which he commanded until 1945. He died in May 1969. Lieutenant Eric Jacobs-Larkcom was another regular officer who remained with the colours, spending much of his time in the Far East. During the Second World War as a lieutenant colonel he served with the British Military Mission to China after which he entered the Foreign Service. He died at Truro in May 1982 aged 87.

For the majority the end of hostilities heralded the long-awaited opportunity to return to civilian life. Eddie Combe, who defended Le Quesnoy and reportedly 'went over the top' on some fifteen occasions, opened the UK office of Clarke Dodge and Co., a leading firm of New York Stockbrokers, in 1924 and later became a partner. He retired to Brighton after forty years in the business and died in June 1967. Lieutenant Colonel John Durnford Crosthwaite was another stockbroker who returned to the family business of Fenn and Crosthwaite. After the fall of France in 1940 he rejoined the army but resigned when he was refused overseas service on account of his age and so, like many old soldiers, he joined the Home Guard. He lived out his final years as a senior partner in the family firm and died in January 1981 aged 89.

Lieutenant Colonel Hugh John Chevalier Peirs, who commanded 8/Queens at Le Verguier, left the army with a further bar to his DSO and continued to practise law until his untimely death in June 1943 aged 57. Captain Harry Kenneth Staddon lived considerably longer and also resumed his law practice. He died in May 1961, four years before Lieutenant Claude Lorraine Piesse of 8/Queens who returned to Australia in 1920 and died in Perth. Like Piesse, Lieutenant Herbert Asquith was greatly affected by the war. He was the second son of Herbert Henry Asquith, the British Prime Minister and younger brother of Raymond Asquith who was killed on the Somme in September 1916. After the war he returned to practise law but is better known for his writing. In 1937 he wrote of his war experiences in *Moments of Memory*, episodes that appeared again in his poetry which included *The Volunteer* and *The Fallen Subaltern*. He died in 1947, aged 66. Another writer was Lieutenant Colonel Rowland Fielding who concluded his war in command of the 1st Battalion Civil Service Rifles after which he returned to mining engineering. He will always be remembered as the author of *War Letters to a Wife* which was published in 1929. During the Second World War he served in the Home Guard and died at Wimbledon in September 1945 aged 74.

Lieutenant Colonel Charles Kenneth Howard-Bury, the grandson of the 16th Earl of Suffolk and Berkshire, was taken prisoner on 21 March having been mentioned in despatches on seven occasions. After escaping from Fürstenberg – he remained at large for nine days almost reaching the Danish frontier – he was recaptured and sent to Clausthal 2,000 feet up in the Hartz Mountains where he remained until he was repatriated. In 1921 he led the first British expedition to Everest, an enterprise which included George Leigh Mallory in its number. The 1921 expedition made Howard-Bury a public figure and in 1922 he won the Conservative seat for Bilston which he lost in 1924. He returned to the House of Commons two years later as MP for Chelmsford, a seat he held for six years. He died in September 1963 aged 82.

The 2/2 Londons commanding officer, Lieutenant Colonel Archibald Read Richardson, was 37-years-old when he was wounded on 21 March, injuries which left him disabled for the rest of his life. After the war he was appointed to the Chair of Mathematics at the University of Swansea in 1920, a position he held until 1940 when he was compelled to resign on account of increasing ill-health. Retiring to South Africa he continued mathematical research up until shortly before his death in November 1954. Lieutenant Colonel Herbert John Wenyon who commanded 8/Royal West Kents, died in August 1944 aged 56. He was a county cricketer who played for Middlesex between 1921 and 1923. In July 1945 his only son, RNVR Lieutenant Louis Wenyon, was killed in a flying accident.

Major Cecil James Hazard who had been the last man to cross the Bristol Bridge at Pèronne, emigrated to Guatamala in 1924 and laid the foundations for the Los Andes coffee growing plantation which is still farmed by the family today. Captain George Arthur Howson retired as a major and devoted the remainder of his life to helping the war disabled by forming the Disabled Society and later by establishing the Royal British Legion Poppy Factory which largely employed disabled soldiers. He died aged 50 in November 1936. Lieutenant Robert Forden Petschler who destroyed No.4 Bridge at Ham resumed his civilian occupation as an electrical engineer. He later retired to run a hotel in Chichester and died in June 1978 aged 85.

Major Alwyn Leslie Raimes survived the war but his younger brother, Captain Lancelot Raimes was killed in action in June 1916; he is buried at Bailleul Communal Cemetery Extension. After the war Alwyn presumably returned to working with the family firm of Raimes and Co. and wrote an account of his battalion at war entitled *The Fifth Battalion Durham Light Infantry, 1914–1918.* By 1948 he was working with the Ministry of Food. When he retired he was living in Dorking and died in November 1967. Second Lieutenant John Crawford Cunningham was awarded the DSO for his gallantry, news of which reached him at Holtzminden Prison Camp where he was joined by five other subalterns from his battalion and Major Marcus Hartigan who was captured at Malaisse Farm. In 1920 Cunningham resumed work in the family business, remaining there until the outbreak of war in 1939 when he became the Factory Defence Officer at the Luton Percival Aircraft factory. In January 1941 he was awarded the George Medal for defusing an unexploded parachute mine during an air raid on the factory where he remained until 1954. He died ten years later.

For others such as Captain James Charles Vanner of 7/Leicesters the ravages of war were responsible for his early death in March 1919 aged only 22. Wounds received in August 1918 effectively ended his war and, weakened from gas poisoning, he gradually deteriorated. Fortunately Private Fred Hodges remained unscathed, returning to civilian life in 1919 where he worked as an accountant in the gas industry for forty-five years and had the distinction of being one of the last few remaining Great War veterans. He died in February 2002. Sadly Lieutenant Colonels Robert Edward Dewing and Christopher 'Kit' Bushell VC were victims of the last months of the war. Dewing was killed in April and Bushel on 8 August 1918 – the first day of the Battle of Amiens.

Father Henry Vincent Gill, the Roman Catholic chaplain to 2/Royal Irish Rifles, was awarded the DSO and Military Cross for his bravery under fire and spent the last thirteen years of his life as a minister at the Leeson Street Jesuit community in Dublin. He died in 1934. The Wesleyan chaplain, Reverend Thomas Westerdale, who wrote of his experiences with the Somerset Light Infantry at St Simon, published a number of books including, *Messages From Mars: A Chaplain's Experiences at the Front.* Westerdale managed to combine his religious duties with that of war correspondent and regularly sent copy to the *Methodist Times.* After the war he continued to write on a variety of subjects and died in Winchester in 1965. Another officer who turned to the church was Tom Witherow of 2/Royal Irish Rifles who was described as a 'most remarkable combination of warrior and man of the cloth'. He died aged 99 in September 1989.

Captain Harry Fine who commanded the garrison at Fort Vendeuil left the army with a Military Cross and is thought to have died in 1948. In 1939 he applied for a Short Service Commission having given his age as 45 but was turned down on health grounds. He was still single at the time and living with his sister in Paddington. Captain Leonard Maurice Harper was awarded a bar to his Military Cross and died in December 1967 aged 74 at Hounslow. The gallant Lieutenant Geoffrey Ewart Lester returned to the Standard Bank of South Africa after his repatriation in 1919 but moved to Kenya in 1922 where he married and continued his career in banking. Returning to England in 1944 he died aged 60 in 1953. Lieutenant David Victor Kelly, the 110 Brigade Intelligence Officer took a different path and joined the Diplomatic Service and became the British Ambassador to Argentina, Turkey and the Soviet Union. He was knighted in 1942 and died in March 1959. He wrote several books including *39 Months with the Tigers 1915–1918.*

The Victoria Cross holders who survived the war all fared well apart from Cecil Leonard Knox who was killed in February 1943 after losing control of his motor cycle. On returning to England in 1919 he had became a Freeman of the Borough of Nuneaton and a director of Haunchwood Brick & Tile Company. In 1940 he took command of the local Home Guard until his untimely death three years later. He was cremated at Gilroes Cemetery, Leicester. Frank Crowther 'Cully' Roberts was appointed GOC of the Poona Brigade in 1938 and briefly commanded the 48th Division in 1939, retiring with the rank of major general. He died in January 1982 and is buried at Bretby Churchyard near Burton-on-Trent. Charles Edwin Stone returned to Derby to work for Rolls Royce, remaining there for the rest of his working life. He died in August 1952 aged 60 and is buried in Belper Cemetery, Derby. Alfred Cecil Herring retired as a major and returned to civilian life as a chartered accountant. In 2006 a public house in Palmer's Green in North London was named after him. He died in August 1966. Jack Davies was possibly the only living recipient of the Victoria Cross to have been first awarded the medal posthumously. Thought to have been killed in action, his postcard from Zagen confirmed he was still alive and had been taken prisoner. Jack returned to work at the Ravenhead Brick and Pipe Works in St Helens and married his sweetheart Beatrice. During the Second World War he was a captain in the Home Guard. He died suddenly in October 1955 aged 60. Alfred Maurice Toye remained in the army and spent six years as chief instructor at the Royal Egyptian Military College, later becoming commandant of the War Office School of Chemical Warfare. For much of the Second World War he was on active service with the 6th Airboirne Division and retired as a brigadier general in 1948. He died in 1955 in his fifty-eighth year and is buried at Tiverton, Devon.

Notes

Introduction
1. Goes, Unter dem Stahlhelm, *Der Tag X*. p. 63.
2. Account by Peirson in CAB 45/193.
3. Wace to Edmonds, CAB 45/193.

Chapter 1
1. Richardson, *39 Months with the Tigers*, p. 91
2. Westropp, *Sixteenth, Seventeenth, Eighteenth & Nineteenth Battalions The Manchester Regiment 1914–1918*, p. 44.
3. Essame, *The Battle For Europe 1918*, p. 11.
4. Ibid, p. 13.

Chapter 2
1. Anglesey, *A History of the British Cavalry, Vol 8*, p. 68.
2. Maze, *A Frenchman in Khaki*, p. 267.
3. Travers, *How the War Was Won*, p. 57.
4. Ibid, p. 63.
5. Account in CAB 45/192.
6. Liddell Hart Military Archive, LH2P/79/1-3 Claude L Piesse.
7. Diary account of Father Henry Gill, p. 179.
8. *Annals of the King's Royal Rifle Corps: 1918*, pp. 285–6.
9. Private Papers of C Miller. IWM Department of Documents, reference 4118.
10. Letter from Mudie to Edmonds in CAB 45/192.
11. Fielding, *War Letters to a Wife*, pp. 258–7
12. Quoted in, *1918, Year of Victory*, p. 42.
13. Private Papers of C Miller. IWM Department of Documents, reference 4118.
14. Ibid, reference 4118.
15. Demolitions, Fifth Army, 1918. *RE Journal March 1933*, p. 18.
16. Ibid, p. 27
17. Liddell Hart Military Archive, LH2P/79/1-3 Claude L Piesse.
18. Demolitions, Fifth Army, 1918. *RE Journal March 1933*, pp. 27–8.
19. Passingham, The German Offensives of 1918, p. 22.
20. *Durch-Bruchmüller* is translated as Breakthrough-Müller.

Chapter 3

1. Lawrence, Echoes of War 1915–1918 (Part 4). *South African Journal of Military Studies* Vol. 8, No4, 1978.
2. *The 2nd London Regiment in the Great War*, p. 292.
3. Ibid, p. 293.
4. Private Papers of Captain M L Harper, IWM Dept. of Documents, reference 7670.
5. George Ansell is commemorated on the Pozières Memorial.
6. Grey, *The 2nd London Regiment in the Great War,* pp. 298–9.
7. Private Papers of Captain M L Harper, IWM Dept. of Documents, reference 7670.
8. *London Gazette*, 1 July 1919.
9. Grimwade, *The War History of the 4th Battalion the London Regiment*, pp. 373–4.

Chapter 4

1. *The 18th Division in the Great War*, p. 259.
2. Nichols, *Pushed and the Return Push*, p. 16.
3. Cited in *The Biscuit Boys* pp. 318.3.
4. Ibid, pp. 318.3–4. John Gordon and Norman Williams are both commemorated on the Pozières Memorial.
5. Ibid, p. 318.4. Stanley Harvey and Douglas Tosetti are both commemorated on the Pozières Memorial.
6. Account by Crosthwaite in CAB 45/192.
7. Ibid.
8. Ibid.
9. 23-year-old Captain Harold Thomas Rapson is buried at Sery-les-Mezieres Communal Cemetery.
10. Account by Crosthwaite in CAB 45/192.
11. MacDonald, *To the Last Man*, p. 98.
12. Ibid, pp. 98–99.
13. Ibid, pp. 99–100. Lieutenant R M Patterson was taken prisoner and repartriated in December 1918.
14. Ibid, p. 100.
15. *The 18th Division in the Great War*, p. 268.
16. Farndale, *The Royal Artillery 1914–1918*, p. 262.
17. Moore, *See How They Run*, p. 88.
18. Goes, Unter dem Stahlhelm, *Der Tag X*. p. 63.
19. GHF Nichols, *Pushed and the Return Push*, p. 20.
20. The Diary of Major H G Paris at http://hampstead-heavies.com/hgpdiary16a.htm.
21. Ibid.
22. Goes, Unter dem Stahlhelm, *Der Tag X*. p. 64.
23. Nichols, *Pushed and the Return Push*, p30. Major Wilfred Dennes MC is commemorated on the Pozières Memorial.
24. Middlebrook, *The Kaiser's Battle*, p. 327.
25. Letter to Edmonds in CAB 45/193.
26. Captain Reginald Singlehurst is remembered on the Pozières Memorial. He was 36-years-old.
27. Hare, *History of the King's Royal Rifle Corps* Vol. 5, pp. 283–4.

28. Ibid, p. 284.
29. Ibid, p. 284.
30. Ibid, account by Major Bowen, p. 282, and letter from Bowen to Edmonds in CAB 45/192.
31. Middlebrook, *The Kaiser's Battle*, p. 215.
32. Letter from Birch to Edmonds in CAB 45/192.
33. Ibid.
34. Account by Llewellyn Davies in CAB 45/193.

Chapter 5
1. Private Papers of C Miller. IWM Department of Documents, reference 4118.
2. Adamson in CAB 45/192.
3. Ibid.
4. Ibid.
5. Ibid.
6. Middlebrook, *The Kaiser's Battle*, p. 267.
7. Goes, Unter dem Stahlhelm, *Der Tag X*. p. 55.
8. Ibid p. 56.
9. Fox, *The Royal Iniskilling Fusiliers in the World War*, pp. 138–9.
10. Ibid, p. 250.
11. Sheperd, *The 2nd Battalion Wiltshire Regiment*, p. 139.
12. Ibid pp. 139–40.
13. Middlebrook, *The Kaiser's Battle*, p. 210.
14. Ibid, p. 140.
15. Captain Arthur Oliver Clayton is commemorated on the Pozières Memorial. He was 23-years-old.
16. Westropp, *The Sixteenth, Seventeenth, Eighteenth, Nineteenth Battalions the Manchester Regiment: A Record 1914–1918*, p. 52.
17. Asquith, *Moments of Memory*, p. 314.
18. Ibid, p. 318.
19. Ibid, pp. 320–21.
20. Westropp, *The Sixteenth, Seventeenth, Eighteenth, Nineteenth Battalions the Manchester Regiment: A Record 1914–1918*, p. 51.
21. H R Hardman, IWM Department of Documents, reference 1847.
22. R F Petschler, IWM Department of Documents, reference 11732.
23. The cottages are marked on the 1918 trench maps in square 4a while the quarry which housed the main defences of the redoubt is in square 4c.
24. *The Oxfordshire and Buckinghamshire Light Infantry Chronicle 1918*, p. 193.
25. Ibid, p. 194.
26. Middlebrook, *The Kaiser's Battle*, p. 190.
27. Ibid, pp. 177–8.
28. *The Oxfordshire and Buckinghamshire Light Infantry Chronicle 1918*, p. 194–5.
29. MacDonald, *To the Last Man*, p. 112.
30. Nicholson, *Behind the Lines*, pp. 148–9.
31. Letter to Edmonds from Davie in CAB 45/192.
32. Captain Thomas McNaughton Davie MC was awarded the DSO in Deptember 1918.
33. Falls, *The Gordon Highlanders in the First World War*, p. 177.

Chapter 6

1. Middlebrook, *The Kaiser's Battle*, p. 367.
2. Ibid, p. 367.
3. *The History of the Eighth Battalion The Queen's Own Royal West Kent Regiment*, pp. 162–3.
4. *Rifle Brigade Chronicle 1918*, pp. 156–7.
5. *The History of the Eighth Battalion The Queen's Own Royal West Kent Regiment*, p. 167.
6. Second Lieutenant John Crawford Buchan is buried at Roisel Communal Cemetery. He was 26-years-old.
7. Lumley, *The History of the Eleventh Hussars*, p. 316.
8. Ibid, pp322–323 and Letter from Lumley to Edmonds in CAB 45/193.
9. Letter from Peirs to Edmonds in CAB 45/193.
10. Surrey History Centre, reference Z/433/1.
11. Surrey History Centre, reference Z/433/1 and Liddell Hart Military Archive, LH2P/79/1-3. John William Sayer died of wounds on 18 April 1918 and is buried at Le Cateau Military Cemetery.
12. Letter from Peirs to Edmonds in CAB 45/193.
13. Letter from Bond to Edmonds in CAB 45/192.
14. Letter from Baillie-Hamilton to Edmonds in CAB 45192. Captain John Brown is commemorated on the Pozières Memorial. He was 29-years-old.
15. Middlebrook, *The Kaiser's Battle*, p. 230.
16. Letter from Fox to Edmonds in CAB 45/192.
17. Letter from Feetham to Edmonds in CAB 45/192.
18. Ibid.
19. Goes, Unter dem Stahlhelm, *Der Tag X*.
20. Letter from Cuncliffe to Edmonds in CAB 45/192
21. Potter and Fothergill, *The History of the 2/6 Lancashire Fusiliers*, p. 115.
22. Ibid, p. 114.

Chapter 7

1. Letter to Edmonds from L C Jackson, GSO 1 of 16th Division, CAB 45/193.
2. Letter from Patman to Edmonds in CAB 45/193 and E A Dixon in CAB 45/193.
3. Letter from Terry to Edmonds in CAB 45/193.
4. Ibid.
5. The War Diary of 2/Royal Irish Regiment, TNA WO 95/1979.
6. Letter from Terry to Edmonds in CAB 45/193.
7. Fielding, *War Letters to a Wife*, p. 264.
8. Ibid, p. 265.
9. Ibid, p. 266 and 6/Connaught Rangers War Diary, TNA WO 95 1970.
10. Fielding, *War Letters to a Wife*, p. 267.
11. Letter of OC 94 Artillery Brigade RFA in TNA CAB 45/192. See also the Supplement to the *London Gazette*, 16 September 1918, No. 30901 p. 10864.
12. Account by Hartigan in CAB 45/192.
13. Ibid, CAB 45/192 and the battalion war diary in TNA WO 95/2837. Lieutenant Patrick Leopold Cahill is buried at Epéhy Wood Farm Cemetery.
14. Account by Peirson in CAB 45/193 and the War Diary of 2/Dublin Fusiliers in TNA WO 95/1974.

15. Account by Hartigan in CAB 45/192.
16. War Diary of 2/Munster Fusilers, TNA WO 95/1974.
17. Account by Hartigan in CAB 45/192.
18. Goes, Unter dem Stahlhelm, *Der Tag X*, p. 37.
19. Kelly, *39 Months with The Tigers*, p. 97 and Cumming, *A Brigadier in France*, p. 103.
20. Middlebrook, *The Kaiser's Battle*, p. 199.
21. Cumming, *A Brigadier in France*, pp. 104–5.
22. Account by Scarfe in CAB 45/193.
23. Account by Borthwick in CAB 45/193.
24. Simpson, *History of the Lincolnshire Regiment*, p. 296.
25. Account by White in CAB 45/193.
26. Croft, *Three Years with The 9th Division*, p. 183.
27. Kelly, *39 Months with The Tigers*, p. 99.
28. Ibid p. 99. Lieutenant Colonel William Norman Stewart is commemorated on the Pozières Memorial. He was 44-years-old.
29. Goes, Unter dem Stahlhelm, *Der Tag X*, p. 39.
30. Bacon, Leicestershire Record Office, 22D63/146.
31. Account by Scarfe in CAB 45/193.
32. Ibid.
33. Roberts, Leicestershire Record Office, P170/4. Lieutenant Stewart Longston Thirlby is commemorated on the Pozières Memorial. He was 25-years-old.
34. Kelly, *39 Months with The Tigers*, pp. 100–101. Captain Archibald McLay is commemorated on the Pozières Memorial. He was 31-years-old. 27-year-old Captain Arthur Lawson commanded the 110th Trench Mortar Battery and is buried at Saulcourt Churchyard Extension.
35. Account by MacMahon in CAB 45/194.
36. Kelly, *39 Months with The Tigers*, p. 103.

Chapter 8
1. Churchill, *The World Crisis 1911–1918*, p. 768.
2. Goes, Unter dem Stahlhelm, *Der Tag X*, p. 38.
3. Ibid, p. 38.
4. Both men are commemorated on the Pozières Memorial.
5. Account by Dawson in WO 95/1779.
6. Ibid.
7. Accounts by Gater and Fisher in CAB 45/192.
8. Letter from Congreve to Edmonds in CAB 45/192.
9. Gough, *The Fifth Army*, pp. 270–1.
10. Cited in Macdonald, *To the Last Man*, p. 197.
11. Croft, *Three Years with the 9th Division*. p. 136.
12. Gillion, *The KOSB in the Great War*, p. 365.
13. Account by Ritson in CAB 45/193.
14. Account by Dawson in WO 95/1779.
15. Ibid.
16. Lawrence, Echoes of War 1915–1918 (Part4). *South African Journal of Military Studies* Vol. 8, No4, 1978.

17. Letter from Ormiston to Tanner, CAB 45/193
18. Account by Dawson in WO 95/1779.
19. Ibid.
20. Ibid.
21. Ibid.
22. Binding, *A Fatalist at War*, p. 207.

Chapter 9
1. Grimwade, *The War History of the 4th Battalion, The London Regiment*, p. 379.
2. Grey, *The 2nd London Regiment in the Great War*, p. 303.
3. Grimwade, *The War History of the 4th Battalion The London Regiment*, pp. 380–1.
4. *London Gazette* 23 July 1918.
5. Nichols, *Pushed, and the Return Push*, p. 12.
6. Account by Snell in CAB 45/193.
7. Ibid, p. 52.
8. Account by Snell in CAB 45/193.
9. Banks and Chell, *With the 10th Essex in France*, p. 360.
10. Account by Chell quoted by Macdonald in, *To the Last Man*, p. 187.
11. Ernst Lange, *Hauptmann Willy Lange*, Verlag Schwert und Schild, Diesdorf 1935.
12. War Diary TNA WO 95/2038.
13. Account by Chell cited by Macdonald in, *To the Last Man*, p. 187.
14. Account by Brookling in CAB 45/192.
15. Account by Batten-Pooll in CAB 45/192.
16. Cited by Mcdonald in, *To the Last Man*, p178.
17. Letter from Birch to Edmonds in CAB 45/192.
18. Ibid.
19. Cited by Macdonald in, *To the Last Man*, p. 179.
20. Account by Brookling in CAB 45/192.
21. Account by Snell in CAB 45/193.
22. From the personal statement made by Alfred Herring, Royal Logistics Corps Archive.
23. Gough, *The Fifth Army*, p. 267.
24. Account by Ling in CAB 45/193.
25. 40-year-old Lieutenant Colonel James Knox was killed on 23 September 1918 and is buried at Granezza British Cemetery near Asiago. His brother, 33-year-old Second Lieutenant Andrew Knox, was killed on 12 December 1915 and is buried at Albert Communal Cemetery Extension.
26. The Diary of TLB Westerdale, IWM Department of Documents, reference 14137.
27. Ibid.
28. Ibid.
29. Private papers of G D J McMurtrie, IWM Department of Documents, reference 6796.
30. The Diary of TLB Westerdale, IWM Department of Documents, reference 14137.
31. Account by Allum in CAB 45/192.
32. Private papers of G D J McMurtrie, IWM Department of Documents, reference 6796. Lieutenant Colonel Burges-Short was wounded and taken prisoner later on 24 March near Villeselve.

Chapter 10

1. Account by Ling in CAB 45/193.
2. Account by Lacey in CAB 45/193.
3. Account by Cousland, Liddell Hart Military Achives, reference GB0099 Cousland.
4. Whether the attack began at 6.00pm is debatable as Lacey tells us he was still in position further east on the Flavy road at 6.30pm before he retired.
5. Account by Wilkins in CAB 45/193. Everard Wyrall in his history of the King's Regiment states that 12/King's held the eastern and north eastern defences of Cugny on the night of 23/24 March. The 61 Brigade War Diary also notes that at 4.00pm on 23 March their brigade major found the 12/King's on the eastern outskirts of Cugny. This does not appear to be corroborated by Wilkins and we can only assume that 12/King's had withdrawn by the evening.
6. Account by Wilkins in CAB 45/193.
7. The account of 2/RIF at Cugny has been partly drawn from accounts contained in the service records held at the National Archives: Strohm WO 339/69183, Thompson WO 399/40568 and Moore WO 339/13908.
8. Ibid.
9. Ibid.
10. Diary account of Father H Gill, p. 189.
11. Bickersteth, *History of the 6th Cavalry Brigade 1914–1918*, p. 84.
12. Quoted in Cusack & Herbert, *Scarlet Fever, A Lifetime with Horses*, p. 74.
13. Ibid.
14. Ibid.
15. William Cubitt is buried at Noyon New British Cemetery and his brother, Alick Cubitt is commemorated on the Cambrai Memorial at Louveral.
16. Carnock, *The History of the 15th The King's Hussars 1914–1922*, pp. 162–3.
17. Ibid.
18. Letter from Major L W Kentish in CAB 45/193.
19. Letter from Rees to Edmonds in CAB 45/193.
20. Gough, *The Fifth Army*, pp. 253–4.
21. Raimes, *The 5th Battalion The Durham Light Infantry*, p. 119.
22. Private Papers of Lieutenant J F Fleming-Bernard, IWM Department of Documents, reference 13793.
23. Raimes, *The 5th Battalion The Durham Light Infantry*, p. 121.
24. War Diaries of 4/Yorkshire Regiment, WO 95/2583 and 5/ and 6/DLI, WO 95/2840. Bernard Charleton is buried at Roisel Communal Cemetery Extension and James Bainbridge is commemorated on the Pozières Memorial.
25. In a letter to Edmonds in CAB 45/193, Watts suggests that the crucial decision taken by the 50th Division on 22 March as to which line the division should retire to was taken by Brigadier General Rees in consultation with the other brigade commanders. There seems to be some suggestion that Stockley had not fully grasped the mantle of divisional command at that point.
26. Raimes, *The 5th Battalion The Durham Light Infantry*, p. 123.
27. Ibid, p. 124.
28. Ainsworth, *The Story of The 6th Battalion The Durham Light Infantry*, p. 45.
29. Letter to Edmonds from Rees in CAB 45/193.

30. The 39th Division was placed at the disposal of Congreve's VII Corps at noon on 21 March. Congreve immediately allotted 116 Infantry Brigade and 174 and 186 Artillery Brigades to support the 16th Division.
31. Fielding, *War Letters to a Wife*, p. 273.

Chapter 11

1. Letter from Brooke in CAB 45/192.
2. Stanley, *The History of the 89th Brigade*, pp. 257–8.
3. Ibid, p. 259. The officer referred to by Stanley was Lieutenant John McHale aged 29. He is buried at Ham British Cemetery.
4. R F Petschler, IWM Department of Documents, reference 11732.
5. Asquith, *Moments of Memory*, pp. 327–8.
6. R F Petschler, IWM Department of Documents, reference 11732.
7. Ibid.
8. Letter from Duncan to Edmonds in CAB 45/192.
9. War Diary of 11/South Lancashire Regiment, TNA WO 95/2323.
10. Ibid.
11. Private Papers of J T Davies, IWM Department of Documents, reference 17153.
12. Reymann, *Das Infantrie-Regiment von Alvensleben Nr. 52 1914–1918*, p. 190.
13. Account by Evans-Lombe in CAB 45/192.
14. Buckland, Demolitions Fifth Army, 1918, *Royal Engineers Journal*, June 1933, p. 204. Lieutenant George Baylay is buried at Pargny British Cemetery.
15. War Diary of 1/Worcestershire Regiment, TNA WO 95/1723.
16. Ibid.
17. Liddell Hart Military Archive, GB0099 KCLMA Jacobs-Larkcom.
18. Atkinson, *The Devonshire Regiment 1914–1918*, Volume 1, pp. 330–1. Lieutenant James Huntingford was commissioned from the ranks on 31 July 1917 and, like Maunder, survived the war.
19. Burne, *Q Battery in the Great War*, p. 28.
20. Private Papers of F R Curtis, IWM Department of Documents, reference 1391.
21. War diary of 2/Middlesex Regiment, TNA WO 95/1713. Captain Hugh Neville Wegg was killed in action on 25 March 1918. He was 36-years-old and is commemorated on the Pozières Memorial.
22. War Diary of 2/Middlesex Regiment, TNA WO 95/1713. Second Lieutenant Alexander Frederick Liversedge was killed in action on 25 March 1918 and is commemorated on the Pozières Memorial.
23. *London Gazette*, 8 May 1918.
24. Raimes, *The 5th Battalion The Durham Light Infantry*, pp. 131–2.
25. Sheffield & Bourne, *Douglas Haig, War Diaries and Letters 1914–1918*, pp. 390–1.
26. Ibid.
27. Travers, *How the War Was Won*, pp. 66–70.
28. Cooper, letter to Edmonds in CAB 45/184.
29. Philpott, *Bloody Victory*, p. 505.
30. Gough, *The Fifth Army*, p. 306.

Chapter 12

1. *The Kings Royal Rifle Corps Chronicle 1918*, p. 304.
2. The Diary of TLB Westerdale, IWM Department of Documents, reference 14137.
3. War Diary of 61 Infantry Brigade Headquarters, TNA WO 95/2125.
4. The Diary of TLB Westerdale, IWM Department of Documents, reference 14137.
5. Account in TNA WO/339/115633.
6. Account in TNA WO 339/2036.
7. 'To the Last Man and the Last Round', *Queen's Royal Surrey Regiment Newsletter, May 1972*, pp. 11–12. Stanley Grant is commemorated on the Pozières Memorial.
8. Gruter et al, *Das 2. Badische Grenadier-Regiment Kaiser Wilhelm I.* p. 229. Godfrey Warre-Dymond MC was a man born for war. He survived his period of captivity and died of a heart attack in 1955 aged 64. The young R C Sherriff served under him during his time as a subaltern with 9/East Surreys and many believe Warre-Dymond was the original template for 'Stanhope' in Sherriff's famous play *Journey's End*.
9. McCance, *History of the Royal Munster Fusiliers*, Vol II, p. 153.
10. Ibid, p. 154.
11. War Diary of 11/Hampshires, TNA WO 95/1495.
12. An unknown officer's account cited in, Wyrall, *The History of the 50th Division*, p. 290.
13. Atkinson, *The Devonshire Regiment 1914–1918*, Vol. I, p. 334.
14. Lieutenant Colonel Cecil Morgan is buried at St Sever Extension Cemetery, Rouen and his son, Second Lieutenant Basil Morgan, is commemorated on the Arras Memorial, Bay 6.
15. Raimes, *The 5th Battalion The Durham Light Infantry*, pp. 137–8.
16. Liddell Hart Military Archive, GB0099 KCLMA Jacobs-Larkcom. The 5.9s mentioned by Jacobs-Larkcom was a reference to the shells fired by the 15cm German field howitzer.
17. Goes, Unter dem Stahlhelm, *Der Tag X*.
18. From the unpublished diary of Edward Riddell, quoted by Raimes in *The 5th Battalion The Durham Light Infantry*, pp. 142–3.
19. Rose, *The Story of the 2/4 Oxford and Buckinghamshire Light Infantry*, pp. 108–9.
20. Goes, Unter dem Stahlhelm, *Der Tag X*.
21. *The Kings Royal Rifle Corps Chronicle 1918*, p. 308.
22. Private Papers of F Warren, IWM Department of Documents, reference 11467.

Chapter 13

1. Gough, *The Fifth Army*, p. 317.
2. Ibid, pp. 317–8.
3. Goes, Unter dem Stahlhelm, *Der Tag X*. p. 169.
4. Windsor Royal Archives RAS/PS/GV/Q 832/302 Gough to Wigram 4 April 1918.
5. Account by Sandilands in CAB 45/193.
6. Maze, *A Frenchman in Khaki*, p. 310.
7. Pitman, The Operations of the Second Cavalry Division in the Defence of Amiens. *The Cavalry Journal* Volume XIII 1923, pp. 360–70.
8. Seely, *Adventure*, p. 299.
9. Ibid, p. 300.
10. Connolly, The Action of the Canadian Cavalry Brigade at Moreuil and Rifle Wood – March and April 1918. *Canadian Defence Quarterly*, Vol. III October 1925, p. 12.
11. Quoted by Grodzinski, *The Battle of Moreuil Wood*, pp. 6–7.

12. Seely, *Adventure*, p. 302.
13. Grodzinski, *The Battle of Moreuil Wood*, p. 8.
14. Goes, Unter dem Stahlhelm, *Der Tag X*. p. 171.
15. Lunt, *Charge To Glory! A Garland of Cavalry Exploits*, p. 237.
16. John Evelyn Carmichael Darley is buried at Moreuil Communal Cemetery Allied Extension. He was 38 years old.
17. Pitman, The Operations of the Second Cavalry Division in the Defence of Amiens. *The Cavalry Journal* Vol. XIII 1923, p. 370.
18. From the diary account of Child-Villiers quoted in, *The Oxfordshire Hussars in the Great War*, p. 284.

Appendix I

Order of Battle – British Expeditionary Force

III Corps – Lieutenant General R H K Butler

58 London Division (Major General A B Cator)	18 (Eastern) Division (Major General R P Lee)	14 (Light) Division (Major General V A Couper)
173 Brigade (Brig Gen R B Worgan)	53 Brigade (Brig Gen H W Higginson)	41 Brigade (Brig Gen P C Skinner)
2/2 London	10/Essex	8/KRRC
3/London	8/Royal Berkshire	7/Rifle Brigade
2/4 London	7/Royal West Kent	8/Rifle Brigade
174 Brigade (Brig Gen C G Higgins)	54 Brigade (Brig Gen Sadleir-Jackson)	42 Brigade (Brig Gen G N Forster)
6/London	11/Royal Fusiliers	5/Ox & Bucks
7/London	7/Bedfordshire	9/KRRC
8/London	6/Northamptonshire	9/Rifle Brigade
175 Brigade (Brig Gen H C Jackson)	55 Brigade (Brig Gen E A Wood)	43 Brigade (Brig Gen R S Tempest)
9/London	7/Queen's	6/Somerset Light Infantry
2/10 London	7/Buffs	9/Scottish Rifles
12/London	8/East Surrey	7/KRRC
Pioneers: 1/4 Suffolk	Pioneers: 8/Royal Sussex	Pioneers: 11/King's Own

XVIII Corps – Lieutenant General Sir Ivor Maxse

36 (Ulster) Division (Major General O S Nugent)	30 Division (Major General W de L Williams)	61 Division (Major General C Mackenzie)
107 Brigade (Brig Gen W M Withycombe)	21 Brigade (Brig Gen G D Goodman)	182 Brigade (Brig Gen W K Evans)
1/Royal Irish Rifles	2/Wiltshires	2/6 Royal Warwicks
2/Royal Irish Rifles	2/Green Howards	2/7 Royal Warwicks
15/Royal Irish Rifles	17/Manchester	2/8 Worcester
108 Brigade (Brig Gen C R Griffiths)	89 Brigade (Brig Gen F C Stanley)	183 Brigade (Brig Gen A H Spooner)
12/Royal Irish Rifles	17/King's Liverpool	9/Royal Scots
1/Royal Irish Fusiliers	18/King's Liverpool	5/Gordon Highlanders
9/Royal Irish Fusiliers	19/King's Liverpool	8/Argyll & Sutherland Highlanders
109 Brigade (Brig Gen W F Hessey)	90 Brigade (Brig Gen H S Poyntz)	184 Brigade (Brig Gen Hon R White)
1/Royal Inniskilling Fusiliers	2/Bedford shire	2/5 Gloucestershire
2/Royal Inniskilling Fusiliers	2/Royal Scots Fusiliers	2/4 Gloucestershire
9/Royal Inniskilling Fusiliers	16/Manchester	2/4 Royal Berkshire
Pioneers: 16/Royal Irish Rifles	Pioneers: 11/South Lancashire	Pioneers: 1/5 Durham Light Infantry

XIX Corps – Lieutenant General Sir H E Watts

24 Division
(Major General A C Daly)

17 Brigade
(Brig Gen P V Stone)
8/Royal West Surrey
1/Royal Fusiliers
3/Rifle Brigade

72 Brigade
(Lt Col L J Wyall – Acting)
9/East Surrey
8/Royal West Kent
1/North Staffs

73 Brigade
(Brig Gen W J Dugan)
9/Royal Sussex
7/Northampton
13/Middlesex

Pioneers: 12/Notts and Derby

66 Division
(Major General N Malcolm)

193 Brigade
(Brig Gen O C Borrett)
6/Lancashire Fusiliers
2/7 Lancashire Fusiliers
2/8 Lancashire Fusiliers

198 Brigade
(Brig Gen A J Hunter)
4/East Lancashire
2/5 East Lancashire
9/Manchester

199 Brigade
(Brig Gen G C Williams)
2/5 Manchester
2/6 Manchester
2/7 Manchester

Pioneers: 5/Border Regiment

VII Corps – Lieutenant General Sir W N Congreve VC

16 (Irish) Division
(Major General Sir C P Hull)

47 Brigade
(Brig Gen H G Gregorie)
6/Connaught Rangers
2/Leinster
1/Royal Munster Fusiliers

48 Brigade
(Brig Gen F W Ramsay)
1/Royal Dublin Fusiliers
2/Royal Dublin Fusiliers
2/Royal Munster Fusiliers

49 Brigade
(Brig Gen P Leveson-Gower)
2/Royal Irish
7/Royal Irish
7/8 Royal Inniskilling Fusiliers

Pioneers: 11/Hampshire

21 Division
(Major General D G Campbell)

62 Brigade
(Brig Gen G H Gator)
12/13 Northumberland Fusiliers
1/Lincolnshire
2/Lincolnshire

64 Brigade
(Brig Gen R H Headlam)
1/East Yorkshire
9/KOYLI
15/Durham Light Infantry

110 Brigade
(Brig Gen H R Cumming)
6/Leicestershire
7/Leicestershire
8/Leicestershire

Pioneers: 14/Northumberland Fusiliers

9 (Scottish) Division
(Brig Gen C R Tudor – Acting)

26 Brigade
(Brig Gen J Kennedy)
8/Black Watch
7/Seaforth Highlanders
5/Cameron highlanders

27 Brigade
(Brig Gen W D Croft)
11/Royal Scots
12/Royal Scots
6/KOSB

South African Brigade
(Brig Gen F S Dawson)
1/South African Regiment
2/South African Regiment
4/South African Regiment

Pioneers: 9/Seaforth Highlanders

Cavalry

1st Cavalry Division (Major General R L Mullens)	2 Cavalry Division (Major General W H Greenly)	3 Cavalry Division (Brigadier General A E Harman)
1 Brigade (Brig Gen E Makins)	3 Brigade (Brig Gen J Bell-Smyth)	6 Brigade (Brig Gen A Seymour)
2/Dragoon Guards	4/Hussars	3/Dragoon Guards
5/Dragoon Guards	5/Lancers	1/Royal Dragoons
11/Hussars	16/Lancers	10/Hussars
2 Brigade (Brig Gen D Beale-Browne)	4 Brigade (Brig Gen T Pitman)	7 Brigade (Brig Gen B P Portal)
4/Dragoon Guards	6/Dragoon Guards	7/Dragoon Guards
9/Lancers	3/Hussars	6/Inniskilling Dragoons
18/Hussars	Oxfordshire Hussars	17/Lancers
9 Brigade (Brig Gen D Legard)	5 Brigade (Lt Col W F Collins)	Canadian Cavalry Brigade (Brig Gen J E Seely)
8/Hussars	Royal Scots Greys	Royal Canadian Dragoons
19/Hussars	12/Lancers	Lord Strathcona's Horse
15/Hussars	20/Hussars	Fort Garry Horse

Reserve Infantry Divisions

20 (Light) Division (Major General W Douglas-Smith)	8 Division. (Major General W C Heneker)	50 Division (Brigadier General A U Stockley – until 24 March) (Major General H Jackson)
59 Brigade (Brig Gen H H Hyslop)	23 Brigade (Brig Gen G W Grogan)	149 Brigade (Brig Gen E P Riddell)
2/Scottish Rifles	2/Devonshire	4/Northumberland Fusiliers
11/KRRC	2/West Yorkshire	5/Northumberland Fusiliers
11/Rifle Brigade	2/Middlesex	6/Northumberland Fusiliers
60 Brigade (Brig Gen F J Duncan)	24 Brigade (Brig Gen R Haig)	150 Brigade (Brig Gen H Rees)
6/KSLI	1/Worcestershire	4/East Yorkshire
12/KRRC	2/Northamptonshire	4/Yorkshire
12/Rifle Brigade	1/Sherwood Foresters	5/Yorkshire
61 Brigade (Brig Gen J K Cochrane)	25 Brigade (Brig Gen C Coffin)	151 Brigade (Brig Gen C T Martin)
12/King's Liverpool	2/Royal Berkshire	5/Durham Light Infantry
7/Somerset Light Infantry	2/East Lancashire	6/Durham Light Infantry
7/DCLI	2/Rifle Brigade	8/Durham Light Infantry
Pioneers: 11/Durham Light Infantry	Pioneers: 22/Durham Light Infantry	Pioneers: 7/Durham Light Infantry

Select Bibliography

The Marquess of Anglesey, *A History of the British Cavalry 1816–1919* (Vol. 7), Leo Cooper,1973–1982.

Herbert Asquith, *Moments of Memory*, Hutchinson, 1937.

Correlli Barnett, *The Sword Bearers – Studies in Supreme Command in the First World Wa*r, Hodder & Stoughton, 1986.

Banks and Chell, *With the 10th Essex in France*, Gay & Handcock, 1924.

J B Bickersteth, *History of the 6th Cavalry Brigade 1914–1918*, Baynard Press, 1921

J H Boraston & C E Bax, *The Eighth Division in War 1914–1919*, Medici Society, 1926.

Lord Carnock, *The History of the 15th The King's Hussars 1914–1922*, Crypt House Press, 1932.

Guy Chapman, *A Passionate Prodigality*, Nicholson and Watson, 1933.

W D Croft, *Three Years with The 9th (Scottish) Division*, John Murray, 1919.

Robert Cumming, *A Brigadier In France 1917–1918*, Jonathan Cape, 1918.

J C Darling, *20th Hussars in the Great War*, Privately published, 1923.

W H Downing, *To the Last Ridge*, H H Champion, 1920.

Sir J E Edmonds, *Military Operations France and Belgium 1918 Vols. 1 and 2*, Macmillan, 1935.

H Essame, *The Battle for Europe 1918*, Batsford, 1972.

John Ewing, *The History Of The Ninth (Scottish) Division 1914–1919*, John Murray, 1921.

General Sir M Farndale, *History of the Royal Regiment of Artillery-Western Front*, Royal Artillery Institution, 1986.

Rowland Fielding, *War Letters to a Wife*, Medici Society, 1929.

Randal Gray, *Kaiserschlacht 1918: The Final German Offensive*, Osprey, 1991.

W E Grey, *2nd City of London Regiment in the Great War 1914–1918*, privately published 1929.

Paddy Griffith, *Battle Tactics of the Western Front*, Yale University Press, 1994.

Stair Gillon, *The KOSB in the Great War*, Thomas Nelson, 1930.

Gerald Gliddon, *VCs Handbook*, Sutton, 2005.

Hubert Gough, *The Fifth Army*, Hodder & Stoughton, 1931.

Peter Hart, *1918 – A Very British Victory*, Weidenfeld & Nicolson, 2008.

Frederick Hodges, *Men of 18 in 1918*, Stockwell, 1988.

V E Ingleford, *The History of the Twentieth (Light) Division*, Nisbet and Co., 1921.

David Kelly, *39 Months With The Tigers*, Ernest Benn, 1930.

David Lloyd-George, *War Memoirs Volume V*, Nicholson & Watson, 1934.

L R Lumley, *History of the Eleventh Hussars*, RUSI, 1926.

Lynn Macdonald, *To the Last Man*, Viking, 1998.

Paul Maze, *A Frenchman in Khaki*, Heinemann, 1934.

Martin Middlebrook, *The Kaiser's Battle, 21 March 1918*, Allen Lane, 1978.

William Moore, *See How They Ran*, Sphere Books, 1975.

George Nichols, *History of the Eighteenth Division*, Blackwood, 1922.

George Nichols, *Pushed and the Return Push*, Blackwood & Sons, 1919.

W N Nicholson, *Behind The Lines*, Jonathan Cape, 1939.

Ian Passingham, *The German Offensives of 1918*, Pen and Sword, 2008.

Alwyn Raimes, *The 5th Battalion The Durham Light Infantry*, Gale and Polden, 1931

James Taylor, *The 2nd Royal Irish Rifles in the Great War*, Four Courts, 2005.

Walter Shaw Sparrow, *The Fifth Army in March 1918*, John Lane, 1921.

W S Shepherd, *2nd Battalion Wiltshire Regiment*, Gale and Polden, 1927.

F C Stanley, *The History of the 89th Brigade*, Liverpool Daily Post, 1919.

Tim Travers, *How the War Was Won*, Routledge, 1992.

Everard Wyrall, *The History of the Duke of Cornwall's Light Infantry 1914–1919*, Methuen & Co.,1932.

Everard Wyrall, *The Diehards in the Great War*, Harrison and Sons, 1926.

Index

Index of Individuals